Influence of Investor Behaviour On Investment Performance

Influence of

Investor Behaviour

On Investment Performance

Jackson Oyaro Ong'eta

EXCELLER BOOKS®
A GLOBAL PRESS

Influence of Investor Behaviour on Investment Performance

Cover by Exceller Books using resources from Pixabay.com

ISBN: 978-93-47397-73-8

First published in India in 2025 by Exceller Books,
An imprint of GE Group

Address: G1, Dream Apartment, Degree College Road, Belgharia,
Kolkata, 700056, India
www.excellerbooks.com

EXCELLER BOOKS®
A GLOBAL PRESS

Dedication

I dedicate this book to my dear wife, Susan Moraa Abuya, our children, Sonia and Jabali, and to my brother in-law Timothy Osebe Abuya

Acknowledgment

This book would not have been completed without the help of research advisors, family members, colleagues, and friends. My appreciation goes to my God for keeping me in good health and enabling me to complete this book. I also extend my heartfelt appreciation to my committee members: Dr. Eric J. Nasution, Dr. Kenneth Swansi, and Dr. Samuel Gaikwad for their enormous contribution in the process of writing this book. I also thank Dr. Leroy Ruhupatty and Dr. Maria Vallejos-Cornejo for the valuable advice they extended to me during this important exercise. Their knowledge, critical analysis, and input made the completion of this book a reality. To my lovely wife, Susan Moraa Abuya, who sacrificed time, resources, and provided the much-needed encouragement to soldier on when the work seemed to weigh me down.

To the University of Eastern Africa Baraton, for the time and support that was extended to me so that I can complete this process. To my daughter, Sonia Nyanchera and son, Jabali Ong'eta who sacrificed their time to be with me, so that I can complete this writing, I hope now I can spend more time with you. To my parents, Moses Ong'eta and Abigael Nyaboke and my parents in-law, Joseph Abuya and Peninah Nyagochi for their prayers and encouragement. To all my brothers and sisters and the in-laws for their prayers and support. To my classmates for the time we shared insights in class as we learned the concepts that helped us acquire the knowledge. Finally, to all my friends for their prayers, support, and encouragement.

Abstract

Investors in the financial markets are expected to act rationally in their investment decisions as postulated by the efficient market hypothesis. This expectation of rational investor behaviour, however, does not always hold true. The individual investors have often been found to be *irrational* in their investment decisions. Researchers have tried to explain this investors' *irrational* behaviour by pointing to behavioural factors such as herding, prospects, and heuristics. To build on what is known from the literature, this study aimed to research on the behavioural and market factors influencing investment performance with an additional indicator of prospect, namely, *escalating the commitment.*

Using a positivist research paradigm, a cross-sectional survey was conducted among individual investors of Nairobi Securities Exchange. Multiple regression analysis was used to analyze the data to determine the influence of the behavioural and market factors on investment performance. The behavioural and market factors explained for 77.4% of the variance in investment performance (R^2 of 77.4). The study found that herding had a negative influence on investment performance (β = -.602, $p < .05$). In addition, market factors also had a negative relationship with the investment performance (β = -.195, $p < .05$). On the other hand, prospect factors influence the investment performance positively (β = .424, $p < .05$). The heuristic factors had a positive relationship with the investment performance (β = .536, $p < .05$). The investment decisions as a control variable had no significant influence on the model.

These results contribute to literature on the influence of behaviourial factors on the investment performance in two important ways: (a) the understanding of the behavioural factors displayed by the individual investors and (b) the identification of the significant influence of the behavioural and market factors on the investment performance. This study stands to benefit future researchers while designing their studies. The implications for practice is that the NSE and Capital Market Authority will be informed to initiate appropriate training programs that will enable the individual investors to mitigate the negative investment performance that they may exhibit.

List of Abbreviations

AB:	Availability Bias
CMA:	Capital Market Authority
EC:	Escalating the Commitment
EI:	Expert Information
EMH:	Efficient Market Hypothesis
HE:	Herding
HUF:	Heuristic Factor
IP:	Investment Performance
IPO:	Initial Public Offering
LA:	Loss Aversion
MF:	Market Factor
NSE:	Nairobi Securities Exchange
OV:	Overconfidence
PF:	Prospect Factor
PI:	Public Information
RA:	Regret Aversion

Table of Contents

Chapter 1 | Introduction

The chapter provides an introduction to the study. It consists of the following sections. First, it highlights the background to the study and states the problem. Second, it presents the purpose of the study, research objectives, research questions, hypotheses, and the significance of the study. Third, the chapter outlines the limitations, delimitations, assumptions of the study, and definition of terms. Fourth, the organization of the study is also provided.

Background of the Study

Investors in the financial markets are expected to act rationally in their investment decisions. This aligns with traditional finance theories such as the Efficient Market Hypothesis (EMH), which postulates that stock markets efficiently provide the necessary information for decision-making by market participants (Sharma, 2014, p. 274). The rational expectations of investors should ensure that no anomalies occur in the securities market. However, this expectation of rational investor behavior does not always hold true. Individual investors have often been found to be irrational in their investment decisions (Aduda, Oduor, & Onwonga, 2012, p. 56). Researchers have attempted to explain this "irrational" behavior by pointing to behavioral factors such as herding, prospect theory, and heuristics (Kharb & Malik, 2014, p. 34; Shiller, 1998, p. 2). Furthermore, the understanding of how and which behavioral factors influence investment decisions remains incomplete (Kumar & Goyal, 2015). To build on existing literature, this study aimed to examine the behavioral factors (herding, prospect, and heuristic) influencing investment decisions, with an additional indicator of prospect—namely, "escalating commitment." In addition, the study determined the influence of behavioral factors on the impact of market efficiencies on investment performance.

Investment decisions by investors in the financial markets have led to anomalies that the EMH could not explain. This motivated researchers to begin exploring human behavior as the missing link (Shiller, 2003). As a result, there has been a rise in research on behavioral finance. Behavioral finance examines how investors and financial markets are influenced by psychology (Sewell, 2010, p. 1). In addition, behavioral finance refers to financial decision-making that incorporates psychology and sociology (Shiller, 2003). Therefore, the study of behavioral finance encompasses the influence of psychosocial factors on financial decisions.

Behavioral factors determine the investment decision-making of individual investors. Individual investors are those who purchase securities under their own names (Kaur & Vohra, 2012). They usually have accounts with brokerage firms, and the decisions on the type, timing, and quantity of securities to buy or sell are made personally. Studies have established that individual investors are prone to errors and biases due to their personal behavior, which often leads to losses on their investments (Jagongo & Mutswenje, 2014; Nyamute, Lishenga, & Oloko, 2015).

Individual investors have been found to exhibit negative performance (Aduda et al., 2012) as a result of behavioral factors influencing their decision-making. This negative performance could be mitigated if the behavioral factors affecting individual investment decisions are identified and, subsequently, the impact of market efficiencies on investment performance is determined. Thus, there is a motivation to investigate the behavioral factors influencing individual investment decisions and the impact of market efficiencies on investment performance. Understanding the influence of behavioral factors on investment decisions is expected to enhance rational decision-making, thereby minimizing or avoiding losses in stock market investments.

Individual investors are influenced by both behavioral and market factors when making investment decisions. The behavioral factors are explained under three major theories: herding behavior theory, heuristic theory, and prospect theory. Several behavioral factors have been identified as influencing individual investors' decisions in the stock market.

One of the behavioral factors is herding. Studies (Aduda et al., 2012; Das, 2012; Jagongo & Mutswenje, 2014; Kengatharan & Kengatharan, 2014; Rekik & Boujelbene, 2013; Vijaya, 2014) have shown that individual investors are influenced by herding behavior. This behavior is exhibited when individual investors make decisions by following the actions of other investors. They are influenced regarding when to buy or sell their stocks, the speed of these transactions, and the volume of stock to trade. Therefore, individual investors are influenced by herding when making investment decisions.

Another behavioral factor is availability bias. The decision-making of individual investors is influenced by readily available information. Stocks that are more visible or available in the market may sway investors' decisions. Moreover, investors are more likely to invest in stocks they are familiar with or that are available locally, rather than in foreign stocks. Therefore, availability bias has been found to influence investment decisions (Chandra & Kumar, 2012; Kengatharan & Kengatharan, 2014; Vijaya, 2014).

Individual investment decisions are also affected by overconfidence. This occurs when individual investors perceive themselves as more experienced in trading and believe they can outperform others. Consequently, they tend to trade excessively, believing they can beat the market. Overconfidence has been identified as a factor influencing investment decisions (Chandra & Kumar, 2012; Das, 2012; Kengatharan & Kengatharan, 2014; Rekik & Boujelbene, 2013; Veeraraghavan & Anbalagan, 2011; Vijaya, 2014).

Market factors also influence investors in the stock market. These may not be behavioral in nature, but they affect the decisions of individual investors and therefore warrant inclusion in the study. For example, market factors include public and expert information (Das, 2012). Individual investors rely on public information available through print and electronic media, as well as published financial statements. Therefore, public information influences investment decisions.

Investors may also consult financial experts, such as investment advisors. A study by Das (2012) identified expert information as a factor influencing investment decisions. Investors may use information about stock performance in the market to inform their decisions. Therefore, expert information influences individual investors because it can be used to guide investment decisions.

Loss aversion is another factor influencing individual investors. This refers to the tendency of investors to make decisions aimed at avoiding losses. Loss aversion has been observed among individual investors (Chandra & Kumar, 2012; Das, 2012; Kengatharan & Kengatharan, 2014; Rekik & Boujelbene, 2013; Vijaya, 2014). According to Sahi, Arora, and Dhameja (2013, p. 100), individual investors "strongly prefer avoiding losses to acquiring gains." Therefore, loss aversion plays a significant role in investment decision-making.

Regret aversion also influences individual investors. Individual investors make investment decisions to avoid regret. Moreover, regret aversion has been identified as influencing investment decisions (Chandra & Kumar, 2012; Kengatharan & Kengatharan, 2014; Vijaya, 2014). In addition, a study noted that individual investors "anticipate that they would make an error and hence end up taking a decision that will not cause them to feel regret later" (Sahi et al., 2013, p. 100). Therefore, individual investors are influenced by regret aversion while making decisions.

The disposition effect also influences individual investors. The disposition effect is "the inclination to possess losing securities too long and to sell gainers too quickly because of loathing to lose" (Sukheja, 2016, p. 78). In addition, the disposition effect can be looked at from the selling of securities on one hand and the buying of securities on the other. A study (Chandra & Kumar, 2012) looked at the disposition effect from the selling side, but limited studies have researched it from the buying side (Lin, Fan, & Chih, 2014), which is referred to as escalation of the commitment. The effect of escalating the commitment has been studied in isolation, and in addition, limited studies have combined escalating the commitment with other indicators of prospect theory.

Escalating the commitment is the tendency by decision-makers to hold on to a decision even if it becomes apparent that it is a bad decision. A study (Lin et al., 2014) confirmed that escalating the commitment has a negative effect on the investment performance of mutual fund managers. Few scholars have studied the influence of escalating the commitment on the investment performance of individual stock market investors. Also, escalating the commitment has not been combined with other indicators of prospect theory. Therefore, escalating the commitment was combined with loss aversion and regret aversion as prospect indicators in this study, along with other behavioural factors—herding and heuristic factors (availability bias and overconfidence)—and market factors (public and expert information), to determine the influence they have on investment performance. Having introduced the study, the statement of the problem will follow.

Statement of the Problem

Investors are expected to be guided by the EMH in making investment decisions to promote their self-interest and maximize their earnings. It has been noted that the efficient market hypothesis guides investment decision-making (Vijaya, 2014). In addition, the EMH facilitates investors in making rational investment decisions. Therefore, individual investors should not be guided by their biases while making investment decisions. As such, there should be no abnormal occurrences in the financial market if investors are guided by the efficient market hypothesis. If that is the case, individual investors are expected to earn the equivalent of the market performance.

This expectation of rational investor behaviour, however, does not always hold true. Individual investors have often been found to be influenced by behavioural factors in their investment decisions (Aduda et al., 2012). Furthermore, anomalies have been reported in the securities market which the efficient market hypothesis could not explain (Latif, Arshad, Fatima, & Farooq, 2011). Therefore, this points to the fact that investment decisions may be influenced by other factors besides the EMH.

This influence of behavioural factors on investors has resulted in anomalies in the securities market, leading to major losses on investments made. In the recent past, it has been noted that equities in the financial market have done well, while individual investors reported losses in the NSE (Vijaya, 2014). A study by Dalbar (2015) conducted in the United States reported that in 2014, equity mutual fund investors underperformed the S&P 500 by earning an average return of 5.50% compared to the 13.69% average return of the S&P 500—a significant margin loss of 8.19%. This clearly indicates the existence of anomalies in the stock market, leading to heavy losses on the part of individual investors against the backdrop of good market performance in the financial market. Further, other negative consequences of investor behaviour are identified as a reduction in the market value of firms, discouraging potential stock market investors, and the underperformance of the financial system.

The underperformance of individual investors, to a large extent, may be due to factors related to individual investors' behaviour and not the performance of the securities market. A deeper investigation of individual investors' behaviour is, thus, warranted. Therefore, this study aimed to research the behavioural factors (herding, prospect, and heuristic) and market factors influencing investment decisions, with an additional indicator of prospect, namely escalating the commitment, and eventually determine the influence of investment decisions on investment performance. The findings of the study are expected to enhance the understanding of stock market investors' behaviour and its influence on investment performance. After providing the statement of the problem, the focus now shifts to stating the purpose of the study, research objectives, research questions, and hypotheses.

Purpose of the Study

The purpose of the study was to assess the behaviour of individual investors in the Nairobi Securities Exchange (NSE). In particular, this study attempted to assess whether individual investors in the NSE display the following behavioural factors (herding, prospect, and heuristic) and market factors (public information and expert information), with an additional indicator of prospect—namely, escalating the commitment. If they do, this study attempted to determine the degree of behavioural factors (herding, prospect, and heuristic) and market factors (public information and expert information) that NSE individual investors display, and eventually determine the influence of behavioural factors (herding, prospect, and heuristic) and market factors (public information and expert information) on investment performance.

Research Objectives

The study was guided by the following research objectives:

1. To determine whether individual investors in the NSE display behavioural factors such as herding, prospect (loss aversion, regret aversion, and escalating the commitment), and heuristic (availability bias and overconfidence).
2. To ascertain the extent of the behavioural factors such as herding, prospect (loss aversion, regret aversion, and escalating the commitment), and heuristic (availability bias and overconfidence) displayed by individual investors in the NSE.
3. To examine whether the following factors—herding, prospect (loss aversion, regret aversion, and escalating the commitment), heuristic (availability bias and overconfidence), and market factors (public information and expert information)—significantly differ by the demographic and psychographic characteristics of individual investors in the NSE.
4. To assess whether the following factors—herding, prospect (loss aversion, regret aversion, and escalating the commitment), heuristic (availability bias and overconfidence), market factors (public information and expert information), and investment decisions—are significantly correlated with each other in the NSE.
5. To establish whether the following behavioural factors—herding, prospect (loss aversion, regret aversion, and escalating the commitment), heuristic (availability bias and overconfidence), and market factors (public information and expert information)—combined together significantly influence investment performance in the NSE.
6. To investigate how the following behavioural factors—herding, prospect (loss aversion, regret aversion, and escalating the commitment), heuristic (availability bias and overconfidence), and market factors (public information and expert information)—combined together significantly influence investment performance with investment decisions as a control variable in the NSE.

Research Questions

The study was guided by the following research questions:

1. What behavioural factors such as herding, prospect (loss aversion, regret aversion, and escalating the commitment), and heuristic (availability bias and overconfidence) are displayed by individual investors in the Nairobi Securities Exchange (NSE)?
2. To what extent are the behavioural factors such as herding, prospect (loss aversion, regret aversion, and escalating the commitment), and heuristic (availability bias and overconfidence) displayed by individual investors in the NSE?
3. Do the following factors—herding, prospect (loss aversion, regret aversion, and escalating the commitment), heuristic (availability bias and overconfidence), and market factors (public information and expert information)—significantly differ by the demographic and psychographic characteristics of individual investors in the NSE?

4. Are the following factors—herding, prospect (loss aversion, regret aversion, and escalating the commitment), heuristic (availability bias and overconfidence), market factors (public information and expert information), and investment decisions—significantly correlated with each other in the NSE?
5. Do the following behavioural factors—herding, prospect (loss aversion, regret aversion, and escalating the commitment), heuristic (availability bias and overconfidence), and market factors (public information and expert information)—combined together significantly influence investment performance in the NSE?
6. Do the following behavioural factors—herding, prospect (loss aversion, regret aversion, and escalating the commitment), heuristic (availability bias and overconfidence), and market factors (public information and expert information)—combined together significantly influence investment performance with investment decisions as a control variable in the NSE?

Research Hypotheses

This study was guided by the following stated research hypotheses:

1. **H01:** The following factors—herding, prospect (loss aversion, regret aversion, and escalating the commitment), heuristic (availability bias and overconfidence), and market factors (public information and expert information)—do not significantly differ by the demographic and psychographic characteristics of individual investors in the NSE.

   H1: The following factors—herding, prospect (loss aversion, regret aversion, and escalating the commitment), heuristic (availability bias and overconfidence), and market factors (public information and expert information)—significantly differ by the demographic and psychographic characteristics of individual investors in the NSE.
2. **H02:** The following factors—herding, prospect (loss aversion, regret aversion, and escalating the commitment), heuristic (availability bias and overconfidence), market factors (public information and expert information), and investment decisions—are not significantly correlated with each other in the NSE.
   H2: The following factors—herding, prospect (loss aversion, regret aversion, and escalating the commitment), heuristic (availability bias and overconfidence), market factors (public information and expert information), and investment decisions—are significantly correlated with each other in the NSE.
3. **H03:** The following behavioural factors—herding, prospect (loss aversion, regret aversion, and escalating the commitment), heuristic (availability bias and overconfidence), and market factors (public information and expert information)—combined together do not significantly influence investment performance in the NSE.

   H3: The following behavioural factors—herding, prospect (loss aversion, regret aversion, and escalating the commitment), heuristic (availability bias and overconfidence), and market factors (public information and expert information)—combined together significantly influence investment performance in the NSE.

4. **H04:** The following behavioural factors—herding, prospect (loss aversion, regret aversion, and escalating the commitment), heuristic (availability bias and overconfidence), and market factors (public information and expert information)—combined together do not significantly influence investment performance with investment decisions as a control variable in the NSE.
   H4: The following behavioural factors—herding, prospect (loss aversion, regret aversion, and escalating the commitment), heuristic (availability bias and overconfidence), and market factors (public information and expert information)—combined together significantly influence investment performance with investment decisions as a control variable in the NSE.

Significance of the Study

This study sought to understand the behaviour of individual investors in the NSE by including one indicator of prospect, which is escalating the commitment, and ultimately, the influence of investment decisions on investment performance. Individual investors stand to benefit from this study since they will be enlightened on the behavioural factors influencing investment performance. Therefore, they will be enabled to make decisions that maximize their investment performance.

Investment advisors also stand to benefit, since the behavioural factors in the NSE were highlighted, enabling them to effectively advise individual investors. The level of behavioural factors also highlights to stock market regulators and NSE management the need to organize awareness initiatives regarding their effect on investment performance. The study findings will also inform policy formulation by the NSE and the Capital Markets Authority. The study will form a basis for future related research by scholars.

The study contributes to the theory of behavioural finance by extending the understanding of which behavioural factors, and to what extent, influence individual investors while making investment decisions. In addition, escalation of commitment was found to affect individual investors' decision-making, thereby extending the understanding of its effect on investment decision-making and investment performance.

Scope, Delimitation, and Limitations of the Study

The scope, delimitation, and limitations of the study are discussed in this section. The purpose is to highlight the extent and the limitations of the study. These concepts are discussed as follows.

Scope of the Study

The study was limited in time; therefore, it was necessary to identify the area of study. The study covered the population of individual investors of the NSE. The respondents were identified from those who have equity trading accounts with brokerage firms registered with offices in Nairobi and Nakuru cities in Kenya. This study was a cross-sectional study because data collection was conducted at one point in time during the year 2018.

Delimitations of the Study

The study had the following delimitations:

1. The study considered the behavioral factors (herding, prospect, heuristic) and market factors influencing the investment performance of the individual investors in the NSE.
2. Cross-sectional data were collected between January and March 2018 from individual investors registered with brokerage firms.
3. The data were collected from individual investors residing within the Nairobi and Nakuru cities in Kenya.

Limitations of the Study

The study had the following limitations:

1. The sample of this study was drawn from investors in the NSE who are registered with brokerage firms in Kenya using convenience sampling; hence, the results may not be generalizable to all individual investors of the NSE. In addition, the findings of this study may be cautiously generalized to other developing countries.
2. The study was limited by time. This is because the time between embarking on the study and its completion was restricted. This limitation affected the amount of data that could be collected and analyzed.
3. The questionnaire instrument was used to collect data. Therefore, other techniques of data collection, such as interviews, were not used. This limited the data collection to that which could be obtained through questionnaires.

Assumptions of the Study

The following assumptions were made while conducting the study. First, the individual investors in the NSE were expected to exhibit behavioral factors while trading in equity shares, which influence individual investment decisions. In the same breath, investor behavior was also expected to influence investment performance. Second, the researcher was assumed to be free from bias while collecting data from the respondents in order to obtain accurate data for analysis to answer the research questions adequately. Third, the analysis was assumed to be conducted objectively, and not subjectively, to achieve accurate findings.

Definition of Terms

Availability bias has been defined as "people assess[ing] the frequency of a class or the probability of an event with the ease with which instances or occurrences can be brought to mind" (Tversky & Kahneman, 1974, p. 1127). The study adopted this definition because individual investors are postulated to make investment decisions using easily available information.

Behavioral finance is "financial decision making that incorporates psychology and sociology" (Shiller, 2003, p. 83). This definition was adopted for this study because it identifies the effect of psychological and sociological factors on financial decision-making.

Investment performance is the perception of individual investors regarding the degree to which market efficiencies (weak, semi-strong, and strong forms) impact their investment performance. This definition was used for this study because market efficiencies are expected to guide individual investors in making investment decisions in the stock market, which will ultimately affect both the stock market and individual investment performance.

Escalating commitment is defined as "the tendency of decision makers to persist with failing courses of action" (Brockner, 1992, p. 39). This definition was adopted for this study because individual investors may continue to invest in equities that are performing poorly.

Expert information has been defined as "the content generated by professional" (Adams, 2004; van Kerkhoff & Lebel, as cited in Weible, 2008, p. 615). This definition was adopted for this study because individual investors may seek and use expert advice when making investment decisions.

Herding behavior is the "intent by investors to copy the behavior of other investors" (Bikhchandani & Sharma, 2001, p. 281). This definition was adopted for this study because individual investors are postulated to copy and imitate the decisions of other investors.

Heuristic behavior is where people "reduce the complex tasks of assessing probabilities and predicting values to simpler judgmental decisions" (Tversky & Kahneman, 1974, p. 1124). Individual investors may use heuristics in decision-making since they are limited in analyzing probabilities to make predictions for decision-making. Therefore, this definition was adopted for this study.

Individual investors are investors who purchase securities under their name (Kaur & Vohra, 2012, p. 10). They normally have accounts with brokerage firms, and decisions on the type, timing, and number of securities to buy or sell are made individually. This definition was adopted for this study.

Investment behaviors are defined as "how the investors judge, predict, analyse and review the procedures for decision making, which includes investment psychology, information gathering, defining and understanding, research and analysis" (Lee, Wang, Kao, Chen, & Zhu, 2010, p. 2). This definition was adopted for this study.

Irrational decision-making is "the deviation from the expected or from the rational decision-making models and, hence, the exhibition of heuristics and biases" (Polič, 2009, p. 81). This study adopted this definition because individual investors are expected to deviate from the rational decision-making process when making investment decisions in the stock market.

Loss aversion is defined as "prefer[ing] the certain prospect (x) to any risky prospect with expected value of x" (Kahneman & Tversky, 1979, p. 264). This definition was adopted for this study. Individual investors make decisions to avoid losses.

Overconfidence is the "overestimation of the precision of private information" (Glaser & Weber, 2007, p. 6). This definition was adopted for this study. Individual investors are expected to overestimate their abilities in trading in the stock market.

Rational decision making is the situation which "requires the decision makers to analyze alternative choices available and then selecting the one that has the highest value to the decision maker" (Oliveira, 2007, p. 12). Therefore, individual investors are expected to make choices between different investment opportunities in the stock market. This definition was adopted for this study.

Regret aversion is defined as the "desire by the decision maker to avoid consequences in the individuals will appear, after the fact, to have made the wrong decision, even if in advance, the decision appeared to be correct with the information available at the time" (Bell, 1982, p. 961). The study adopted this definition. This is because individual investors are expected to make decisions to avoid regretting later.

Prospect behavior is the decision making that takes into account the anticipated gains and losses (Kahneman & Tversky, 1979, p. 264). This meaning of prospect was adopted for this definition. This is because the study anticipated individual investors would consider the expected gains and losses before making decisions.

Public information is "the information shared by everyone" (Morris & Shin, 2002, p. 1521). This definition was adopted for the study. This is because public information is in the public domain and can be used for decision making by individual investors.

Organization of the Study

This book is organized into five chapters. Chapter 1 presents the background of the study, the problem statement, purpose, research questions, research hypotheses, and significance of the study. The chapter concludes with limitations, delimitations, and definitions of terms. Chapter 2 presents the review of related literature.

Chapter 3 presents the research methodology employed in the study. Chapter 4 describes the findings of the study. Chapter 5 presents the discussion and conclusions of the research and offers recommendations for further research. The discussion is based on the significant findings of the study. The chapter that follows provides the related literature that was reviewed for the study.

2 | Review of Related Literature

This chapter provided a review of the relevant literature and the theories that guided the study. The literature review was facilitated by the preparation of a literature review matrix on the influence of investor behavior on investment decisions and the degree of market efficiency's impact on investment performance. The development of the variable synthesis matrix was done to aid the writing process of the literature review. This chapter discussed efficient market theory and behavioral finance theories as the foundation of investor behavior.

Introduction

A review of related literature is essential for any research to uncover what has been previously studied and to identify emerging trends (Saunders, Lewis, & Thornhill, 2007), which become the foundation of the study. Further, the literature review critically analyzes the work of other authors (Jankowicz, as cited in Saunders et al., 2007, p. 60). This study used the funnel method of literature review as proposed by Saunders et al. (2007), which starts with a general-level literature review, followed by narrowing down to studies related to the study, and finally critiquing the previous related studies. The general-level literature review enabled the researcher to acquire key ideas and themes of investor behavior, investment decisions, and investment performance. Narrowing down to studies related to the current study enabled the researcher to identify the findings and trends in the topic of interest. Critiquing journal articles from past studies enabled the researcher to highlight the gaps that the current study intended to address.

General Level Review of Literature

This review required a search for studies on behavioral finance across disciplines to identify major contributors and the theories supporting the topic. The literature search using keywords was conducted through online databases including Google Scholar, ProQuest, and EBSCOhost. The online articles were also beneficial in the literature review process. A literature review search summary matrix showing the databases searched, search terms used, results, and relevant articles was provided as Appendix E.

Narrowed Literature Review

This stage was important in determining and focusing the research proposal. Journal article abstracts, research questions, theories, methodologies, findings, conclusions, and recommendations were read and compared with the research topic. Those that were found to be relevant had their full texts downloaded and filed in folders according to the study variables. The relevant articles were determined by their relation to the topic and their focus on behavioral factors of investor behavior and investment performance. Another criterion for inclusion was that the publications had to be recent—within the last ten years, that is, from 2008 to the current year. Articles published more than ten years ago were included only if they were considered important for situating the study regarding theoretical development by key authorities in the area. Another inclusion criterion was that the journal articles had to be peer-reviewed. The downloaded journal articles were uploaded into the Mendeley application for easy retrieval, citation, and referencing. A backup of the files was maintained on an external hard disk and Google Drive.

Critical Review of Relevant Literature

Finally, both theoretical and empirical studies were reviewed critically. The major ideas from past studies on each variable were synthesized and summarized. The propositions and findings of the studies were analyzed critically, evidenced, and cited using APA style. The literature review matrix, variable matrix, and variable synthesis matrix were prepared. This search enabled the researcher to identify gaps in the literature, thereby focusing the current study.

A review of literature on individual investors' behavior and investment performance was conducted. The literature review started with investment performance as the dependent variable. The review followed the following steps: the concept, situating the concept historically, definitions, philosophical foundations, biblical perspective, theories, benefits and costs, and the indicators.

Concept of Investment Performance

Investment is the commitment of resources in the current period by individual investors for a period with the expectation of earning a return (Bodie, Kane, & Marcus, 2014). In other words, individual investors postpone current consumption of funds for future consumption. There are many investment vehicles, which are classified into real assets and financial assets. Real assets are those used in the production of goods and services—for example, land and buildings (Bodie et al., 2014). On the other hand, financial assets are claims on the real assets. Therefore, the owners of financial assets share the returns generated by the real assets. Individual investors buying stocks invest in the real assets.

Investment performance is measured by the return generated by the investment. The return earned by investment has received significant attention because of the scarcity of resources and the need to direct investments to ventures with higher returns. An individual investor compares the risks of investments and their rewards to make investment choices (Nwude, 2012). Therefore, the importance of measuring investment performance. The two types of performance measures include financial and non-financial. Individual investors are more interested in the financial measurement of investment performance. Financial measurement is quantifiable and easily comparable across investments. The actual performance of an investment is the return that the investment realizes (Ranjbar, Abedini, & Jamali, 2014, p. 82). Individual investors measure the performance of the investment by the actual return realized.

There are several methods of evaluating the performance of an investment. Some of these methods include return on assets, return on capital, return on equity, and earnings yield (Bodie et al., 2014). Earnings yield would be of interest to individual investors in the stock market. Stock investment performance (earnings yield) is determined by the increase in share price (capital gains) and the dividends paid by the stock, which together give the total return from the stock investment. When the total return per stock is divided by the price paid per stock, it gives the return. Investors in the stock market may possess a single stock or several stocks from which they expect to earn a satisfactory return. Individual investors' performance may be influenced by market-related factors and individual investor behavior (Ngoc, 2013). In addition, stock market investment performance may also depend on the efficiency of the market in providing information that is relevant for investment decision-making.

Investor behavior may lead investors to make irrational decisions (Aduda et al., 2012), which may result in losses in the stock market (Vijaya, 2014). Therefore, investors are likely to underperform relative to market performance. In fact, they may earn a return that is less than what the market earns—for example, the average return in the NSE. Individual investor underperformance has been related to the transaction costs of excessive trading and poor stock-picking skills (Park & Kim, 2014).

Situating the Concept of Investment Performance Historically

Economist Adam Smith, in the 17th century, noted that economic behavior is the result of self-interest (Ashraf, Camerer, & Loewenstein, 2005). Individuals and nations get involved in economic activities because they want to promote their self-interest. Promoting self-interest was enhanced by investment of resources in economic activities so as to earn returns. This wealth creation ensured that the self-interest of individuals and nations was promoted since poverty levels were reduced. Keynes and Fisher postulated that investments should generate future cash flows (Eklund, 2013). Keynes and Fisher went on to say that investment should be done until the present value of the future cash flows is equal to the cost of the investment. This gave rise to the need to measure the performance of investments so as to make investment decisions

Individual investors are interested in increasing their wealth by making good investment decisions. These good decisions depend on the available information, especially the returns that investments promise to earn. Adam Smith talked about the growth of economies through increasing returns to scale, hence initiating the investment performance. In addition, Keynes and Fisher postulated that as long as the revenues generated are higher than the opportunity cost of capital, investors should continue to commit their resources to investments (Eklund, 2013). When the revenues generated equal the opportunity cost of capital, the investment should be stopped. Therefore, if losses are realized, then that is not a good investment.

Ratios have evolved, dating back to 300 B.C., when Euclid conducted an analysis of ratios (Anjum, 2011). However, the actual use of ratios to measure investment performance started in the 1900s. It appeared towards the maturity period of the Industrial Revolution in America. From that time, more ratios have been developed to measure investment performance.

The development of ratios has seen them categorized into accounting ratios and market ratios (Al-Matari, Al-Swidi, & Fadzil, 2014). The accounting-based ratios include return on assets, return on equity, return on investment, and earnings per share. On the other hand, the market-based ratios include Tobin's Q, dividend yield, and price-earnings ratio. These ratios have become important in measuring investment performance. There are many ratios investors may use, and the ratio to use in measuring investment performance will depend on the objective of the user. Investors in the stock market want to know whether their investments are earning sufficient return. Stock market investors are likely to use return on investment, earnings per share, dividend yield, and price-earnings ratio.

The EMH influences investment performance because the available information in the market may dictate the decisions that individual investors will make. If the stock market is not efficient in readily providing the available information, individual investors may become noise traders and hence influence the performance of the stock market, which will affect their own investment performance. The EMH postulates that stock market prices should incorporate all available information about the stock and hence, it is not possible to beat the market. Moreover, price changes cannot be predicted since they are influenced by information. This information is expected to arrive randomly, giving it the name "random walk." With this regard, market efficiency is divided into weak, semi-strong, and strong forms of market efficiency. The market where the stock prices incorporate all past information is referred to as weak-form efficiency and, therefore, the analysis of past information may not help predict future price movements. As a result, investors will not be able to outperform the market. In addition, the semi-strong form of efficiency in the market postulates that stock prices incorporate publicly available information. Furthermore, stock prices instantaneously adjust to arriving news. The strong form of market efficiency states that stock prices incorporate both public and private available information (Fama, 1970).

In the weak-form EMH, stock prices fully reflect all available historical information, such as data on the trading volume of stocks and their rates of return. In addition, the rates of return are independent and hence have no relationship with past rates of return and other historical market data. As a result, investors cannot make excess returns by making decisions to buy or sell using past information (Fama, 1970).

For the semi-strong form EMH, security prices are expected to rapidly change with the release of all information that is in the public domain. In other words, current stock prices fully reflect all public information. In addition, the weak-form hypothesis is included in the semi-strong EMH since all public information is incorporated in the stock prices. The strong-form EMH states that stock prices fully incorporate both private and public information. In addition, no investor will have a monopoly on access to information that will enable them to earn excess returns over the market return. Therefore, no investor can earn rates of return that are above the adjusted average risk (Fama, 1970).

The EMH is very important to investors in providing information for evaluating investment opportunities and, ultimately, making investment choices. This may be the reason that investors tend to concentrate on popular stocks. Furthermore, investors' decisions are influenced by the captivating happenings in the securities market, although they may not be aware of whether these events will result in good investment returns in the future or not (Barber & Odean, 2000).

The stock market may display some inefficiency in the provision of available information. This inefficiency is caused by anomalies arising from technical, fundamental, and calendar factors. For example, anomalies that are fundamental relate to the semi-strong form of EMH. Fundamental analysis postulates that some stocks outperform others and are hence good for investments.

The EMH is theoretically based on three key concepts: investors are rational, rational traders would cancel out the effect of irrational traders, and discrepancies in stock prices are eliminated. Moreover, investors should only be guided by the available information when making investment decisions. In contrast, stock prices should not change if there is no new information being made available by the stock market (Fama, 1970). The EMH has key implications for individual investors. Information is instantly incorporated into stock prices and, hence, analyzing the available information will not help investors to beat the market.

The NSE is a securities market in Kenya, started in 1954 when it was registered as a society formed by a group of stockbrokers. At that time, there was no framework for dealing with buying and selling of shares. In 1990, the Capital Markets Authority (CMA) was formed to promote and facilitate the development of capital markets in Kenya. The NSE trades in equities and bonds, but recently, trading in derivatives was introduced.

Trading in the NSE is automated. The composition of traders in the NSE comprises 65.41% institutions, 13% East African individuals, and 21.64% foreign investors. The number of local individual investors stood at 1,229,886, holding 42,395,118,270 shares, representing 52.39% of the value of equities, while the number of local individual bondholders is 3,936, holding Kenya shillings 4,614,896,162 billion, representing 5.24% (Capital Market Authority, 2015). Furthermore, the number of local individual investors was 1,196,995 in 2017 (Capital Market Authority, 2017). This figure indicates that interest in trading in stocks has increased suddenly. In addition, several cases of oversubscription for companies that have floated their initial subscription of shares (IPO) show the increase in interest in trading in stocks. The growing interest in investing in the stock market shows the increasing importance of measurement of investment performance.

Definitions of Investment Performance

Investment performance is measured by the return it generates for the individual investor. Return has been measured using both accounting-based and market-based metrics. Return can represent several measures of profitability (Al-Matari et al., 2014). Some of these measures are listed as follows:

1. Return on assets (ROA), which represents the net income divided by net assets for a given period.
2. Return on equity (ROE), calculated as the net profit minus tax divided by the value of shares outstanding at the end of a trading period.
3. Return on investment (ROI), which is the return divided by the cost of investment.
4. Earnings per share (EPS), representing the net income divided by the total number of outstanding shares.
5. Return on capital employed (ROCE), defined as the profit before tax divided by the capital issued.
6. Tobin's Q, defined as the market capitalization plus total debt divided by the total assets of the firm.

7. Dividend yield, which defines return as the dividend per share divided by the price per share.

In this study, investment performance was viewed as the degree of market efficiency's impact on investment performance. It was measured by the perception of individual investors' agreement on the degree to which market efficiencies (weak, semi-strong, and strong forms) impact their investment performance. This is because market efficiencies are expected to guide individual investors in making investment decisions in the stock market, which ultimately affect both the performance of the stock market and the individual's investment performance.

Individual investors who do not make their investment decisions using information available in the stock market through the Efficient Market Hypothesis (EMH) will exhibit irrationality, which negatively affects their investment performance. Therefore, they will earn a return that is not equivalent to the market's return. On the other hand, investors who use the information provided by the EMH can potentially benefit. Fama (1998) noted that individuals in the stock market tend to overreact to past information, which reverses the performance of past stock winners and losers. This means that stocks which were winners in the past period will become losers, and those that were losers will become winners.

Philosophical Foundations of Investment Performance

Philosophy guides the generation of knowledge. This study employed a positivist paradigm to investigate investment performance (Saunders et al., 2007). This approach was appropriate since the study began by reviewing existing theories in order to explain the antecedents of investment performance. Philosophy can be discussed under the following categories: metaphysics, ontology, epistemology, and axiology.

Metaphysics deals with what is real (Saunders et al., 2007). In other words, what causes things to happen in the world? Additionally, nothing happens without being caused; therefore, there is a force behind every occurrence. Investment performance was postulated to be caused by irrational factors.

Ontology examines the nature of existence, which can be internal or external (Saunders et al., 2007). This study postulated that knowledge exists external to the researcher. Epistemology considers the nature of truth. In this study, truth was represented by facts that can be realized through objective observation. Axiology is concerned with values. In this study, the researcher maintained a value-free stance so that actual facts could be realized from the data collected and analyzed.

Aristotle was one of the greatest philosophers and significantly influenced the philosophical foundations of investment performance. He discussed how irrationality influences human decisions. The current study postulated that investment performance is affected by the irrationality of individual investors. First, Aristotle noted that human beings are rational in their capacity for speech, making them social beings (Reed & Johnson, 2012). However, he also observed that humans possess elements of irrationality, similar to animals. Therefore, individuals are expected to make rational investment decisions by evaluating various options and selecting those that provide the highest return, thereby promoting their self-interest.

Aristotle supported empirical inquiry, leading him to reject some of Plato's work (Reed & Johnson, 2012). Empirical studies are necessary to either reject or support emerging theories. This study was empirical and thus supported by Aristotelian philosophy, as it aimed to collect data to determine the influence of investor behavior on investment performance.

In order to make sound investment decisions and realize strong investment performance, individual investors should follow logical reasoning. Aristotle, considered the father of logic (Reed & Johnson, 2012), developed a formal system of reasoning. This reasoning is expected to enhance the quality of investment decision-making, thereby improving investment performance.

Furthermore, Aristotle postulated that managing a household requires the acquisition of wealth (Reed & Johnson, 2012). He stated that wealth is not acquired for its own sake, but for the use to which it is put. This philosophical view supported the rationale for this study, as individual investors seek to increase their wealth through stock market investments. These investments aim to improve their well-being. Therefore, individual investors should ensure that their wealth is used for the benefit of their family and society at large. As Aristotle noted, individuals possess both rationality and irrationality, which may affect their reasoning and, in turn, their investment performance (Reed & Johnson, 2012).

A study by Tversky and Kahneman (1986) describes the normative model, in which people are expected to use logic to make decisions under risk, but this does not always represent actual behavior. This implies that people may not be fully rational and may exhibit irrational behavior. This study also aligns with that philosophical view. In another study, Kahneman (2003) highlighted that people may not be fully rational due to limitations in the information they possess. In conclusion, this study was well grounded in philosophical underpinnings.

Biblical Perspectives of Investment Performance

Trust is one of the themes in the Bible whereby man is supposed to be accountable to God for the resources that have been placed under his care. This trust is expected to be portrayed by individual investors' behavior in decision-making. Furthermore, investment decisions are important in determining the investment performance that investors are likely to achieve from their investments. Therefore, God presumes that man should utilize the resources prudently, the way He would have done. Genesis 1:26 records that God created man in His image and placed him as the manager of all the creation of God. This shows that everything on earth belongs to God the Creator.

This created a relationship of creator and steward between God and man. The parable of the talents shows how God expects us to handle the resources He has placed under our care (Matthew 25:15). The Bible narrates a story of a person who went on a long journey. He gave the workers talents according to their ability: five talents to the first, two talents to the second, and one talent to the third.

The ones who received five and two talents immediately set out to invest the talents and received a return on their investments. The one who received one talent hid it and, hence, earned no return. The person was pleased with the ones who invested the talents and earned some return, but was disappointed with the one who did not earn any return because he did not invest the talent. This shows that God expects individual investors to invest and make good returns.

The story of the talents shows how God places importance on the prudent use of resources. The behavior of an individual influences how prudently the individual utilizes those resources. Proverbs 21:5 notes that "hasty leads only to want." The term *hasty* clearly indicates that the behavior of an individual influences him to make decisions that may lead to the incurring of losses. Therefore, individuals should check their behavior so that they can reduce the losses which may result from biases. This is the biblical basis of investor behavior. Therefore, there is a clear relationship between the biblical worldview and the proposed topic of the influence of investor behavior on investment performance.

Theoretical Foundations of Investment Performance

The theories of investment performance began evolving when economists, led by Adam Smith, examined the investment of scarce resources to promote economic growth. This led to the development of methods for measuring investment outcomes. Some of the theories that have contributed to the development of investment performance are discussed in the following sections.

Economic Growth Theory

Adam Smith, in his book *The Wealth of Nations*, postulated that nations can increase their growth by investing the resources they have (Ashraf et al., 2005). Therefore, a country with resources that does not invest them will not create wealth. This means that investment was to be measured by the resulting economic growth. This principle can also be applied to individual investors. Individual investors should invest the resources they have to earn a return. This theory did not consider how investments should be evaluated for the ultimate choice of investment opportunities.

Q Theory of Investment

Tobin's Q theory was postulated by Brainard and Tobin in 1968. The theory states that investors would continue to invest up to the point where "the market value of assets is equal to the replacement costs of the assets" (Eklund, 2013, p. 8). In other words, Tobin's Q is the market-to-book ratio. Therefore, the market value of assets is divided by the book value of those assets. This theory has a limitation due to the potential measurement errors in market and book values, which can render the Q value inaccurate. Nevertheless, Tobin's Q is very useful in measuring investment opportunities. It is noted that listed firms may be valued differently from their actual value. This can be addressed by adding an error term to the market value of the firm's assets. Therefore, if the Efficient Market Hypothesis (EMH) is true, the market value of the assets will "contain all historical, public and private information" (Eklund, 2013, p. 10).

Efficient Market Theory

Fama (1970) postulated that an efficient market should incorporate the available information in stock prices. This gave rise to three forms of market efficiency. The three forms of the Efficient Market Hypothesis (EMH) were distinguished by the kind of information available in the stock market.

- First, the weak form fully reflects all the available past information in stock prices (Fama, 1970). Therefore, investors cannot earn an excess return by evaluating past information about stocks.
- Second, the semi-strong form fully reflects all available past and public information in stock prices. Hence, investors may not earn above-market returns from investing based on the evaluation of past and public information.
- Third, the strong form fully reflects all past, public, and insider information in stock prices. In that case, investors would not earn above-market returns by investing based on past, public, and private information. Therefore, a market will be efficient to the extent of the information available within it.

In the early stages of the EMH, the assertion that stocks fully reflect the available information indicated that "successive price changes are independent" of past stock prices (Fama, 1970, p. 386). In addition, future price changes or returns would be identically distributed. These two conditions explained the concept of a random walk. During the early stages of the EMH, the supporting evidence was extensive, with limited and contrary findings.

However, in a meta-analysis conducted on African stock markets, Gyamfi, Kyei, and Gill (2017) found that the EMH could not be validated as it was in its early years. Publication bias affected information market efficiency, while the type of test conducted, data collected, and location of the study did not affect the conclusions. This study found that the weak form of EMH had a positive but not statistically significant result. Regarding the semi-strong form, the study found that markets were considered inefficient. This may be due to some investors being privy to public information that others are not. These findings indicate that African stock markets may report some form of weak efficiency, but semi-strong and strong forms of efficiency are unlikely.

The efficient market hypothesis assumes that financial markets are efficient since security prices incorporate all relevant information. This implies that all investors have the same set of information, and therefore, no investor has an advantage over others regarding investment decision-making. This symmetry of information ensures that stock prices in the securities market reflect the fundamental values of those securities. Hence, efficiency in the market, combined with well-informed investors, ensures that no bubbles will form in the stock market (Abreu & Brunnermeier, 2003). The argument is that informed investors would exploit any arbitrage opportunity through buying and selling, thereby eliminating discrepancies in stock pricing.

Although stock markets were expected to be efficient with no anomalies, studies have shown that anomalies do occur in the stock market (Malkiel, 1989). Over time, financial markets have experienced anomalies that cannot be explained by the EMH. This has led to growing interest in behavioral finance. The persistence of anomalies in financial markets may be due to investors influenced by behavioral factors (Abreu & Brunnermeier, 2003). Investor performance is influenced by stock market efficiency. In the absence of efficient markets, behavioral factors become critical in investment decision-making. Konstantinidis, Katarachia, Borovas, and Voutsa (2012) highlighted the weaknesses of the EMH and proposed that behavioral finance should guide profitable investing. In other words, investors may use behavioral finance to maximize their investment performance.

Benefits and Costs of Investment Performance

Investment performance is critical for both individuals and firms. It enables individual investors to monitor increases or reductions in their wealth. Since individual investors are interested in increasing wealth for future consumption, investment performance is vital. It allows investors to decide which investments to retain and which to discard from their portfolios. As noted by Al-Matari et al. (2014), it is not possible for individual investors to improve their investment process without measuring outcomes.

While it is beneficial to measure investment performance, it comes with costs. First, individual investors must expend resources, such as money, to acquire the necessary statistics to determine investment returns. Second, some investors may find it difficult to understand performance measures because the information is technical. Third, the information may be incorrect due to the use of inaccurate data in deriving performance measures.

Indicators of Investment Performance

Performance measurement is of interest to a firm's stakeholders. That is why stock market investors care about the performance of their stock investments. They invest with the expectation of achieving higher future returns. Traditionally, financial measures have been used to indicate investment performance (Wadongo, Odhuno, Kambona, & Othuon, 2010). Over time, performance measurement has come to include non-financial indicators.

The financial indicators of performance used by stock market investors include return on investment, earnings per share, and the price-earnings ratio. Non-financial measures include innovation and learning, quality improvement, and customer satisfaction (Bhatti & Awan, 2014). Financial performance indicators are considered short-term, while non-financial indicators are long-term oriented. Therefore, long-term performance indicators are important in guiding firms to achieve their strategic objectives. Financial performance indicators are used by stock market investors to make investment decisions. However, stock market performance may be determined by the kind of information available to market participants and how they use that information in making stock investment decisions.

Efficient market performance may be measured by the kind of information available to investors in the stock market. The forms of market efficiency include the strong form, semi-strong form, and weak form (Fama, 1998). Rational investors are expected to use the available information provided by the EMH and, therefore, earn returns equivalent to market performance. Thus, there will be neither excess returns nor underperformance.

This study measured stock market investment performance using individual investors' perceptions of the impact of market efficiency on investment performance. The weak market efficiency form postulates that past information is incorporated into stock prices; therefore, analyzing past information for investment decisions may not earn investors excess returns over market returns (Fama, 1970). The semi-strong form of market efficiency posits that stock prices reflect past and all publicly available information. Public information may include published financial statements, announced annual earnings, dividends, and stock splits.

The strong form of market efficiency indicates that stock prices incorporate all available public and private information (Fama, 1970). Stock prices will reflect all information, including insider information, thereby ensuring that no investor has a monopoly on information. Consequently, no investor can earn excess returns based on insider information.

The sections that follow discuss the antecedents of investment performance. The antecedents are discussed in the following order: behavioural antecedents (herding, prospect, and heuristic) and market antecedents (public and expert information). The discussion begins with concepts, definitions, theories, and indicators, and concludes with the relationship between each antecedent and investment performance.

Antecedents of Investment Performance

Investment performance is influenced by both behavioral and market factors. Investor behavior is influenced by the fact that individual investors are not fully rational. This leads them to exhibit heuristics and biases that affect their investment performance. On the other hand, the market provides information that influences individual investors in making investment decisions. The Efficient Market Hypothesis (EMH) postulates that an efficient stock market should reflect all available information in stock prices. Hence, if investors use this information to make investment decisions, their investment performance will be equal to the stock market performance. Therefore, market factors may also affect individual investors' investment performance. The antecedents of investment performance are discussed under behavioral factors and market factors in the following sections.

Behavioral Factors

The growth of behavioral finance aimed to address the limitations of the traditional finance paradigm, especially EMH. Furthermore, behavioral finance argued that investment decisions are not always made using full rationality. In addition, it attempted to explain financial decisions by removing the two foundations of traditional finance. First, agents do not correctly change their beliefs. Second, agents are not following the normative process while making investment choices (Barberis & Thaler, 2003).

There are three foundations of behavioral finance. One is limits to arbitrage, which assumes that rational traders lack the ability to use arbitrage to eliminate the mispricing caused by irrational traders (Barberis & Thaler, 2003). Therefore, arbitrage opportunities will continue to exist and have an impact on security prices. Behavioral finance uses cognitive psychology and biases to explain investor irrationality. This arises when people form beliefs and preferences that influence their decision-making (Barberis & Thaler, 2003).

The second foundation is psychology. This shows how individuals are influenced by biases in forming their beliefs and preferences, which ultimately affect their decision-making. The third foundation is sociology. Sociology shows how the social interactions of investors influence them in decision-making. This contradicts the postulate of EMH, which emphasizes that individuals make decisions on their own without external influences.

Two approaches to understanding human behavior in investment decision-making include traditional finance and behavioral finance. Traditional finance postulates that investors are rational by considering all available information to make decisions that will maximize their wealth (Fama, 1970). As such, prices are right, meaning that stocks reflect all available information, ensuring no free lunch. This means that investors will not earn a rate of return different from the market return of the stock. In addition, the stock markets are efficient, and stock prices represent their true value. Further, investors should react quickly to any new information. Therefore, stock prices will be updated instantaneously.

Behavioral finance was founded on psycho-social factors that contradict the notions of EMH. EMH assumes investors to be rational in decision-making. On the other hand, behavioral finance studies how psycho-social factors determine investment decisions. As noted by Sewell (2010), behavioral finance examines how psychology affects investors and the influence it has on the stock markets. There are two sets of psychological factors that influence behavioral finance: cognitive and emotional. Cognition refers to the way people think, while emotion represents the way people feel. Limits to arbitrage make markets inefficient. Therefore, investors do not use all the available information but instead select the information that appears important to them. Psycho-social factors influence investors while making investment decisions, which makes them irrational. This is because they do not use all available information in decision-making.

Financial theories assume that investors will be rational, in that they will use all available information for investment purposes. Further, investors will use the available information to make investment decisions. On the contrary, the behavior of individual investors influences their investment decisions in the stock market (Barberis & Thaler, 2003). Therefore, the rationality of individual investors in decision-making is negated by their individual behavior.

Shefrin (2001) noted that behavioral finance explains the effect of psychology on investment decisions. In addition, behavioral finance is financial decision-making that incorporates psychology and sociology (Shiller, 2003). This study adopts the definition of behavioral finance by Shiller (2003) because the study intends to determine the psychological and social factors that influence investment decisions. Behavioral finance explains the reasons why markets are inefficient (Sewell, 2010). Further, it indicates the effect of psychology in decision-making.

Herding Behavior

Herding behavior is one of the behavioral antecedents of investment performance. This factor looks at how people behave in groups. It is postulated that it affects investment decisions, which determine investment performance.

Concept of Herding Behavior

Market efficiency has, for quite some time, guided decision-making in the financial markets. In addition, there has been a debate on EMH for quite some time. The debate concerns whether the financial markets are fully efficient as postulated by EMH (Malkiel, 1989). The existence of irrational investors promotes the inefficiency of stock markets because of the unpredictability of their investment decisions. The irrational behavior of individual investors may distort the fundamental values of financial assets in the financial markets and, hence, make the financial markets inefficient (Kofarbai & Zubairu, 2016). Moreover, individuals should recognize the mistakes they make, the reasons for the mistakes, and ways of avoiding the mistakes. The irrationality of individual investors is influenced by the following behavioral factors: herding, prospect, and heuristic.

Definitions of Herding Behavior

Scholars have defined herding behavior in different ways (see Table 1). Bikhchandani and Sharma (2001) posit that herding behavior is the "intent by investors to copy the behavior of other investors" (p. 281). Individual investors copy what others are doing in the financial markets. According to Christie and Huang (1995), herding is when "investors are drawn to the consensus of the market" (p. 32). Herding is a situation where "economic agents are imitating each other's actions and/or base their decisions upon the actions of others" (Spyrou, 2013, p. 175). In the words of Cipriani and Guarino (2014), herding is when "a trader trades against his own private information in order to conform to the information contained in the history of trades" (p. 232). In this study, herding is conceptualized as copying other investors, imitating other investors, and conforming to the actions of other investors.

Author	Theme	Definition	No. of Citations
Bikhchandani and Sharma (2001)	Copy	"Intent by investors to copy the behavior of other investors" (p. 281)	87
Christie and Huang (1995)	Consensus	"Investors are drawn to the consensus of the market" (p. 32)	75
Spyrou (2013)	Imitating	"Economic agents are imitating each other actions and/or base their decisions upon the actions of others" (p. 175)	7
Cipriani and Guarino (2014)	Conform	"A trader herds when he trades against his own private information in order to conform to the information contained in the history of trades" (p. 232)	5

Table 1: Definitions of Herding

Theory of Herding Behaviour

A theory is "a set of interrelated concepts, which structure a systematic view of [a] phenomenon for the purpose of explaining or predicting" (Imenda, 2014). Also, a theory has been defined as "a set of interrelated constructs (variables), definitions, and propositions that presents a systematic [view] of phenomena by specifying relations among variables, with the purpose of explaining natural phenomena" (Kerlinger, 1979, as cited in Creswell,

2009). Therefore, theories form the basis of a study from which concepts that explain the phenomenon can be established. The independent and dependent variables are formulated to establish the relationships. This study used five theories, which were explained under each concept, starting with the herding theory.

A group of people is influenced by group psychology while making individual investment decisions. Furthermore, the behaviour of people differs when making decisions as a group compared to when they make decisions as individuals. This work on group behaviour gave birth to the thinking on herding. The work on group behaviour was pioneered by Mackay (1841), who showed the impact of groups on individuals while making personal decisions. Another work by Le Bon (1896) explained the relationship between the group and social psychology. Also, he showed how individuals are impacted by groups in decision making.

Herding is the habit of following or imitating the decision of other individuals in the group (Bikhchandani & Sharma, 2001). For example, investors are in a group, and investors will herd when they follow the decisions of other investors. Also, individuals may support group decisions, but when the decisions turn out to be bad, they retreat to safer havens as individuals (Mackay, 1841). There are two types of herding: spurious herding and intentional herding. Spurious herding occurs when people make similar decisions because they have the same set of information. If the investors are rational and have the same set of information, they are likely to arrive at the same decisions. On the other hand, intentional herding involves following the decisions of other individuals without taking into consideration any information. However, differentiating empirically between spurious and intentional herding is difficult (Bikhchandani & Sharma, 2001).

Individuals may herd for several reasons, which include investors believing that other investors have information that they may not have and conforming to other individual investors' decisions. Also, herding arises from the intentional copying of other investors' behaviour (Bikhchandani & Sharma, 2001). Therefore, they follow the decision of their peers (Vijaya, 2014). This will influence the decisions they take because they want to be like the other investors. The investors who herd may also quickly follow the decisions of other investors regarding the speed of buying, speed of selling stocks, and the volume of trading in stocks (Vijaya, 2014).

Herding effect is exhibited in a variety of different market conditions (Almeida et al., 2017). Actually, there will be different levels of herding between high trading volume days and low trading volume days. Moreover, Almeida et al. (2017) found herding to be present during periods of high trading volume in some areas, while others showed herding during low trading volume days. The methodologies adopted in Almeida et al. (2017) attempted to detect indications of herd behaviour in stock markets by determining the relationship between the dispersions of returns on individual assets and the average return of the market.

Indicators of Herding Behaviour

An indicator is used when concepts or dimensions of concepts cannot be directly measured. Therefore, the formulation of indicators of a concept enables its measurement in a practical way. Indicators "infer the value of actual phenomena of interest" (Singer, 1982, p. 12). The discussion of indicators was discussed under each concept, starting with herding behaviour.

Some studies (Aduda et al., 2012; Jagongo & Mutswenje, 2014; Kengatharan & Kengatharan, 2014; Rekik & Boujelbene, 2013; Vijaya, 2014) have confirmed the existence of herding behaviour. The individual investors were found to trade in the same direction, influenced by the decision of friends and colleagues and also by the popular opinion of the majority of investors. The effect of herding on the individual investors was found to be varied and, hence, not conclusive.

Herding has been measured by using the perception of individual investors on how the actions of other investors influence their own decision making. This is because herding is when investors imitate the actions of others (Rekik & Boujelbene, 2013). Individual investors will indicate herding by following the actions of other investors concerning when and how much to buy of the stocks. Vijaya (2014) noted that individual investors follow the decisions of others when they change their portfolio so as to be like them. In addition, Mackay (1841) postulated that individual investors will retreat to safer havens when the decision they had imitated turns out to be bad.

Herding behaviour was first noted by Selden (1912) when he pointed out that public opinion largely influences share prices. Public opinion influences how individual investors behave in the stock market. The individual investor will follow the decisions of other investors on the assumption that it is the correct decision since the majority of the population is supporting it. The decision will be whether to sell, buy, or hold onto a security as a result of the general public opinion. It has also been noted that the view of the majority of the stockholders influences investment decisions (Das, 2012). The questions on the questionnaire were derived from the aforementioned indicators.

Relationship between Herding Behaviour and Investment Performance

Researchers agree that investors exhibit herding behaviour, which affects their investment decisions. This herding behaviour exists at different levels of impact and usually affects investment performance (Goel, 2014; Khan, 2014). Herding was found to have low, moderate, and high impact levels. In addition, different economies exhibited different levels of impact. In a study, Chen (2013) found developed markets to have the strongest levels of herding, followed by frontier markets, and lastly, emerging markets. This indicated that herding affects investment decisions at different levels. In contrast, Ton and Dao (2014) found that herding did not affect investment decisions. Therefore, the findings of various studies are not conclusive on the level of impact of herding behaviour. Also, there is no consensus on the existence of herding among investors. There are also limited studies on herding among individual investors (Kumar & Goyal, 2015).

Herding behaviour influences the investment decisions of individual investors, thereby affecting investment performance. Also, herding has an influence on investment performance, although the performance is lower than the market return (Goel, 2014). This indicates that investors who exhibited herding underperformed compared to market performance. A study conducted on 128 stockholders of the Colombo Stock Exchange found herding to have a positive effect on investment performance ($\beta = 0.113$, $p \leq .05$; Kengatharan & Kengatharan, 2014).

Also, Ranjbar et al. (2014) conducted a study on 148 respondents of the Tehran Stock Exchange and found that herding had a significant effect on investment performance ($\beta = 0.21$, $p \leq .05$). Likewise, the effect of herding on investment performance was found to be significant by Nyamute et al. (2015), where $\beta = 0.182$, $p \leq .05$, in a study on 385 respondents of the NSE in Kenya. Khan (2014) also conducted a study on 150 respondents of the Karachi Stock Exchange and found the effect of herding on investment performance to be significant ($\beta = 0.49$, $p \leq .05$). Likewise, Luong, Thu Ha, and Owe (2011) found that there was a significant positive relationship between herding and investment performance.

In another study, Javed, Bagh, and Razzaq (2017) conducted research on the Pakistani Stock Exchange with 220 individual investors and found herding to have a significant positive relationship with investment performance ($\beta = .283$, $p < .05$). In addition, findings from a study of 200 individual investors in the Malaysian Stock Exchange showed a negative relationship with investment performance ($\beta = -.067$, $p < .05$). The results from these studies show that herding may have a significant but varying level of impact on investment performance. This study conceptualizes the relationship between herding and investment performance to be positive. Table 2 shows the summary of the relationship between herding and investment performance.

Prospect Behaviour

Prospect behaviour is another factor that influences investment performance. Prospect behaviour deals with what goes on in the minds of people when making decisions.

Concept of Prospect Behaviour

In their study, Kahneman and Tversky (1979) showed how people make decisions under risk and uncertainty. They noted that individuals are not consistently risk-averse. That is to say, for gains, they are risk-averse, while for losses, they are risk-takers. In other words, people value more the outcomes that are perceived to be certain than those that are considered less sure. This is known as the *certainty effect*.

Prospect theory postulates that investors will behave differently concerning prospective gains and losses. As such, investors will be more distressed by the prospect of losses than they will be happy about the equivalent gains they are likely to earn. In addition, investors will consider losing one dollar to be more painful than the pleasure of receiving a gain of one dollar.

Relationship	Nyamute et al. (2015)	Khan (2014)	Ranjbar et al. (2014	Kengatharan and Kengatharan (2014)	Luong et al. (2011)	Javed, Bagh, and Razzaq, (2017)	(Bakar & Yi, 2016)
HE-IP	β = 0.182, p ≤ .05	β = 0.49, p ≤ .05	β = 0.21, p ≤ .05	β = 0.113, p ≤ .05	β = 0.11, p ≤ .05	β = 0.283, p ≤ .05	β = -.067, p ≤ .05

Table 2: Relationship between Herding and Investment Performance
Note: HE: herding; IP: investment performance

Definition of Prospect Behaviour

There are a number of definitions that have been put forward for prospect behaviour. Kahneman and Tversky (1979) postulated prospect as the decision-making process that takes into account anticipated gains and losses. This causes individual investors to exhibit the following behaviours: loss aversion, regret aversion, and escalating commitment. These prospect dimensions are defined as follows.

Kahneman and Tversky (1979) defined loss aversion as when an individual "prefer[s] the certain prospect (x) to any risky prospect with expected value of x" (p. 264). Therefore, although the gains and losses may be equal, the individual will value gains more highly since they are certain when compared to losses. Also, loss aversion is when "people interpret outcomes as gains and losses relative to a reference point and are more sensitive to losses than to absolute commensurate gains" (Abdellaoui, Bleichrodt, & Paraschiv, 2007, p. 1659). Likewise, Barberis (2013) defined loss aversion as "the idea that people are much more sensitive to losses—even small losses—than to gains of the same magnitude" (p. 175). In addition, Ert and Erev (2003) defined loss aversion as "the absolute subjective value of a specific loss is larger than the absolute subjective value of an equivalent gain" (p. 214).

In this study, loss aversion was conceptualized as individual investors making decisions to avoid losses, becoming more risk-seeking with a positive return, and being more risk-averse with a negative return. Loss aversion has been defined in different ways as shown in Table 3.

Author	Theme	Definition	No. of Citations
Kahneman and Tversky (1979)	Preference	"Prefer the certain prospect (x) to any risky prospect with expected value of x" (p. 264)	9,942
Abdellaoui, Bleichrodt, and Paraschiv (2007)	Sensitivity	"People interpret outcomes as gains and losses relative to a reference point and are more sensitive to losses than to absolute commensurate gains" (p. 1659)	163
Barberis (2013)	Sensitivity	"The idea that people are much more sensitive to losses-even small losses-than to gains of the same magnitude" (p. 175)	90
Ert and Erev (2003)		"The absolute subjective value of a specific loss is larger than the absolute subjective value of an equivalent gain" (p. 214)	44

Table 3: Definitions of Loss Aversions

Regret aversion is also a prospect dimension. Several scholars have proposed definitions for this behaviour (see Table 4). Regret aversion has been defined by Loomes and Sugden (1982) as the "reflection on how much better his [her] position would have been, had he [she] chosen differently, and this reflection may reduce the pleasure he [she] derives from [the current position]" (p. 808). Another definition states that it is the "desire by the decision maker to avoid consequences in [which] the individual will appear, after the fact, to have made the wrong decision, even if in advance, the decision appeared to be correct with the information available at the time" (Bell, 1982, p. 961). In addition, Zeelenberg (1999) defined regret aversion as "a negative, cognitively based emotion that we experience when realizing or imagining that our present situation would have been better, had we decided differently" (p. 93). In this study, regret aversion was conceptualized as being more willing to sell those stocks whose prices have increased, less willing to sell those stocks whose prices have decreased, and feeling bad when the stocks not bought perform better. Also, the performance of the investment depends on luck and buying stocks that other investors are buying to avoid regretting alone.

Author	Theme	Definition	No. of Citations
Loomes and Sugden (1982)	Pleasure	"Reflect on how much better his [her] position would have been, had he [she]chosen differently, and this reflection may reduce the pleasure he [she] derives from [the current position]" (p. 808)	3,624
Bell (1982)		"Desire by the decision maker to avoid consequences in the individuals will appear, after the fact, to have made the wrong decision, even if in advance, the decision appeared to be correct with the information available at the time" (p. 961)	2,818
Zeelenberg (1999)	Experience	"A negative, cognitively based emotion that we experience when realizing or imagining that our present situation would have been better, had we decided differently" (p. 93)	317

Table 4: Definitions of Regret Aversion

The dimension of escalating the commitment has been defined by various scholars (see Table 5). Brockner (1992) defined escalating the commitment as "the tendency of decision makers to persist with failing courses of action" (p. 39). Escalating the commitment occurs when individual investors consider that "even if there is a wrong decision and the consequences confirm this, still there is an insistence for continuing and it intensifies the case" (p. 237). In addition, Kirkman and Shapiro (1998) considered escalating the commitment to be when "an individual pursues an investment strategy of increasing investment in a stock when prices are falling" (p. 166). On the other hand, escalating the commitment is when "a firm continues to invest in its previous course of action" (p. 83). Rutledge (1994) defined escalating the commitment as "an increased total investment can occur even when the project shows poor economic performance" (p. 12). In this study, escalating the commitment was conceptualized as continuing to invest even if losses were incurred in the previous period from the stock, continuing to invest even if unsure of attaining the goal, and continuing to invest even if the investment is known to be bad.

Author	Theme	Definition	No. of Citations
Brockner (1992)	Self-justification	"The tendency of decision makers to persist with failing courses of action" (p. 39)	365
(Sadi et al., 2011)		"Even if there is a wrong decision and the consequences confirm this, still there is an insist for continuing and it intensifies the case"(p. 237)	41
Kirkman and Shapiro (1998)	Self-justification	"An individual pursues an investment strategy of increasing investment in a stock when prices are falling" (p. 166)	10
Tang (1998)		"A firm continues to in its previous course of action" (p. 83)	9
Rutledge (1994)	Rationalization	"Increased total investment can occur even when the project shows poor economic performance" (p. 12)	8

Table 5: Definitions of Escalating the Commitment

Theories of Prospect Behaviour

This theory explains how the state of mind of investors affects their decision-making. This theory was postulated by Tversky and Kahneman (1979), providing an alternative to expected utility theory. Prospect theory notes that "people underweight outcomes that are merely probable in comparison with outcomes that are obtained with certainty" (Kahneman & Tversky, 1979, p. 263). This is called the *certainty effect,* which makes people risk-averse when it comes to certain gains and risk-seeking in the face of sure losses. The dimensions of prospect theory include loss aversion, regret aversion, and mental accounting.

One of the theories under prospect theory is loss aversion. Loss aversion refers to the tendency of individuals to make decisions aimed at avoiding losses. Prospect theory shows that people are "less willing to gamble with profit than with losses" (Vijaya, 2014, p. 298). Therefore, they will prioritize avoiding losses when making investment decisions.

The theory of regret aversion postulates that individuals desire to avoid the regret of making decisions that produce a less-than-expected return. Regret is a state of mind after realizing that a mistake has been committed (Luong et al., 2011). Therefore, what goes on in the minds of individual investors influences their decision-making. In addition, regret aversion shapes investors' decisions as they seek to avoid future regret about potential outcomes.

The theory of escalating commitment explains one aspect of prospect theory. Escalating commitment occurs when individuals continue to invest more resources into losing strategies (Lin et al., 2014; Lunenburg, 2010). Investors may continue to invest because they do not want to admit they made a wrong decision. Additionally, they may hope that the future will change the situation for the better.

Indicators of Prospect Behaviour

In their study, Kahneman and Tversky (1979) demonstrated how people make decisions under risk and uncertainty. They noted that individuals are not consistently risk-averse. That is to say, they are risk-averse when it comes to gains and risk-seeking when facing losses. In other words, people value outcomes perceived as certain more than those perceived as uncertain. This is known as the *certainty effect.*

Prospect theory postulates that investors behave differently when facing potential gains versus potential losses. As such, investors are more distressed by the prospect of losses than they are pleased by the equivalent gains they are likely to earn. In addition, investors may consider losing one dollar more painful than the pleasure of gaining one dollar. Prospect theory shows that people "are risk-averse in gains but risk-takers in losses" (Kishore, 1979, p. 12). This gives rise to loss aversion and regret aversion.

Loss aversion refers to the tendency of investors to "underweight outcomes that are merely probable in comparison with outcomes that are certain" (Kahneman & Tversky, 1979, p. 263). Therefore, there is a tendency for investors to strongly desire avoiding losses rather than striving for gains (Kahneman & Tversky, 1979). Indicators of loss aversion among individual investors include a high risk-taking attitude after positive stock returns, and more risk aversion after negative stock returns. Investors may avoid investments that promise higher gains but are uncertain and instead invest in options that are certain, even if the gains are smaller. In this case, investors overweight the value of certain investments. Studies (Kengatharan & Kengatharan, 2014; Sahi et al., 2013; Vijaya, 2014) have confirmed that loss aversion influences individual investors' decision-making. Therefore, loss aversion plays a significant role in shaping investors' decisions.

Regret aversion also influences investment decisions. Regret aversion is "the emotion that occurs after people make mistakes" (Vijaya, 2014, p. 299). Its indicators include investors' unwillingness to sell stocks that have decreased in value, and a readiness to sell stocks that have increased in value (Vijaya, 2014). Regret aversion occurs when investors make decisions aimed at avoiding regret over the outcomes of those decisions. As noted by Kishore (1979), people tend to feel the pain or fear of regret due to making errors. A study by Kengatharan and Kengatharan (2014) found that regret aversion influences individual investors' decisions. The fear of regret may influence investors to make errors in their investment decisions.

Escalating commitment refers to the tendency of decision-makers to persist with a decision even when it becomes clear that it is a poor one (Brockner, 1992). Escalation of commitment involves the continued allocation of resources to a failing investment decision. Escalating commitment has been found to influence decision-making and the persistence of those decisions (Lunenburg, 2010). Since escalating commitment has been found to influence decision-making in other domains, it is proposed that it may also affect investor decision-making. Indicators of escalating commitment include continuing to invest despite losses in a previous period, continuing to invest even when unsure of achieving the goal, and continuing to invest even when the investment is known to be poor.

Relationship between Prospect Behaviour and Investment Performance

A study by Luong et al. (2011) among 300 respondents on the Ho Chi Minh Stock Exchange found that the dimensions of prospect theory (regret aversion, loss aversion, and mental accounting) have a moderate effect on investment decisions, with a negative impact on investment performance ($\beta = -0.12$, $p \leq .05$). This indicates that investors who engage in disposition effects may exhibit poorer investment performance. Table 6 shows the relationship between prospect dimensions and investment performance.

Loss aversion and mental accounting have been found to negatively affect investment performance (Ranjbar et al., 2014), in a study conducted among 148 stock investors on the Tehran Stock Exchange. Kengatharan and Kengatharan (2014), in research involving 128 investors on the Colombo Stock Exchange, found loss aversion to have a negative but not statistically significant effect on investment performance ($\beta = -0.031$, $p > .05$). From the literature review, the relationship between loss aversion and investment performance is conceptualized as negative.

Relationship	Ranjbar et al. (2014)	Kengatharan and Kengatharan (2014)	Luong et al. (2011)	Turino and Soetjipto (2012)	Lin et al. (2014)
LA & MA-IP	$\beta = -.16$, $p \leq .05$				
LA-IP		$\beta = -.031$, $p > .05$			
RA-IP		$\beta = .104$, $p > .05$			
LA, RA & MA-IP			$\beta = -.12$, $p \leq .05$		
EC-IP				BE: $t = -.49$, $p > .05$ BU: $t = .70$, $P > .05$	$\beta = -.89$, $p \leq .10$

Table 6: Relationship between Prospect and Investment Performance

Note: LA: loss aversion; MA: mental accounting; IP: investment performance; RA: regret aversion; EC: escalating the commitment; BE: bearish period; BU: bullish period.

This indicates that investors who sell stocks to avoid losses are more likely to report negative outcomes in their investment performance. Regret aversion occurs when investors sell stocks to avoid losses. A study (Kengatharan & Kengatharan, 2014) found that regret aversion has a low positive but not significant influence on investment performance ($\beta = 0.104$, $p > 0.05$). Therefore, the effect of regret aversion on investment performance is low but not significant. The study conceptualized a positive relationship between regret aversion and investment performance.

Escalating the commitment is an indicator of the disposition effect but from the buying side. However, there is a lacuna in the literature on the escalation of the commitment dimension. A study (Lin et al., 2014) confirmed that escalating the commitment has a negative influence ($\beta = -0.89$, $p \leq 0.10$) on the investment performance of 250 mutual fund managers in the Taiwan Stock Exchange. Turino and Soetjipto (2012) conducted a study with 229 individual investors of the Indonesia Stock Exchange. The findings showed that escalating the commitment and performance of the individual investors had a negative relationship ($t = -0.49$) during the bearish period, but had a positive relationship ($t = 0.70$) that was not significant ($p > 0.01$). This study postulated a negative relationship between the escalation of the commitment and investment performance. There is a need to study the effect of escalating the commitment on investment decisions by individual investors and, ultimately, its effect on investment performance. This is because this dimension of prospect theory is understudied.

Heuristic Behaviour

Heuristics also influence investment performance. The heuristics factor refers to the mental shortcuts that people use to make decisions.

Concept of Heuristic Behaviour

Scholars have tried to define heuristics from the behavioural point of view. Heuristic has been defined as the reliance on mental shortcuts to make decisions (Tversky & Kahneman, 1974). In other words, individual investors simplify tasks in order to make quick decisions. The reasons for individual investors using mental shortcuts for decision-making include a shortage of time to analyse the available information and an inability to process that information. In addition, individual investors may lack the skills required to analyse investment opportunities.

Definitions of Heuristic Behaviour

Heuristic is where people "reduce the complex tasks of assessing probabilities and predicting values to simpler judgmental decisions" (Tversky & Kahneman, 1974, p. 1124). Individual investors may use heuristics in decision-making since they are limited in analysing the probabilities required to make predictions. There are several dimensions of heuristics, but the definitions of those that will be used for the study are provided.

Several definitions have been put forward (see Table 7) for availability bias. Tversky and Kahneman (1974) define availability bias as when "people assess the frequency of a class or the probability of an event with the ease with which instances or occurrences can be brought to mind" (p. 1127). This encourages people to use readily available information. Sewell (2010) defined availability bias as "a cognitive heuristic in which a decision maker relies upon knowledge that is readily available rather than examine other alternatives or procedures" (p. 8). On the other hand, availability bias is defined as "considering the easily recalled events more probable than those they can hardly imagine or perceive" (Sadi, Asl, Rostami, Gholipour, & Gholipour, 2011, p. 236). In this study, availability bias was conceptualized as individual investors investing in local companies, well-performing companies, and easily recalled names. In addition, individual investors buy the stock of companies with information in the public domain. They also do not change their portfolio.

Author	Theme	Definition	No. of Citations
Tversky and Kahneman (1974)	Ease	"People assess the frequency of a class or the probability of an event with the ease with which instances or occurrences can be brought to mind" (p. 1127)	45,514
Sewell (2010)		" A cognitive heuristic in which a decision maker relies upon knowledge that is readily available rather than examine other alternatives or procedures" (p. 8)	204
Sadi, Asl, Rostami, Gholipour, and Gholipour (2011)		"Consider[ing] the easily recalled events more probable than those they can hardly imagine of perceive" (p. 236)	41

Table 7: Definitions of Availability Bias

Overconfidence is another dimension of heuristic behaviour. There is no specific definition of overconfidence (Glaser & Weber, 2007). Some of the definitions are shown in Table 8. Glaser and Weber (2007) defined overconfidence as the "overestimation of the precision of private information" (p. 6). In the words of Biais, Hilton, Mazurier, and Pouget (2005), overconfidence is "the tendency to overestimate the precision of one's information" (p. 295). Overconfidence is when individual investors consider that "their knowledge is more accurate than it really is and that their forecasts are more precise than their experience should validate" (Baker & Nofsinger, 2002, p. 103).

Overconfidence has also been defined as "an inappropriate belief toward a witnessed reasoning, judgment, and the person's cognitive abilities" (Sadi et al., 2011, p. 236). This study conceptualized overconfidence as individual investors considering themselves better in terms of stock trading skills, forecasting stock prices accurately, and stock selection skills. They also believe they are able to trade stocks easily. Individual investors consider themselves to have the ability to trade without incurring significant risks.

Author	Theme	Definition	No. of Citations
Glaser and Weber (2007)	Miscalibration, too tight volatility estimates and better than average effect	"Overestimation of the precision of private information" (p. 6)	85
Biais, Hilton, Mazurier, and Pouget (2005)	Miscalibration	"The tendency to overestimate the precision of one's information" (p. 295)	75
Baker and Nofsinger (2002)	Illusion of knowledge and Illusion of control	"Their knowledge is more accurate than it really is and	42

		that their forecasts are more precise than their experience should validate" (p. 103)	
Sadi, Asl, Rostami, Gholipour, and Gholipour (2011)		"An inappropriate belief toward a witnessed reasoning, judgment, and the person's cognitive abilities" (p. 236)	41

Table 1: Definitions of Overconfidence

Theories of Heuristic Behaviour

The heuristic theory is when individuals simplify tasks so that decisions can be made quickly (Tversky & Kahneman, 1974). There are four heuristics that individuals can utilize. They include representativeness, availability, anchoring, and overconfidence.

Availability bias theory postulates that people will make decisions by taking into account the instances of easy retrieval of information on the occurrences of events (Tversky & Kahneman, 1974). Individual investors will relate to the information they can easily and quickly recall. Therefore, people will excessively use the easily available information (Luong et al., 2011). For example, investors may be influenced in decision-making by local companies which they can easily recall.

The theory on overconfidence notes that investors consider themselves to be more skillful at trading stocks than other investors and hence, eventually earn above-market returns (Ngoc, 2013). This heuristic causes individual investors to trade more in stocks than others. Indicators include miscalibration, overly narrow volatility estimates, and the better-than-average effect.

Indicators of Heuristic Behaviour

Individual investors are normally faced with complex situations during uncertainty that require them to make decisions. In addition, individual investors may not have the knowledge, capacity, or time to analyze the different scenarios to make decisions based on the fundamentals of the assets. Therefore, they may be forced to use shortcuts. Heuristics are where individuals develop rules by trial and error that guide them in processing data, which eventually enables them to make investment decisions (Águila, 2009). A study (Tversky & Kahneman, 1974) noted that individuals may use heuristics that turn complex situations into simpler decision-making ones. They normally employ mental shortcuts that are useful during complex situations. Tversky and Kahneman (1974) postulated that mental shortcuts may be useful in reducing the complexity of situations to simple decision-making processes, but individual investors may be biased in their decision-making. Consequently, they make investment decisions that are shrouded in error, leading them to incur losses.

Indicators of availability bias include using the available information in decision-making. In addition, Tversky and Kahneman (1974) noted that people use information they can easily remember to make financial decisions. Individual investors may use any of the following types of availability (Tversky & Kahneman, 1974). First, **retrievability** of the information—this is where individual investors use easily retrievable information to make investment decisions. The second is **categorization**—in this case, individual investors try to fit new information into the categories of information they already possess. The third is **narrow range of experience**—this is where individual investors refer to a limited set of information to make investment decisions. The fourth is **resonance**—this is when individual investors use information that matches their personal characteristics to make investment decisions.

The indicators of overconfidence show how individual investors make decisions based on their perceived abilities. The first indicator of overconfidence is **miscalibration**—the tendency of investors to perceive themselves as more skillful (Rekik & Boujelbene, 2013; Ton & Dao, 2014). This leads them to overestimate their trading capabilities. The second is the **better-than-average effect**, which postulates that they can make better decisions than other individual investors (Águila, 2009; Ton & Dao, 2014). The third is the **illusion of control**, where individual investors believe they are able to determine the outcome of an investment. Therefore, they believe they will make better investment decisions and hence, perform better than other investors. This belief exposes them to making errors. There is an influence of overconfidence on investment decisions (Vijaya, 2014).

Relationship between Heuristic Behaviour and Investment Performance

Availability bias influences investment decisions, which will ultimately have an impact on investment performance. A study by Javed et al. (2017) found that availability bias had a significant positive relationship with investment performance ($\beta = 0.285$, $p \leq .05$). Javed et al. (2017) conducted their study among 220 individual investors of the Pakistani stock exchange. In another study (Bakar & Yi, 2016), conducted among 200 individual investors of the Malaysian stock exchange, the relationship between availability bias and investment performance was also found to be significantly positive ($\beta = 0.466$, $p \leq .05$). Therefore, the findings of these studies confirm that availability bias influences investment decisions and, ultimately, investment performance. As such, there is a need to study availability bias further to understand its impact on investment decisions. This study postulated a positive relationship between availability bias and investment performance.

Investment decisions by overconfident investors will affect the outcome of investment performance. This is because overconfident investors will trade excessively, leading them to incur higher costs that may offset the returns earned. Studies have mixed findings on the influence of overconfidence on investment performance. Ranjbar et al. (2014) found that overconfidence and anchoring combined had a positive impact on investment performance ($\beta = 0.59$, $p \leq .05$). Ranjbar et al. (2014) conducted their study among 148 individual investors of the Tehran stock exchange. Further, a study by Luong et al. (2011), done with 300 individual investors of the Ho Chi Minh stock exchange, showed that overconfidence and the gambler's fallacy combined had a high positive impact on investment performance ($\beta = .68$, $p \leq .05$).

In another study (Javed et al., 2017), conducted with 220 individual investors of the Pakistani stock exchange, a significant positive relationship was found between overconfidence and investment performance ($\beta = .274$, $p \leq .05$). Also, Bakar and Yi (2016) determined the relationship between overconfidence and investment performance to be

significantly positive (β = .466, $p \leq .05$). This study by Bakar and Yi (2016) was conducted among 200 individual investors of the Malaysian stock exchange.
However, Kengatharan and Kengatharan (2014) conducted a study on 128 individual investors of the Colombo stock exchange in Sri Lanka and determined the relationship between overconfidence and investment performance to be significantly negative (β = -.356, $p \leq .05$). Similarly, Nyamute et al. (2015), conducting a study among 385 individual investors of the NSE, found that overconfidence had a significantly negative relationship with portfolio performance (β = -.134, $p \leq .05$). These findings indicate that the results are not conclusive on the direction and strength of the impact of overconfidence on investment performance. Therefore, more studies should be conducted on overconfidence so that its impact on investment performance can be confirmed. This study conceptualized the relationship between overconfidence and investment performance to be positive. Table 9 shows the relationship between heuristic dimensions and investor performance.

Relationship	Ranjbar et al. (2014)	Kengatharan and Kengatharan (2014)	Nyamute et al. (2015)	Luong et al. (2011)	Javed et al. (2017)	Bakar and Yi (2016)
AB-IP					β = 0.285, $p \leq .05$	β = 0.568, $p \leq .05$
OV & AN-IP	β = 0.59, $p \leq .05$					
OV-IP		β = -.356, $p \leq .05$	β = -.154, $p \leq .05$		β = 0.274, $p \leq .05$	β = 0.466, $p \leq .05$
OV & GF-IP				β = .68, $p \leq .05$		

Table 2: Relationship between Heuristic and Investment Performance

Note: AB: Availability Bias; IP: Investment Performance; OV: Overconfidence; AN: Anchoring; GF: Gamblers Fallacy.

Market Factors

The market factors are the environment under which stock investment decisions are undertaken. These factors may include information about stocks. It is postulated that they influence investment decisions.

Concept of Market Factors

Market factors constitute the environment under which stock market investors trade. The stock market factors affect the decisions individual investors make with regard to the stocks to buy and the ones to sell. The semi-strong form of EMH postulates that information is incorporated into the stock price (Fama, 1998). Therefore, the prices of stocks fluctuate with the information received in the stock market.

Information flow is critical for investors because of investment decision-making (Chandra & Kumar, 2012). This information may be available in the public domain, such as financial statements, the reputation of the firm in the industry, and the status of the firm. Moreover, Khan, Naz, Qureshi, & Ghafoor (2017) noted that investors might be influenced by the information that is available to them. For example, they may be influenced by advertising and investment advisors without researching to establish whether the stocks they are buying are good.

A study (Fleming & Remolona, 1999) noted that public information affects stock prices and the volume of stocks traded. When the prices of stocks are affected, the returns of individual investors in the stock market will be affected. Therefore, public information will influence the behaviour of investors and, hence, affect stock market prices. In addition, behavioural factors cause changes in stock prices, market information, and customer preferences, affecting investors' decisions in the stock market (Kengatharan & Kengatharan, 2014).

As noted by Chandra and Kumar (2012), "Investors while making investment decisions are relying on [the] judgment or best-guess heuristics to draw [the] inference from financial information available in the public domain" (p. 155). Therefore, the financial information available in the market will influence investors to behave in a certain way while making investment decisions in the stock market. Investors consider financial statements, public information, and accounting information while making investment decisions in the stock exchange (Das, 2012).

The availability of public information may lead investors to overweight its importance in decision-making, leading to excessive trading (Hammond, 2015), consequently causing stock prices to deviate from their fundamental value (Hammond, 2015). This movement away from the fundamental value of stock prices will affect the investment performance of individual investors.

Expert advice is postulated to be a case of asymmetric information (Valsecchi, 2013). This is because the expert possesses information about the stock markets that is not possessed by non-experts. Therefore, non-experts who need advice on investment opportunities seek it from experts. A study (Kramer & Lensink, 2012) identified the benefits of financial advice (expert advice) as improving equity returns, reducing risks, and reducing the frequency of trades. Since market factors influence investors' decision-making processes, a study of them was important. This study included public information and expert information as the dimensions of market factors.

Definitions of the Concept of Market Factors

There are few scholars who have tried to define the two market dimensions: public information and expert information. Public information is "the information shared by everyone" (Morris & Shin, 2002, p. 1521). This information is available to all because there is no cost associated with it, or the cost may be low.

Experts are prevalent in all areas where expertise is required. The stock market is an area that requires expert information for those who want to invest. However, there is a problem in identifying those experts who are reliable (Valsecchi, 2013). This is because prominent companies have collapsed after being given a clean bill by auditors. Therefore, the reliability of expertise is doubted.

Expert information has been defined as "the content generated by professionals" (Adams, 2004; van Kerkhoff & Lebel, as cited in Weible, 2008, p. 615). In the stock market, professionals are the investment advisors who do research on the investment opportunities available so that they can offer advice for a fee.

Model of Market Factors

One model that this study will use is Wilson's model of information seeking. This model was proposed by Wilson in 1981 (Wilson, 1999). The model is based on two propositions: information seeking is a secondary need, and the individual will encounter barriers while seeking information. The stock market is affected by the information that is available to individual stock market investors. This information may be in the public domain, for example, in the print media and on television. Therefore, the model by Wilson (1981) presumes that individual investors will seek information as a secondary need because they want to satisfy their primary need of investing in the stock market (Wilson, 1999).

Also, the information may be possessed by investment experts (Weible, 2008), and investors will need to pay a fee to access this information. The investors will react to this information by evaluating how it is likely to affect their investments in stocks. If the information is favourable, they may be encouraged to buy stocks that promise better returns. However, if the information is not favourable, they may withhold the decision to invest. Therefore, market factors are likely to affect the decisions of investors in the stock market (Das, 2012; Kengatharan & Kengatharan, 2014).

Indicators of Market Factors

Public information is the information that is in the public domain about a particular company. This information can be in the form of published financial statements in both the print and electronic media. The published information includes income statements and balance sheets, which influence investment decisions. For example, accounting information has been found to influence investment decisions. The reputation of the firm, management profile, and the status of the firm in the industry influence the investment decisions of individual investors (Das, 2012). The indicators of public information included using the following to make investment decisions: published financial statements, reputation of the firm, and status of the firm.

Expert information also influences investment decisions. Expert information is the information provided by investment experts based on the analysis of stock trading. Some of this information is available only to subscribed members and, therefore, requires a fee to access. A study conducted by Das (2012) found that expert information influences investment decisions. This factor is understudied and, hence, there is a need to include it in the study to determine the influence it has on investment performance. The indicators of expert information included: seeking, reading, and using expert information to make investment decisions.

Relationship between Market Factors and Investment Performance

In a study, Kengatharan and Kengatharan (2014) found that there was no significant relationship between public information and investment performance, where $\beta = .087$, $p > .05$. A positive relationship was postulated between public information and investment performance. Das (2012) found that investors consult experts for information that they can use to make investment decisions. However, only a small percentage (28%) of the respondents reported having asked experts for information on investment decisions. Investors may obtain expert information by consulting experts, accessing published information in print media, or using information published on the internet. The low percentage of investors who use expert information is probably due to the cost involved in accessing such information. This study postulated a positive relationship between expert information and investment performance.

Additionally, investors may find it difficult to understand the technical language involved. This may lead to the existence of information asymmetry in the stock market, where some investors have more information than others about investment opportunities. As such, it enables some investors to access expert information to make investment decisions. Therefore, expert information will influence individual investors' portfolio performance. Kramer and Lensink (2012) conducted a study in the Netherlands on 5,661 individual customers and found a significant influence of expert advice on investment performance, where $\beta = .022$, $p < .01$. After a discussion on antecedents of investment performance, the following section discusses investment decisions as a control factor.

Control Factor

Previous studies have treated investment decisions as a dependent variable. In other words, the studies examined the effect of behavioral factors on investment decisions. This study, however, employed investment decisions as a control factor. The purpose was to establish the influence that behavioral and market factors have on investment performance after controlling for investment decisions. Investment decisions as a control factor are discussed in the sections that follow.

Investment Decisions

Individual investors make investment decisions in order to earn a return. Therefore, they must make investment decisions that yield higher returns compared to other alternatives. The discussion on investment decisions follows this order: concept, definitions, theories, indicators, and relationship with investment performance.

Concept of Investment Decision-Making

Decision-making is an important part of people's lives because they have goals they want to achieve. To achieve these goals, they must make several decisions. Studies have been conducted on the theories of decision-making and the factors that influence it (Dietrich, 2010).

There are two types of decision-making models. The first type is normative (rational) models, which postulate that individual decision-makers are rational beings. The second type is descriptive (psychological) models, which incorporate the influence of psychology in decision-making (Oliveira, 2007). Rational decision-makers make decisions that maximize their self-interest. Therefore, individual investors who make decisions that maximize their self-interest are presumed to be rational.

Rational decision-making occurs when investors utilize either technical or fundamental analysis. Technical analysis uses past information, such as prices, to make investment decisions (Bodie et al., 2014). Investors study the patterns in stock price movements to guide their decisions. If stock prices do not incorporate past information, investors may earn above-average returns. Conversely, if stock prices incorporate past information, investing in such stocks will only enable investors to earn average market returns.

In fundamental analysis, individual investors use future earnings and dividends of a firm to make investment decisions (Bodie et al., 2014). This analysis aims to establish future prospects of the firm that the market has not yet recognized. Investors should buy stocks that are undervalued by the market or sell those that are overvalued. Fundamental values differ from market stock prices when past and present stock information is not fully incorporated, thus providing opportunities for above-average returns.

The failure of the Efficient Market Hypothesis (EMH) to provide information for updating stock prices may render both fundamental and technical analyses less useful for investment decision-making. This may result in market inefficiencies and cause investors to behave irrationally. Additionally, investors may attempt to beat the market by exploiting discrepancies in the fundamental values of stocks (Masry, 2017). Petrusheva and Jordanoski (2016) noted that investors may benefit more by combining both technical and fundamental analyses. Fundamental analysis is useful for determining intrinsic values, while technical analysis is helpful for deciding the timing of buying or selling stocks.

Individual investors who make decisions that do not maximize their self-interest are considered irrational. These irrational investors are influenced by behavioral factors, which lead to biases and errors in investment decisions. Furthermore, such decisions affect their investment performance.

Definitions of Investment Decisions

Decision-making is "the act or process of deciding something" (Decision-making, 2018). It is the activity of choosing a course of action from alternative options. Additionally, decision-making is a process that starts with identifying a need and ends with choosing an action to satisfy that need. As noted by Oliveira (2007), "a decision is a response to a situation and comprehends judgments, expectations, and evaluations" (p. 16). Therefore, investment decisions involve considering alternatives, choosing those that maximize self-interest, and evaluating the outcomes. Understanding the process of decision-making may promote good decisions and reduce the likelihood of poor ones (Polič, 2009). Individual investors are expected to make sound investment decisions to enhance their self-interests.

Theories of Decision Making

Rationality is the "compatibility between choice and value" (Oliveira, 2007, p. 13). In addition, rational decision-making is the "maximization of expected value or expected utility" (Gigerenzer, 2001, p. 1). Rational decision-making requires decision makers to analyze the alternative choices available and then select the one that has the highest value to them (Oliveira, 2007). Therefore, individuals with a problem who are required to make a decision will rank the possible actions according to their outcomes. They will then choose the actions that give the best outcomes, as this will maximize their value, which is known as optimization. These individuals will use the available alternatives to solve their problem. This has been explained by the expected utility theory, which argues that individuals are influenced in decision-making by the expected outcomes of various actions. The alternative with the highest possible outcome will be chosen (Gigerenzer, 2001; Oliveira, 2007).

The subjective expected utility theory postulated that individuals will make choices among alternatives when faced with risk (Ahmed, Bwisa, Otieno, & Karanja, 2014). This was based on the premise that the decision maker tends to seek pleasure and avoid pain. However, the decision maker may not evaluate all possible alternatives. This failure to evaluate all alternatives when making decisions may lead individuals to behave irrationally. Kahneman and Tversky developed heuristic and prospect theories to address the limitations of the expected utility theory (Kahneman, 2003).

Individual decision makers may not always follow models that guide rational decision-making. They may use simplified mechanisms to make decisions, as elucidated by heuristic and prospect theories. This gave rise to individual differences in decision-making (Oliveira, 2007). This has led to interest in cognitive psychology, which explains that decision makers may deviate from rational decision-making models. The deviation from rationality is referred to as heuristics and biases (Polič, 2009).

Bounded rationality, pioneered by Herbert Simon, reinforced the growth of cognitive psychology and, hence, led to the development of the concept of irrational decision-making (Polič, 2009). Bounded rationality is the concept that outlines that individuals can only be rational to the extent of the information available for decision-making, the time available to evaluate alternatives, and their capacity to process information.

Kahneman and Tversky (1979) developed prospect theory, which showed how attitudes toward risk (gains or losses) influence decision-making. Therefore, prospect theory borrowed from expected utility theory to explain attitudes toward risk. Individual investors will make decisions based on the expected outcome. For example, if individual investors expect losses, they will refrain from investing in stocks. However, prospect theory may lead individuals to exhibit biases and heuristics, causing them to make suboptimal investment decisions.

Indicators of Stock Investment Decisions

The disposition effect affects individual investor selling decisions by decreasing the likelihood of selling stocks that have recorded a loss due to a decline in their current price compared to the initial purchase price (Shefrin & Statman, 1985). Investors are unwilling to sell shares that have decreased in price because they are reluctant to realize the loss, while at the same time being more than willing to sell stocks whose prices have increased. Individual investors sell stocks that have increased in price and avoid selling those that have decreased because lower prices may lead to higher transaction costs (Odean, 1998).

As noted by Luong et al. (2011), momentum in stock returns also influences investors to sell stocks that have gained capital. In addition, the pressure to sell may reduce the share price but increase returns later. In contrast, an investor may sell stocks based on an expected price increase, which may ultimately reduce returns.

Prior winning and losing stocks may influence investors' stock purchase decisions (Odean, as cited by Luong et al., 2011). Odean (as cited by Luong et al., 2011) notes that stock purchases may result from the attention effect, where investors, unable to find a good stock to buy, may purchase one that has caught their interest. This attention may come from past performance, whether good or bad (Luong et al., 2011). Additionally, attention may also come from stocks that many investors are currently trading, stocks with high trading volumes, and those frequently mentioned in the news. These trading activities are easily noticeable and may influence investors' decisions to purchase certain stocks.

Making decisions using the fundamental values of assets is not an easy task (Ariely, Loewenstein, & Prelec, 2006). Therefore, individual investors may rely on past prices to make investment decisions—a situation known as anchoring. Likewise, Barber, Odean, and Zhu (2009) noted that individual investors are likely to purchase stocks that attract their attention because they are featured in the news. This is because individual investors can easily recall them.

According to Khan et al. (2017), investors who are biased due to anchoring may be influenced to purchase stocks that do not meet their expectations. This is confirmed by Odean (1998), who noted that individual investors may hold onto stocks that have decreased in price for too long. Investors may also be anchored to once-successful companies that are now underperforming. Additionally, individual investors may purchase unsuitable stocks due to relying on insufficient past information. Furthermore, they may deal with stocks of companies that have market presence due to advertising.

Relationships between Stock Investment Decisions and Investment Performance

Stock market investment decisions are postulated to affect investment performance. Generally, individual investors buy and sell different stocks with varying levels of performance. Therefore, the performance of the stocks held by individual investors will differ. Specifically, individual investors make different investment decisions that influence their investment performance to varying degrees. These investment decisions will be conceptualized as the control variables of the study to establish the influence they have on investment performance. The following section provides the conceptual framework that emerged from the literature review.

Conceptual Framework of the Study

The theories that guided the study included herding, prospect, heuristic, information seeking, and EMH. These five theories enabled the conceptualization of the theoretical framework. A theoretical framework is the "application of a theory or a set of concepts drawn from one and the same theory, to offer an explanation of an event, or shed some light on a particular phenomenon or research problem" (Imenda, 2014, p. 189).

The conceptual framework shown in Figure 1 is a product of the review of literature that shows the relationships among the variables. A conceptual framework is the "end result of bringing together a number of related concepts to explain or predict a given event, or give a broader understanding of the phenomenon of interest" (Imenda, 2014, p. 189). Behavioural factors are the independent variables, with investment decisions as a control variable and investment performance as the dependent variable. The behavioural factors included herding, prospect (loss aversion, regret aversion, and escalating commitment), heuristic (availability bias and overconfidence), and market factors (public information and expert information). The behavioural factors were postulated to influence investment performance.

The market factors were included in the study because they may influence the behaviour of individual investors in the stock market. Public information includes the published financial statements of the firms. Individual investors use public information in making decisions on the stocks to buy (Das, 2012). Das (2012) found that individual investors consult with experts while making investment decisions. Therefore, this study postulated that market factors would influence the investment behaviour of investors. This prompted their inclusion in the study. See Table 2 for the summary of the literature references supporting the relationships in Figure 1.

Relationship among the Variables

Table 10 shows the relationships among the variables. The independent variables consisted of the behavioural and market factors. The dependent variable was investment performance. The independent variables influence the outcome (Creswell, 2009). In this study, the independent variables (behavioural and market factors) were postulated to influence investment performance. The dependent variable is expected to be influenced by the independent variables. Investment decisions were the control variable. A control variable is "a special type of independent variable that researchers measure because they potentially influence the dependent variable" (Creswell, 2009, p. 60). Investment decisions were postulated as a control variable since they are influenced by investor behaviour.

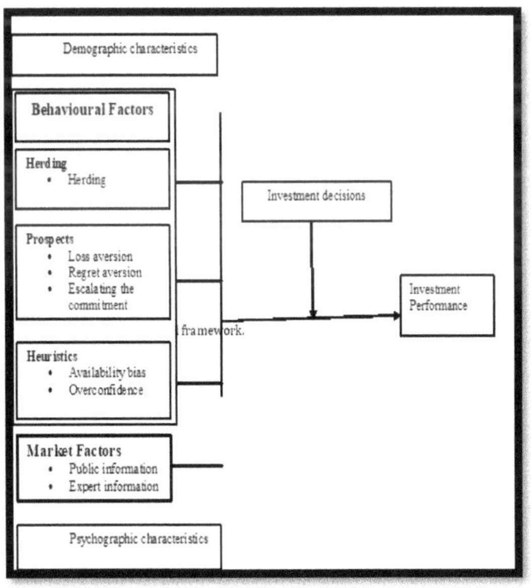

Figure 1: Proposed Conceptual Framework

Variables	References
Herding behaviour and investment decisions	Das, 2012; Jagongo & Mutswenje, 2014; Aduda, Oduor, & Onuonga,2012; Kengatharan & Kengatharan, 2014; Vijaya, 2014; Rekik & Boujelbene, 2013
Loss aversion and investment decisions	Das, 2012; Kengatharan & Kengatharan, 2014; Vijaya, 2014; Chandra & Kumar, 2012; Rekik & Boujelbene, 2013
Regret aversion and investment decisions	Kengatharan & Kengatharan, 2014; Vijaya, 2014; Chandra & Kumar, 2012
Escalating the commitment and investment decisions	Lin et al., 2014
Availability bias and investment decisions	Kengatharan & Kengatharan, 2014; Vijaya, 2014; Chandra & Kumar, 2012
Variables	**References**
Overconfidence and investments decisions	Das, 2012; Kengatharan & Kengatharan, 2014; Vijaya, 2014; Chandra & Kumar, 2012; Veeraragh & Anbalaga, 2011; Rekik & Boujelbene, 2013
Public information and investment decisions	Das, 2012; Chandra & Kumar; 2012
Expert information and investment decisions	Satti, Din, & Ali, 2013
Herding behavior and Investment performance	Bakar & Yi, 2016; Javed et al. 2017; Khan, 2014; Kengatharan & Kengatharan, 2014; Luong et al., 2011; Nyamute et al., 2015; Ranjbar et al., 2014
Loss aversion and investment performance	Ranjbar et al., 2014; Kengatharan & Kengatharan, 2014; Luong et al., 2011
Regret aversion and investment performance	Kengatharan & Kengatharan, 2014; Luong et al., 2011
Escalating commitment and investment performance	Lin et al., 2014; Turino & Soetjipto, 2012
Availability bias and investment performance	Bakar & Yi, 2016; Javed et al. 2017; Luong et al., 2011
Overconfidence and investment performance	Bakar & Yi, 2016; Javed et al. 2017; Ranjbar et al., 2014; Luong et al., 2011; Kengatharan & Kengatharan, 2014; Nyamute et al., 2015
Public information and investment performance	Kengatharan & Kengatharan, 2014
Expert information and investment performance	Kramer & Lensink, 2012

Table 3: Relationship among Variables in the Conceptual Framework

Chapter 3 | Methodology

This chapter provides the methodology that the researcher employed in carrying out the study so as to achieve the set objectives. Good methodology ensures that the right data is collected from respondents with the relevant information and that the correct analysis is done to answer the research questions. First, the chapter discusses research philosophy and paradigm, research approach, research strategy, research choices, and time horizons. Second, it presents the population and sampling, research instrument, validity and reliability, and data collection procedures. Third, it provides data analysis and ethical considerations.

Research Design

Research design is critical in enabling the researcher to achieve the intended objectives of the study. A quantitative approach was adopted for this study. This is because the study was intended to test relationships among the variables, as recommended by Creswell (2009). This study was intended to determine the influence of the behavioural (herding, prospect, and heuristic) and the market factors on investment performance. The descriptive and correlational design was employed. The survey method was used to collect data using a self-administered questionnaire from the study respondents. This design was useful since it was appropriate for establishing the relationships among the variables in the study. The discussion in this section followed the "onion" as proposed by Saunders et al. (2007). Therefore, the flow of the discussion follows the layers as indicated in Figure 2.

Research Philosophy and Paradigm

Epistemology is what the researchers consider to be acceptable knowledge (Saunders et al., 2007). Epistemology includes positivism, realism, and interpretivism. This study assumed positivism on the epistemological front since the study used existing theories to develop hypotheses which were to be tested. Therefore, data was collected to confirm or refute the hypotheses.

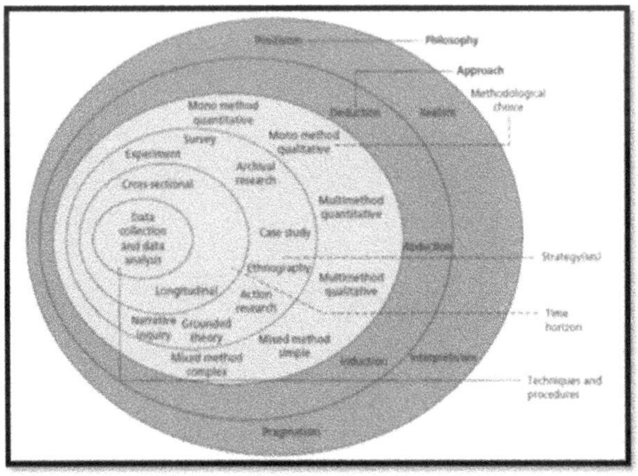

Figure 2: The Research "Onion."

Note: From *Research Methods for Business Students* (4th ed.) (p. 102), by M. Saunders, P. Lewis & A. Thornhill, 2007. England: Prentice Hall.

There are two ontological viewpoints: objectivism and subjectivism (Saunders et al., 2007). The ontological assumption of this study was objectivism. This is because objectivism assumes that social reality, as constructed by the researcher, is external and therefore independent of the researcher. This study was intended to establish the behavioural factors influencing investment decisions, which are external to the researcher's mind. Therefore, objectivism was more appropriate for this study than subjectivism. This is because subjectivism assumes that social reality is in the researchers' minds and hence internal, meaning that social reality is subjective.

Axiology is the value that researchers hold that guides their actions (Saunders et al., 2007). The value that I held while conducting this study was that there is one God and therefore, the reality out there is one. Therefore, this study was conducted with the assumption that there is a single reality on investor behaviour and its influence on investment performance.

Research Approach

There are two research approaches that can be used to guide a study: deductive and inductive approaches (Saunders et al., 2007). The deductive approach was employed since the study started with reviewing the existing theories that are likely to explain investors' behaviour. From the theories, hypotheses to be tested were formulated and either confirmed or refuted.

Research Strategy

This study employed a survey strategy. Survey strategy facilitates the collection of data from a large sample size in a cheaper and more effective way (Saunders et al., 2007). In order to establish the perception of the respondents on the behavioural factors of the individual investors of NSE, a larger sample size was essential. Data was collected from the sample and then the results were generalized to the population of individual investors of NSE. Therefore, the survey method was appropriate for this study.

Research Choices

This study adopted a mono-method. This is where a study does not mix the methods of data collection and analysis (Saunders et al., 2007). The study used only quantitative methods. The study was intended to establish investor behaviour and its influence on the investment performance of individual investors. There was a need to explain the existing relationships among the variables. Therefore, explanatory research was appropriate for this study.

Research Time Horizons

The cross-sectional design was used in this study (Saunders et al., 2007). The time for conducting this study was limited because there were set targets to achieve in order to complete the work. Therefore, there was a need to collect data from the respondents within a short period of time. This encouraged the choice of a cross-sectional design. However, a longitudinal design takes longer to collect data and hence was not appropriate for this study. A cross-sectional design takes a shorter time span to collect data because data collection is done at one point in time.

Population and Sampling

The population of the study included all local individual investors in the NSE, which stood at 1,196,995 (Capital Market Authority, 2017). The local individual investors included only those registered with the brokerage firms trading in equities in the NSE. Sampling techniques "provide a range of methods that enable you to reduce the amount of data you need to collect by considering the data only from a subgroup rather than all possible cases or elements" (Saunders et al., 2007, p. 204). Slovin's formula can be used to estimate the sample size of a population that will be representative (Kalima, Shukla, & Mbabazize, 2016). The formula is given as follows:

$$n = \frac{N}{1+Ne^2}$$

Where: n = Sample size

N = Total population

e = Error margin (0.05)

$$n= \frac{1,196,995}{1 + 1,196,995(0.05)^2}$$

$$n= \frac{1,196,995}{2993.4875}$$

n= 399.87

Therefore, the sample size was 400. However, on the advice of the ERB of AIIAS, the researcher aimed for a sample size of 500. A stratified sampling method was used to identify the brokerage firms. The stratification was based on the brokerage firms listed with the NSE. This sample size was distributed equally to the selected brokerage firms. Convenient sampling was used to identify the 500 respondents from the selected brokerage firms.

There are 40 registered brokerage firms in the NSE. The study did not use all the brokerage firms to access the respondents. From the list of registered brokerage firms, all those with odd position numbers were used. Therefore, the total number of brokerage firms that were sampled was 20. In order to get the 500 respondents, convenient sampling was used to identify 25 respondents from each brokerage firm. Convenient sampling is where cases are selected from a population that can be easily accessed, are geographically reachable, and include willing respondents for the study (Etikan, 2016; Saunders et al., 2007). This method was selected due to time constraints, and the population did not have significant variation in their behavioural aspects. The distribution of the sample size among the brokerage firms is indicated in Table 11.

Research Instrument

The study used primary data. A structured questionnaire with closed-ended questions was used to collect primary data from individual investors in the stock exchange. The instrument had three parts: the first part contained questions on the respondents' demographic characteristics. The second part contained questions on psychographic characteristics. The third part had questions on behavioural factors, investment decisions, and the degree of market efficiency's impact on investment performance. The questionnaire was constructed with the help of academic experts. The questionnaire was administered personally to the sampled respondents. The questions for the instrument were constructed based on the following theories to measure behavioural factors of individual investors and the degree of market efficiency's impact on investment performance: herding theory, prospect theory, heuristic theory, and efficient market theory.

No	Brokerage firm	Sample size
1	ABC Bank	25
2	Dyer and Blair Investment Bank Ltd	25
3	Nyaga Stockbrokers	25
4	Suntra Investment Bank Ltd	25
5	CFC Stanbic Financial Services Ltd	25
6	Afrika Investment Bank Ltd	25
7	Sterling Investment Bank Ltd	25
8	Faida Investment Bank Ltd	25
9	Genghis Capital Ltd	25
10	Kestrel Capital Investment Bank	25
11	African Alliance Kenya Securities	25
12	CBA Capital Ltd	25
13	Standard Investment Bank	25
14	Sterling Investment Bank	25
15	Co-operative Bank	25
16	Investment & Mortgages Bank Ltd	25
17	National Bank	25
18	NIC Bank	25
19	Equity Bank	25
20	Standard Chartered Bank	25
Total		500

Table 4: Sample Size Distribution

Herding was measured using six items. These items were developed using studies that have researched herding (Bikhchandani & Sharma, 2001; Das, 2012; Mackay, 1841; Selden, 1912). The items were measured using a 5-point scale. The scale ranged from 1 = strongly disagree, 2 = disagree, 3 = neutral, 4 = agree, and 5 = strongly agree. The questions to measure herding included the following:

1. I follow the decisions of other investors while making investment decisions.
2. I follow the decisions of other investors without doing any analysis.
3. I follow the decisions of other investors so that I can be like them.
4. I immediately follow the decisions of other investors whenever they make changes in their portfolio.
5. I follow the popular opinion in the selection of my stocks.
6. If my decision turns out bad, I immediately retreat to safer investments.

Prospect was measured by its three dimensions: loss aversion, regret aversion, and escalation of commitment. The questions measured the degree of agreement or disagreement regarding investors' perceptions of the prospect dimensions. Loss aversion was measured using three items. These items were developed using studies that have researched loss aversion (Kahneman & Tversky, 1979; Vijaya, 2014). The items were measured using a 5-point scale. The scale ranged from 1 = strongly disagree, 2 = disagree, 3 = neutral, 4 = agree, and 5 = strongly agree. The questions to measure the loss aversion dimension included the following:

1. I make investment decisions that enable me to avoid losses.
2. A positive return in the past leads me to be more risk-seeking.
3. A negative return in the past leads me to adopt a more risk-averse attitude towards stock investments.

Regret aversion was measured using five items. These items were developed using studies that have researched regret aversion (Kahneman & Tversky, 1979; Luong et al., 2011). The items were measured using a 5-point scale. The scale ranged from 1 = strongly disagree, 2 = disagree, 3 = neutral, 4 = agree, and 5 = strongly agree. The questions to measure the regret aversion dimension included the following:

1. I am more than willing to sell stocks whose prices are increasing.
2. I am less willing to sell stocks whose prices are decreasing.
3. I feel bad when stocks that I did not choose perform better.
4. I believe that successful stock investments depend more on luck than on skill.
5. I buy stocks that other people are buying to avoid regretting alone if they perform poorly.

Escalation of commitment was measured using three items. These items were developed using studies that have researched escalation of commitment (Lin et al., 2014). The items were measured using a 5-point scale. The scale ranged from 1 = strongly disagree, 2 = disagree, 3 = neutral, 4 = agree, and 5 = strongly agree. The questions to measure the escalation of commitment dimension included the following:

1. I will continue to invest in stocks even if I incurred losses in the previous period.
2. Even if I am not sure of attaining my goal, I will still invest in stocks.
3. I will continue to invest in a stock even if I become aware of it being a bad investment.

Heuristic was measured in terms of its two dimensions: availability bias and overconfidence. The questions measured the degree of agreement or disagreement regarding investors' perceptions of the heuristic dimensions. Availability bias was measured using five items. These items were developed using studies that have researched availability bias (Luong et al., 2011; Tversky & Kahneman, 1974). The items were measured using a 5-point scale. The scale ranged from 1 = strongly disagree, 2 = disagree, 3 = neutral, 4 = agree, and 5 = strongly agree. The questions to measure the availability bias dimension included the following:

1. I prefer investing in stocks of local companies rather than foreign ones.
2. I invest in stocks that have performed well in the recent past.
3. I invest in stocks of companies whose names I can easily recall.

4. I like investing in stocks whose information is publicly available.
5. I do not change my stock investment portfolio once I have invested in it.

Overconfidence was measured using six items. These items were developed using studies that have researched overconfidence (Ngoc, 2013; Tversky & Kahneman, 1974). The items were measured using a 5-point scale. The scale ranged from 1 = strongly disagree, 2 = disagree, 3 = neutral, 4 = agree, and 5 = strongly agree. The questions to measure the overconfidence dimension included the following:

1. My stock portfolio performs better than others' because of my superior skills.
2. I believe that stocks I invested in previously performed poorly due to bad luck.
3. I can forecast future stock prices accurately.
4. I am better positioned than other investors to select high-performing stocks.
5. I find it easy to trade in stocks.
6. I can trade in stocks without incurring many risks.

Market factors were measured in terms of two dimensions: public information and expert information. The questions measured the degree of agreement or disagreement regarding investors' perceptions of the market factor dimensions. Public information was measured using four items. These items were developed using studies that have researched public information (Vijaya, 2014). The items were measured using a 5-point scale. The scale ranged from 1 = strongly disagree, 2 = disagree, 3 = neutral, 4 = agree, and 5 = strongly agree. The questions to measure the public information dimension included the following:

1. I look at the printed financial statements of a firm before buying its shares.
2. I check the electronic financial statements of a firm before buying its shares.
3. I purchase shares of firms with a good reputation in the industry.
4. I consider the status of the firm when deciding whether to buy its shares.

Expert information was measured using three items. These items were developed using studies that have researched expert information (Satti et al., 2013). The items were measured using a 5-point scale. The scale ranged from 1 = strongly disagree, 2 = disagree, 3 = neutral, 4 = agree, and 5 = strongly agree. The questions to measure the expert information dimension included the following:

1. I like to read expert information before making investment decisions.
2. I like to read expert information from the web before making investment decisions.
3. Expert information is helpful in making investment decisions.
4. Investment decisions were measured using ten items. These items were developed based on studies that have researched investment decisions (Luong et al., 2011; Odean, 1998; Shefrin & Statman, 1985). The items were measured using a 5-point scale. The scale ranged from 1 = strongly disagree, 2 = disagree, 3 = neutral, 4 = agree, and 5 = strongly agree. The questions to measure investment decisions included the following:

I believe that my investment decision is made on the basis of trading:

1. Stocks whose prices have always increased.
2. Stocks whose prices have always decreased.
3. Stocks other investors are also trading.
4. Stocks with relatively high returns.

5. Stocks with relatively low returns.
6. Stocks that have had good performance in the past.
7. Stocks that have had poor performance in the past.
8. Stocks based on the need to diversify them for risk reduction.
9. Stocks with relatively high trading volumes.
10. Stocks that have been frequently announced in the news.

The degree of market efficiency's impact on investment performance was measured using seven items. These items were developed based on studies that have researched efficient market theory (Fama, 1970). The items were measured using a 5-point scale. The scale ranged from 1 = strongly disagree, 2 = disagree, 3 = neutral, 4 = agree, and 5 = strongly agree. The questions to measure the degree of market efficiency's impact on investment performance included the following:

I believe that investment performance is influenced by my investment decision due to the following factors:

1. Stock prices reflect only past information.
2. Stock investments earn abnormal profits based on past information analysis.
3. Stock prices reflect both past and available public information.
4. Stock investments earn abnormal profits based on financial statement analysis.
5. Stock investments earn abnormal profits based on the fundamentals of the company.
6. Stock prices reflect all information from public and private sources.
7. Stock prices even reflect hidden insider information.

Validity and Reliability

A useful survey instrument should measure the constructs it is supposed to measure (Saunders et al., 2007). This study considered construct validity, face validity, and content validity. Consultations were done with the research advisors of AIIAS Graduate School. The questionnaire was constructed in consultation with the research advisors, ensuring that it measured the constructs of the study. Face validity was achieved by consulting with the research advisors. This questionnaire was given to the research advisors to go through and evaluate whether the language used was appropriate.

To achieve content validity, the researcher consulted with the research advisor, who is a specialist in finance, to ensure that the questions were relevant to behavioral factors, investment decisions, and EMH. A reliable instrument should provide consistent outcomes across different times and conditions (Saunders et al., 2007). This reliability was determined by the coefficient of Cronbach's alpha. A pilot study was conducted with a sample of 100 respondents from two brokerage firms. These respondents were excluded from the main data collection sample. A Cronbach's alpha of at least 0.7 was considered acceptable.

Data Collection Procedures

Permission was sought from AIIAS Graduate School upon approval of the research proposal to collect data. Permission was also sought from the ERB of AIIAS for the data collection. AIIAS School of Graduate Studies provided an introductory letter for data collection.

Afterward, permission was sought from the National Council for Science, Technology, and Innovation (NACOSTI) in Kenya, the brokerage firms, and the individual investors before data collection.

The individual investors were accessed through the brokerage firms. The brokerage firms were contacted to assist in identifying and contacting the respondents. Convenient sampling was used to identify respondents from the list of individual investors in the brokerage firms. The individual investors were contacted by phone or email, and the purpose of the study was explained to them.

For those who agreed to participate, the questionnaires were sent by delivery, and other respondents were met at the brokerage firm offices. Those who did not agree to participate were replaced with others from the list of individual investors. The respondents were given 3 days to complete the questionnaires, after which a polite follow-up was conducted. The completed questionnaires were coded and kept safely until being input into the SPSS program for analysis.

Pilot Test of the Instruments

A pilot survey was conducted among 100 individual investors in the NSE. The sample used in this survey was drawn from individual investors of two brokerage firms, who were excluded from the main data collection sample. Table 12 shows the results from the pilot tests. From the results, the instrument was reliable since it met the minimum threshold of .07 that is required. The reliability test for the survey instrument showed that the overall Cronbach's alpha was .898, indicating that the instrument was reliable for data collection. The variable with the highest Cronbach's alpha value was the public information variable, with a value of .912, and the variable with the least Cronbach's alpha value was overconfidence, with a value of .893.

Variable	No. of Items	No. of Respondents	Cronbach alpha
Herding	6	100	.895
Loss aversion	3	100	.896
Regret aversion	5	100	.897
Escalating the commitment	3	100	.896
Availability bias	5	100	.894
Overconfidence	6	100	.893
Public information	4	100	.912
Expert information	3	100	.910
Investment decisions	10	100	.895
Investment performance	7	100	.895

Table 5: Reliability Estimates of the Variable from Pilot Test Result

Data Analysis

The data collected was coded into the SPSS program for analysis in order to answer the research questions. Pre-analysis data screening was done before conducting the main analysis. Pre-analysis data screening is concerned with checking the quality of data collected before conducting the actual analysis (Mertler & Vannatta, 2013). This is important because quality data will assure us that the main analysis will produce credible results for interpretation. Pre-analysis data screening was done for the following purposes:

1. Checking for the accuracy of the data collected.
2. Checking for missing information.
3. Checking for extreme values (outliers).
4. Checking for the fit between the data collected and assumptions for the regression procedure. This involves checking for normality, linearity, and homoscedasticity.

Accuracy of the data was checked using frequency distributions and descriptive statistics. The means, the standard deviations, and the range of values were checked. In addition, the coded values were checked to ensure that correct codes had been used for categorical data (Mertler & Vannatta, 2013).

Missing data was checked using frequencies. If the frequencies indicated that there were missing values, the percentage of missing data was estimated. If the missing values were less than 5%, they were either replaced or left unreplaced. In case replacement was decided, the mean of the other values was used to replace the missing values.

Outliers are cases of extreme values in a sample. In order to check for outliers, Mahalanobis distance was employed because the study used multivariate data and, therefore, this test was appropriate. The reason for the outliers should be noted. If the outlier is due to an error in data entry, then the error should be corrected. However, if the outlier is due to an error in instrumentation or if the response is simply different from the others, the solution is to remove the case from the analysis (Mertler & Vannatta, 2013).

Since the study had continuous data, normality was checked. Normality is ascertained by checking the skewness and kurtosis of the data. If the data is normal, it should have a skewness value of 0, but normality is assumed if the skewness value is less than 2, whether positively or negatively skewed. Normality is assumed if the kurtosis value is less than 2, whether positive or negative. If the data fails to meet the normality test, data transformation will be considered. Data transformation "involve[s] the application of mathematical procedures to the data in order to make them appear more normal" (Mertler & Vannatta, 2013, p. 33). There are various methods that can be used to transform the data depending on the shape of the skewness, such as square root, inverse, and logarithm.

After data screening was completed, data analysis was conducted to answer the research question of the study. Table 13 below shows the research questions, research hypotheses, and the statistical tools that were employed to answer the research questions.

Research Question 1, "What behavioural factors such as herding, prospect (loss aversion, regret aversion, and escalating the commitment), and heuristic (availability bias and overconfidence) are displayed by the individual investors in the NSE?" was answered using descriptive statistics such as means.

No.	Research questions	Hypotheses	Statistical tools
1.	What behavioural factors such as herding, prospect (loss aversion, regret aversion, and escalating the commitment), and heuristic (availability bias and overconfidence) are displayed by the individual investors in the Nairobi securities exchange (NSE)?	None	Means
2.	To what extent are the behavioural factors such as herding, prospect (loss aversion, regret aversion, and escalating the commitment), and heuristic (availability bias and overconfidence) displayed by the individual investors in the NSE?	None	Means
3.	Do the following factors- herding, prospect (loss aversion, regret aversion and escalating the commitment), heuristic (availability bias and overconfidence), and market factors (public information and expert information)-significantly differ by the demographic and psychographic characteristics of individual investors in the NSE?	H_{01}: The following factors- herding, prospect (loss aversion, regret aversion and escalating the commitment), heuristic (availability bias and overconfidence), and market factors (public information and expert information)-do not significantly differ by demographic and psychographic characteristics of individual investors in the NSE.	*t*-tests and one way ANOVA
4.	Are the following factors- herding, prospect (loss aversion, regret aversion and escalating the commitment), heuristic (availability bias and overconfidence), market factors (public information and expert information), and investment decisions- significantly correlated with each other in the NSE?	H_{02}: The following factors- herding, prospect (loss aversion, regret aversion and escalating the commitment), heuristic (availability bias and overconfidence), market factors (public information and expert information), and investment decisions-are not significantly correlated with each other in the NSE.	Correlation analysis
5	Do the following behavioural	H_{03}: The following behavioural	Multiple

	factors-herding, prospect (loss aversion, regret aversion and escalating the commitment), heuristic (availability bias and overconfidence), and market factors (public information and expert information)-combined together significantly influence investment performance in the NSE?	factors-herding, prospect (loss aversion, regret aversion and escalating the commitment), heuristic (availability bias and overconfidence), and market factors (public information and expert information)-combined together do not significantly influence investment performance in the NSE.	regression
6.	Do the following behavioural factors- herding, prospect (loss aversion, regret aversion and escalating the commitment), heuristic (availability bias and overconfidence), and market factors (public information and expert information)-combined together significantly influence the investment performance with investment decisions as a control variable in the NSE?	H_{05}: The following behavioural factors-herding, prospect (loss aversion, regret aversion and escalating the commitment), heuristic (availability bias and overconfidence), and market factors (public information and expert information)-combined together do not significantly influence the investment performance with investment decisions as a control variable in the NSE.	Multiple regression

Table 6: Research Questions, Hypotheses and Statistical Tools

Research Question 2, "To what extent are the behavioural factors such as herding, prospect (loss aversion, regret aversion, and escalating the commitment), and heuristic (availability bias and overconfidence) displayed by the individual investors in the NSE?" was answered using descriptive statistics such as means.

Research Question 3, "Do the following factors—herding, prospect (loss aversion, regret aversion, and escalating the commitment), heuristic (availability bias and overconfidence), and market factors (public information and expert information)—significantly differ by the demographic and psychographic characteristics of individual investors in the NSE?" was answered by testing the following null hypothesis 1, HO1: "The following factors—herding, prospect (loss aversion, regret aversion, and escalating the commitment), heuristic (availability bias and overconfidence), and market factors (public information and expert information)—do not significantly differ by demographic and psychographic characteristics of individual investors in the NSE." HO1 was tested against alternate hypothesis 1, H1: "The following factors—herding, prospect (loss aversion, regret aversion, and escalating the commitment), heuristic (availability bias and overconfidence), and market factors (public information and expert information)—significantly differ by demographic and psychographic characteristics of individual investors in the NSE."

The one-way analysis of variance and t-tests were used to determine whether to accept or reject the null hypothesis at a 95% degree of confidence. If the significance level from the SPSS output is > 0.05, then the null hypothesis 1, HO1, "The following factors—herding, prospect (loss aversion, regret aversion, and escalating the commitment), heuristic (availability bias and overconfidence), and market factors (public information and expert information)—do not significantly differ by demographic and psychographic characteristics of individual investors in the NSE," cannot be rejected. However, where the significance level from the SPSS output is ≤ 0.05, then the null hypothesis 1 can be rejected and the alternate hypothesis 1, H1, "The following factors—herding, prospect (loss aversion, regret aversion, and escalating the commitment), heuristic (availability bias and overconfidence), and market factors (public information and expert information)—significantly differ by demographic and psychographic characteristics of individual investors in the NSE," is accepted.

Research Question 4, "Are the following factors—herding, prospect (loss aversion, regret aversion, and escalating the commitment), heuristic (availability bias and overconfidence), market factors (public information and expert information), and investment decisions—significantly correlated with each other in the NSE?" was answered by testing the following null hypothesis 2, H02: "The following factors—herding, prospect (loss aversion, regret aversion, and escalating the commitment), heuristic (availability bias and overconfidence), market factors (public information and expert information), and investment decisions—are not significantly correlated with each other in the NSE." H02 was tested against alternate hypothesis 2, H2: "The following factors—herding, prospect (loss aversion, regret aversion, and escalating the commitment), heuristic (availability bias and overconfidence), market factors (public information and expert information), and investment decisions—are significantly correlated with each other in the NSE."

The correlation analysis was used to determine whether to accept or reject the null hypothesis at a 95% degree of confidence. If the significance level from the SPSS output is > 0.05, then the null hypothesis 2, H02, "The following factors—herding, prospect (loss aversion, regret aversion, and escalating the commitment), heuristic (availability bias and overconfidence), market factors (public information and expert information), and investment decisions—are not significantly correlated with each other in the NSE," cannot be rejected. However, where the significance level is ≤ 0.05, then the null hypothesis, H02, can be rejected and the alternate hypothesis 2, H2, "The following factors—herding, prospect (loss aversion, regret aversion, and escalating the commitment), heuristic (availability bias and overconfidence), market factors (public information and expert information), and investment decisions—are significantly correlated with each other in the NSE," is accepted.

Research Question 5, "Do the following behavioural factors—herding, prospect (loss aversion, regret aversion, and escalating the commitment), heuristic (availability bias and overconfidence), and market factors (public information and expert information)—combined together significantly influence investment performance in the NSE?" was answered by testing the null hypothesis 3, H03: "The following behavioural factors—herding, prospect (loss aversion, regret aversion, and escalating the commitment), heuristic (availability bias and overconfidence), and market factors (public information and expert information)—combined together do not significantly influence investment performance in the NSE." H03 was tested against alternate hypothesis 3, H3: "The following behavioural factors—herding, prospect (loss aversion, regret aversion, and escalating the commitment), heuristic (availability bias and overconfidence), and market factors (public information and expert information)—combined together significantly influence investment performance in the NSE."

The multiple regression analysis was used to test null hypothesis 3, H_{03}. The following multiple regression model was used. The multiple regression analysis was used to test null hypothesis 3, H_{03}.

The following multiple regression model was used.

$IP = \propto + \beta_1 HE + \beta_2 LA + \beta_3 RA + \beta_4 EC + \beta_5 AB + \beta_6 OV + \beta_7 PI + \beta_8 E + \varepsilon$

Where:

IP =	Investment Performance
α =	Intercept
β =	Regression coefficients
HE=	Herding
LA=	Loss Aversion
RA=	Regret Aversion
EC=	Escalating the Commitment
AB=	Availability Bias
OV=	Overconfidence
PI=	Public Information
EI=	Expert Information
ε =	Error term

$\beta_1, \beta_2, \beta_3, \beta_4, \beta_5, \beta_6, \beta_7, \beta_8$, represents coefficients

The null hypothesis three can be expressed as follows,

$\beta_1, \beta_2, \beta_3, \beta_4, \beta_5, \beta_6, \beta_7, \beta_8, = 0$

This meant that the independent variables have no significant influence on the dependent variable, IP. The ANOVA was used to test this hypothesis. If the significant p value is > 0.05, therefore, null hypothesis three for the independent variables cannot be rejected. This means that the coefficient β for that independent variable is significantly different from zero and therefore, the independent variable has a significant influence on the dependent variable, IP.

Research Question 6, "Do the following behavioural factors-herding, prospect (loss aversion, regret aversion, and escalating the commitment), heuristic (availability bias and overconfidence), and market factors (public information and expert information)-combined together significantly influence the investment performance with investment decisions as a control variable in the NSE?" was answered by testing the null hypothesis 4, H_{04}, "the following behavioural factors-herding, prospect (loss aversion, regret aversion, and escalating the commitment), heuristic (availability bias and overconfidence), and market factors (public information and expert information)-combined together do not significantly influence the investment performance with investment decisions as a control variable in the

NSE." H_{04}, was tested against alternate hypothesis 4, H_4, "the following behavioural factors-herding, prospect (loss aversion, regret aversion, and escalating the commitment), heuristic (availability bias and overconfidence), and market factors (public information and expert information)-combined together significantly influence the investment performance with investment decisions as a control variable in the NSE.'

The multiple regression was used to test null hypothesis 4, H_4. The following regression model was used. The following multiple regression model was derived.

$$IP = \propto + \beta_1 HF + \beta_2 PF + \beta_3 HUF + \beta_4 MF + \beta_5 ID + \varepsilon$$

Where:

IP	=	Investment Performance
α	=	Intercept
β	=	Regression coefficients
HF	=	Herding Factor
PF	=	Prospect Factor
HUF	=	Heuristic Factor
MF	=	Market Factor
ID	=	Investment decisions
ε	=	Error term

$\beta_1, \beta_2, \beta_3, \beta_4, \beta_5,$ Represents coefficients

The null hypothesis four can be expressed as follows,

$\beta_1, \beta_2, \beta_3, \beta_4, \beta_5, = 0$

This meant that the independent variables do not have a significant influence on the dependent variable, IP. The ANOVA will be used to test this hypothesis. If the significant p-value is > 0.05, the null hypothesis five for the independent variables cannot be rejected. This meant that the coefficient β for that independent variable is not significantly different from zero, and therefore, the independent variable does not have a significant influence on the dependent variable, IP. The null hypothesis was rejected when the significant value was ≤ 0.05, and the alternate hypothesis five, H5, was accepted: "The following behavioral factors—herding, prospect (loss aversion, regret aversion, and escalating commitment), heuristic (availability bias and overconfidence), and market factors (public information and expert information)—combined together significantly influence the investment performance, with investment decisions as a control variable in the NSE." This discussion of the research design is followed by the ethical considerations.

Ethical Considerations

Ethical considerations are issues the researcher needs to take into account while conducting the study to avoid infringing on the rights of the participants. The necessary permissions were also obtained from the relevant authorities. This study was conducted while taking into account the following ethical issues:

Permission

Before collecting data, permission was obtained from the AIIAS Ethics Review Board (ERB) of the AIIAS Graduate School. This authorization by AIIAS enabled the researcher to collect data for the study from the sampled respondents. Authorization was also sought from the National Council for Science, Technology and Innovation (NACOSTI). Permission was also obtained from the brokerage firms for data collection from individual investors.

Informed Consent

The purpose of the study was explained to the respondents, and their consent to participate was sought. The researcher ensured that the respondents gave their informed consent before participating in the study. The respondents were required to give consent by signing agreement forms indicating that they agreed to participate in the study. They were also informed that they could withdraw from participating in the study without any consequences.

Anonymity and Confidentiality

The respondents were informed that the information provided would be confidential and that their identity would not be revealed to anyone. Therefore, data was collected while maintaining the confidentiality of the respondents. The respondents were not required to write their names on the questionnaire, and the researcher handled the completed questionnaires with confidentiality. The questionnaires were coded to conceal the identities of the respondents and their brokerage firms. They were also stored securely to prevent unauthorized access.

Avoidance of Risk or Harm

The respondents were informed that there was no known harm in participating in the study. The participants were informed that their participation was voluntary and that they could withdraw at any time. They were also informed of their right to withdraw from the study even after starting the process of completing the questionnaire, without any harm or prejudice.

Academic Integrity and Objectivity

The researcher gave credit to the work of other researchers cited in the study. To avoid plagiarism, all citations were referenced using the APA style, and AIIAS ethical procedures were followed. During the process of data collection, objectivity was maintained by collecting data accurately and completely. This was important in ensuring that objective data was obtained to answer the research objectives. The chapter that follows presents data analysis and the findings.

Chapter 4 | Data Analysis and Presentation of Findings

The purpose of this chapter was to discuss the findings on the behaviour of individual investors in the NSE. It started with a brief overview of the responses received and described the process of data screening employed. This was followed by the demographic and psychographic characteristics of the respondents, descriptive statistics of behavioural factors, investment decisions, and investment performance. At the end of the chapter, the relationship between the behaviour of individual investors, investment decisions, and investment performance was conceptualized. The researcher distributed 500 questionnaires to individual investors in the NSE; 499 questionnaires were filled out by the individual investors and collected.

The objectives of the study were addressed through the following research questions:

1. What behavioural factors, such as herding, prospect (loss aversion, regret aversion, and escalating commitment), and heuristic (availability bias and overconfidence), are displayed by individual investors in the NSE?
2. To what extent are the behavioural factors, such as herding, prospect (loss aversion, regret aversion, and escalating commitment), and heuristic (availability bias and overconfidence), displayed by individual investors in the NSE?
3. Do the following factors—herding; prospect (loss aversion, regret aversion, and escalating commitment); heuristic (availability bias and overconfidence); and market factors (public information and expert information)—significantly differ by the demographic and psychographic characteristics of individual investors in the NSE?
4. Are the following factors—herding; prospect (loss aversion, regret aversion, and escalating commitment); heuristic (availability bias and overconfidence); market factors (public information and expert information); and investment decisions—significantly correlated with each other in the NSE?
5. Do the following behavioural factors—herding; prospect (loss aversion, regret aversion, and escalating commitment); heuristic (availability bias and overconfidence); and market factors (public information and expert information)—combined together significantly influence investment performance in the NSE?
6. Do the following behavioural factors—herding; prospect (loss aversion, regret aversion, and escalating commitment); heuristic (availability bias and overconfidence); and market factors (public information and expert information)—combined together significantly influence investment performance when investment decisions are used as a control variable in the NSE?

Data Screening

The following section discusses missing values, outliers, normality, and tests for linearity. The data collected was coded into the SPSS program for analysis to answer the research questions of the study. Pre-analysis data screening was conducted before the main analysis. Pre-analysis data screening involves checking the quality of the data collected before conducting the actual analysis (Mertler & Vannatta, 2013). This is important because quality data ensures that the main analysis will produce credible results for interpretation. Pre-analysis data screening was done to check for the accuracy of the data collected, missing information, extreme values (outliers), and the fit between the data and the assumptions for regression procedures, which include checks for normality, linearity, and homoscedasticity.

The accuracy of the data was checked using frequency distributions and descriptive statistics. The means, standard deviations, and range of values were examined. In addition, the coded values were checked to ensure that correct codes had been used for categorical data (Mertler & Vannatta, 2013). The data collected was found to be accurate and complete.

Missing Data

Missing data was checked using frequencies. If the frequencies indicated that there were missing values, then the percentage of missing data would be estimated. If the missing values were less than 5%, they could either be replaced or left without replacement. In this case, no missing data was detected, and hence the researcher used all 499 questionnaires received from the respondents.

Outliers

After checking for missing data, the next step was to check for outliers. Outliers are normally removed from further analysis because they can distort the findings. Mahalanobis distance was used to identify outliers. In this case, there were eight independent variables, one controlling variable, and one dependent variable, giving a total of ten degrees of freedom. Therefore, the critical value of Mahalanobis distance was 29.588. Any case with values greater than 29.588 was eliminated casewise from the dataset. Consequently, one case was deleted (case number 22), and 498 cases remained for further analysis.

Normality Test

This section presents the data normality tests (see Table 14) in preparation for testing the relationships between investors' behaviours (herding, prospect, and heuristic), market factors (public information and expert information), and investment decisions with investment performance. Values for skewness and kurtosis between -2 and +2 are acceptable, though values between -1 and +1 are preferable. The results for this study are shown in Table 5, and all the skewness and kurtosis values were between -2 and +2, which indicated that the data was normal.

Another test for normality is the Kolmogorov-Smirnov test. According to this test, if the results show $p \leq .05$, then the data is significantly different from a normal distribution. The results from this study indicated that all the variables had significant results; hence, normality was violated. However, since the skewness and kurtosis values supported the assumption of normality, the researcher considered the data fit for further analysis.

	N	Min	Max	Mean	SD	Skewness		Kurtosis	
Herding	498	1.50	5.00	3.9766	.85946	-1.415	.109	1.022	.218
Loss aversion	498	1.67	5.00	3.9859	.87006	-1.202	.109	1.359	.218
Regret aversion	498	1.40	4.80	3.5157	.74593	-1.092	.109	.538	.218
Escalating com	498	1.67	5.00	3.7859	.86406	-1.202	.109	1.359	.218
Availability bias	498	2.00	5.00	3.9916	.81909	-1.057	.109	.228	.218
Overconfidence	498	1.67	5.00	4.0311	1.03649	-1.579	.109	.923	.218
Public inform	498	1.00	5.00	2.0602	1.19255	1.612	.109	.977	.218
Expert inform	498	1.00	5.00	2.1452	1.02271	1.643	.109	1.470	.218
Investment decisions	498	1.60	4.40	3.7388	.70271	-1.599	.109	1.290	.218
Investment perform	498	2.29	4.86	3.9785	.67652	-1.136	.109	.397	.218

Table 7: Skewness and Kurtosis Descriptive Statistics

The researcher continued with the data analysis for the study since some violation may be overlooked. This was because the sample size greater than 200 reduces or cancels out the effect of nonnormality (Hair, Black, Babin, & Anderson, 2014). In addition, when group difference are done the large sample sizes may cancel out the effects of nonnormality.

Test for Linearity

Linearity postulates that the variables under study can be represented in a straight line. This study used the scatter plots to determine whether there is linear relationship between the independent variables and the dependent variable. The variables were measured on a continuous scale and hence, suitable for regression analysis. The scatterplot of zresid against zpred indicated a violation of linearity because the data did not form an eclipse like shape but had two shape formed to the far right and left. Also Kolmogorov-Smirnov test indicated a violation of linearity assumption.

Homoscedasticity Test

Homoscedasticity enables the researcher to measure the variability of one continuous variable which should be similar for all continuous independent variables (Tabachnick & Fidell, 2013). The variance should be the same for all the independent variables for the data to be homoscedasticity. The data collected for this study violated homoscedasticity. This violation of homoscedasticity is not fatal to the analysis of ungrouped data (Tabachnick & Fidell, 2013). In addition, the analysis captures the linear relationship of the variables. Furthermore, predictability of the model is maintained if heteroscedasticity is accounted for. However, if the heteroscedasticity is not accounted for, then, "the analysis will only be weakened but not invalidated" (Tabachnick & Fidell, 2013, p. 85).

Multicollinearity Test

Table 15 shows the results of multicollinearity normality test of the data. Multicollinearity is considered to exist when Variance Inflation Factor is < 1 or > 10 and the Tolerance level is > 1. The Tolerance level was < 1 for all the variables and hence there was no multicollinearity.

Model		Unstandardized Coefficients		Standardized Coefficients	t	Sig.	Collinearity Statistics	
		B	Std. Error	Beta			Tolerance	VIF
1	(Constant)	3.378	.307		11.001	.000		
	Regret aversion	.109	.114	.120	.956	.340	.029	34.787
	Escalating com	.754	.144	.970	5.241	.000	.013	75.929
	Availability bias	.622	.105	.753	5.907	.000	.028	35.999
	Overconfidence	.129	.050	.198	2.565	.011	.076	13.212
	Public inform	-.287	.068	-.507	-4.223	.000	.031	31.911
	Expert inform	.038	.071	.058	.542	.588	.039	25.397
	Investment decisions	-.095	.076	-.098	-1.240	.215	.072	13.952
	Herding	-1.239	.257	-1.573	-4.811	.000	.004	237.177
a. Dependent Variable: Investment performance								

Table 8: Multicollinearity Coefficients

Demographic Characteristics

After data screening, this section presents the results of the analysis of the respondents demographic characteristics (see Table 16) including: respondents' gender, age bracket, marital status, occupation, highest level of education, monthly income and experience investing in stock. Individual investors' demographic analyzed data was presented in Table 16, based on the analyzed data. The study established that majority of respondents 90.8% (452) were male compared to 9.2% (46) who were female. This finding indicated that investment in NSE is dominated by men compared to women. Concerning investors' age bracket, the study established that majority of respondents 85.5% (426) were in the age bracket of 36-52 years and14.5% (72) were in the age bracket of 18-35 years. The finding indicated that the individual investors in NSE were of middle age. Findings on marital status revealed that majority of the respondents

Variable	Data Set	Frequency	Percentage
Gender	Male	452	90.8
	Female	46	9.20
	Total	498	100%
Age Bracket	18-35 years	72	14.5
	36-52 years	426	85.5
Variable	**Data Set**	**Frequency**	**Percentage**
	Total	498	100%
Marital Status	Single	46	9.20
	Married	429	86.1
	Divorced	23	4.6
	Total	498	100%

Occupation	Employed	87	17.5
	Business	411	82.5
	Total	498	100%
Highest Level of Education	High school	172	34.5
	College	302	60.6
	Post graduate	24	4.8
	Total	498	100%
Monthly Income	Up to Kshs. 50,000	122	24.5
	Kshs. 50,001-100,000	331	66.5
	Over Kshs. 100,000	45	9.0
	Total	498	100%
Experience Investing in Stock	Up to 5 years	22	4.4
	6-10 years	463	93.0
	11 years and above	13	2.6
	Total	498	100%

Table 9: Demographic Characteristics of Individual Investors

86.1% (429) were married, 9.2% (46) were single and 4.6% (23) were divorced. This findings indicated that investment in NSE was mostly done by married families.

The purpose of this chapter was to discuss the findings on the behaviour of individual investors in the NSE. It started with a brief overview of the responses received and described the process of data screening employed. This was followed by the demographic and psychographic characteristics of the respondents, descriptive statistics of behavioural factors, investment decisions, and investment performance. At the end of the chapter, the relationship between the behaviour of individual investors, investment decisions, and investment performance was conceptualized. The researcher distributed 500 questionnaires to individual investors in the NSE; 499 questionnaires were filled out by the individual investors and collected.

The objectives of the study were addressed through the following research questions:

- What behavioural factors, such as herding, prospect (loss aversion, regret aversion, and escalating commitment), and heuristic (availability bias and overconfidence), are displayed by individual investors in the NSE?
- To what extent are the behavioural factors, such as herding, prospect (loss aversion, regret aversion, and escalating commitment), and heuristic (availability bias and overconfidence), displayed by individual investors in the NSE?
- Do the following factors—herding; prospect (loss aversion, regret aversion, and escalating commitment); heuristic (availability bias and overconfidence); and market factors (public information and expert information)—significantly differ by the demographic and psychographic characteristics of individual investors in the NSE?
- Are the following factors—herding; prospect (loss aversion, regret aversion, and escalating commitment); heuristic (availability bias and overconfidence); market factors (public information and expert information); and investment decisions—significantly correlated with each other in the NSE?

- Do the following behavioural factors—herding; prospect (loss aversion, regret aversion, and escalating commitment); heuristic (availability bias and overconfidence); and market factors (public information and expert information)—combined together significantly influence investment performance in the NSE?
- Do the following behavioural factors—herding; prospect (loss aversion, regret aversion, and escalating commitment); heuristic (availability bias and overconfidence); and market factors (public information and expert information)—combined together significantly influence investment performance when investment decisions are used as a control variable in the NSE?

Data Screening

The following section discusses missing values, outliers, normality, and tests for linearity. The data collected were coded into the SPSS program for analysis to answer the research questions of the study. Pre-analysis data screening was conducted before the main analysis. Pre-analysis data screening involves checking the quality of the data collected before conducting the actual analysis (Mertler & Vannatta, 2013). This is important because quality data ensure that the main analysis will produce credible results for interpretation. Pre-analysis data screening was done to check for the accuracy of the data collected, missing information, extreme values (outliers), and the fit between the data and the assumptions for regression procedures, which include checks for normality, linearity, and homoscedasticity.

The accuracy of the data was checked using frequency distributions and descriptive statistics. The means, standard deviations, and range of values were examined. In addition, the coded values were checked to ensure that correct codes had been used for categorical data (Mertler & Vannatta, 2013). The data collected were found to be accurate and complete.

Missing Data

Missing data were checked using frequencies. If the frequencies indicated that there were missing values, then the percentage of missing data would be estimated. If the missing values were less than 5%, they could either be replaced or left without replacement. In this case, no missing data were detected, and hence the researcher used all 499 questionnaires received from the respondents.

Outliers

After checking for missing data, the next step was to check for outliers. Outliers are normally removed from further analysis because they can distort the findings. Mahalanobis distance was used to identify outliers. In this case, there were eight independent variables, one controlling variable, and one dependent variable, giving a total of ten degrees of freedom. Therefore, the critical value of Mahalanobis distance was 29.588. Any case with values greater than 29.588 was eliminated casewise from the dataset. Consequently, one case was deleted (case number 22), and 498 cases remained for further analysis.

Normality Test

This section presents the data normality tests (see Table 14) in preparation for testing the relationships between investors' behaviours (herding, prospect, and heuristic), market factors (public information and expert information), and investment decisions with investment performance. Values for skewness and kurtosis between -2 and +2 are acceptable, though values between -1 and +1 are preferable. The results for this study are shown in Table 5, and all the skewness and kurtosis values were between -2 and +2, which indicated that the data were normal.

Another test for normality is the Kolmogorov-Smirnov test. According to this test, if the results show $p \leq .05$, then the data are significantly different from a normal distribution. The results from this study indicated that all the variables had significant results; hence, normality was violated. However, since the skewness and kurtosis values supported the assumption of normality, the researcher considered the data fit for further analysis.

The study established that majority of respondents 96.4% (480) invested in stock at NSE with long term plan, 2.6% (13) invested with medium term plan objective whereas only 1% (5) of the individual investors had a short term objective of investment. This finding revealed that majority of individual investors in NSE had a long term plan in their mind when investing so that they get their investment returns much later.

Variable	Data Set	Frequency	Percentage
Investment Objective	Short-term	5	1.0
	Medium-term	13	2.6
	Long-term	480	96.4
	Total	498	100%
Frequency of Investing	Daily	7	1.4
	Weekly	35	7.0
	Monthly	456	91.6
	Total	498	100
Investment Size	100-200	446	89.6
(No. of Shares)	201-1000	52	10.4
	Total	498	100
Sector of Investment	Banking	90	18.1
	Commercial	394	79.1
	Others	14	2.8
	Total	498	100
Type of Stock	Blue chip	221	44.4
	Income Stock	42	8.4
	Actively Traded	235	47.2
	Total	498	100

Table 10: Psychographic Characteristics of Individual Investors

The study established that majority of respondents 91.6% (456) invested in NSE on monthly basis, 7% (35) invested weekly and 1.4% (7) invested daily. This findings reveals that the investors in NSE focussed on investing on a monthly basis. The study established that majority of respondents 89.6% (446) of individual investors in NSE who bought 100-200 shares compared to just 10.4% (52) who bought 201-1,000 shares. This finding indicated that most individual investors in NSE have a mindset of buying small amount of shares in NSE.

The study established that the majority of respondents, 79.1% (394), invested heavily in the Commercial and Services segment of the NSE. This segment includes the following listed companies: Express Limited, Kenya Airways, Nation Media Group, Standard Group, TPS Eastern Africa (Serena), Scangroup Ltd, Uchumi Supermarket, Longhorn Publishers, Atlas Development and Support Services, Deacons (EA) PLC, and Nairobi Ventures Ltd. Another 18.1% (90) of the investors invested in the Banking segment, which includes the following companies: Barclays Ltd, Stanbic Holding PLC, I&M Holding Ltd, Diamond Trust Bank Ltd, HF Group Ltd, KCB Group Ltd, NIC Group Ltd, Standard Chartered Bank Ltd, Equity Group Holding Ltd, and the Co-operative Bank of Kenya Ltd. In comparison, only 2.8% (14) invested in other segments of the NSE.

The study established that the majority of respondents, 47.2% (235), invested in actively traded stocks due to the belief that such stocks can be easily sold by individual investors. Another 44.4% (221) of the respondents traded in stocks sold by blue-chip companies. About 8.4% (42) of the respondents traded in income stocks, which are equity securities that pay regular, often steadily increasing dividends, and offer a high yield that may generate the majority of overall returns.

Having presented the descriptive statistics of demographics and psychographics, the following sections present the findings of the study in the order of the research questions.

Findings on Research Question One

This section addresses research question one: What behavioural factors—such as herding; prospect (loss aversion, regret aversion, and escalation of commitment); and heuristic (availability bias and overconfidence)—are displayed by individual investors in the NSE? The findings of the descriptive statistics of behavioural factors, including herding; prospect (loss aversion, regret aversion, and escalation of commitment); and heuristic (availability bias and overconfidence), are presented. This is followed by market factors (public information and expert information).

Descriptive Statistics of Herding Behaviour

This section presents the descriptive statistics of herding behaviour that influences individual investors' investment decisions in the NSE. Table 18 shows the level of herding among individual investors in the NSE. The findings showed that herding behaviour was prevalent among individual investors in the NSE.

Variable	N	M	SD
Herding	498	3.98	.859

Table 11: Descriptive Statistics of Herding Behaviour

The level of herding had a mean and standard deviation of (M = 3.98, SD = .859), respectively. The findings indicated a high level of herding among individual investors at the NSE. This is inferred to mean that they follow the decisions of other investors while making investment decisions without conducting their own analysis, follow the popular opinion of others, and immediately retreat to safer investments when their decisions turn out poorly.

Descriptive Statistics of Prospect Behaviour

This section presents the descriptive statistics of prospect behaviour that influences individual investors' investment decisions at the NSE. The results in Table 19 show the level of prospect behaviour (loss aversion, regret aversion, and escalating the commitment) among individual investors at the NSE. The findings indicate that loss aversion had a mean and standard deviation of (M = 3.99, SD = .870). This showed that the level of loss aversion was high, indicating that individual investors at the NSE make investment decisions to avoid losses. A positive return in the past leads them to become more risk-seeking, while a negative return in the past leads them to become more risk-averse.

Variable	N	M	SD
Loss Aversion	498	3.99	.870
Regret Aversion	498	3.52	.746
Escalating the Commitment	498	3.79	.864

Table 12: Descriptive Statistics of Prospecting Behaviour

On escalating the commitment, the findings showed a mean and standard deviation of (M = 3.79, SD = .864) among individual investors at the NSE, indicating a high level of escalation of commitment. This could be inferred to mean that they continue to invest in stocks even after incurring losses, even if they are unsure of attaining their goals. They continue to invest even when aware that the investment may be bad. This could be true if investors believe the losses are temporary and that the stocks which have lost value will eventually recover. Therefore, if they continue holding the shares, they expect to reap high returns when the stocks recover in value.

Regret aversion also had a high index level of (M = 3.52, SD = .746). This could be inferred to mean that they are more willing to sell stocks whose prices are increasing, less willing to sell stocks whose prices are decreasing, and feel bad when stocks they did not choose perform better. This means that individual investors make decisions based on avoiding future regret.

Descriptive Statistics of Heuristic Behavior

This study sought to identify the extent to which individual investors are influenced by their heuristic behaviour while making investment decisions. This section presents the descriptive statistics of heuristic behaviour (availability bias and overconfidence).

Variable	N	M	SD
Availability Bias	498	3.99	.819
Overconfidence	498	4.03	1.036

Table 13: Descriptive Statistics of Heuristic Behavior

Availability bias and overconfidence had means and standard deviations of (M = 3.99, SD = .819) and (M = 4.03, SD = 1.036), respectively. These levels were considered to be high. This can be inferred to mean that individual investors at the NSE tend to invest in local companies, companies whose names are easy to recall, those with publicly available information, and those that have performed well.

Regarding overconfidence, individual investors considered themselves better positioned than others to earn superior returns, believed they could forecast future stock prices more accurately, and found it easy to trade in stocks. This clearly indicates that individual investors at the NSE are influenced by overconfidence when making investment decisions.

Descriptive Statistics of Market Factors

The study sought to establish the levels of market factors influencing individual investors at the NSE. These levels were presented using means and standard deviations. This section presents the descriptive statistics of market behaviour (public information and expert information) that influences individual investors' decisions at the NSE. Table 21 shows the level of market factors among individual investors at the NSE.

Variable	N	M	SD
Public Information	498	2.06	1.193
Expert Information	498	2.15	1.023

Table 14: Descriptive Statistics of Market Behavior

Descriptive Statistics of Investment Decisions

This section presents the descriptive statistics on how investment decisions were perceived in response to various behavioural profiles of individual investors at the NSE (see Table 22). The level was high, with a mean and standard deviation of (M = 3.74, SD = .703). This indicates that individual investors were influenced in their decision-making by stock prices, stock returns, stocks that other traders are trading, past performance of stocks, the need for diversification, stock trading volumes, and stocks with frequently announced news.

Variable	N	M	SD
Investment Decisions	498	3.74	.703

Table 15: Descriptive Statistics of Investment Decisions

Descriptive Statistics of Investment Performance

The study also sought to determine the level of the degree of market efficiencies impact on investment performance. The levels were presented in the form of means and standard deviation. This indicated the level of agreement by the individual investors on the effect of market efficiencies (weak form, semi-strong form, and strong form). The study also sought to determine the level of the degree of market efficiencies impact on investment performance.

The levels were presented in the form of means and standard deviation. This indicated the level of agreement by the individual investors on the effect of market efficiencies (weak form, semi-strong form, and strong form) on investment performance. Table 23 shows the level of investment performance as indicated by the individual investors. The level was high with a mean and standard deviation of (M = 3.98, SD = .677). This can be inferred to mean that the individual investors agreed that the market efficiencies has an impact on their investment performance.

Findings on Research Question Two

This section addresses research question two: to what extent are the behavioural factors such as herding, prospect (loss aversion, regret aversion, and escalating the commitment), and heuristic (availability bias and overconfidence) displayed by the individual investors in the NSE? The section presents the descriptive statistics of behavioural factors, including their ranks that are embedded in those presented in Table 24.

Variable	N	M	SD
Investment Performance	498	3.98	.677

Table 16: Descriptive Statistics of Investment Performance

Among the six behavioural factors overconfidence ranks highest with a mean and standard deviation of (M = 4.031, SD = 1.036) and regret aversion ranks lowest with mean and standard deviation of (M = 3.516, SD = .746).

The other behavioural variables are ranked as follows: in the second place is availability bias, the third is loss aversion, the fourth is the herding and the fifth is the escalating commitment variable with means and standard deviations of (M = 3.992, SD = .819), (M = 3.986, SD = .870), (M = 3.977, SD = .859), and (M = 3.786, SD = .864) respectively. This means that a majority of the investors in the NSE are influenced by the behavioural factors when making investment decisions in the order shown in Table 24.

Variable	N	M	SD
Overconfidence	498	4.031	1.04
Availability Bias	498	3.992	.819
Loss Aversion	498	3.986	.870
Herding	498	3.977	.859
Escalating Commitment	498	3.786	.864
Regret Aversion	498	3.516	.746

Table 17: The Rank of the Behavioral Factors

These findings are supported by Waweru, Mwangi, and Parkinson (2014), who also found high levels of behavioural factors among property investors of the estate agents. Waweru et al. (2014) found that real estate investors were affected by loss aversion, regret aversion, overconfidence, and availability bias, with (M = 3.02), (M = 3.62), (M = 3.44), and (M = 3.65) respectively. These levels are not exactly the same as those found in this study, but they show the existence of behavioural factors in both cases. These findings are also supported by Ngoc (2013), who found that herding (M = 3.63), loss aversion (M = 3.83), regret aversion (M = 3.76), and overconfidence (M = 3.66) existed among individual investors. In addition, escalating the commitment has been found to affect mutual fund managers in another study (Lin et al., 2014), which supports my findings, although the level is not indicated. The next section presents findings of Research Question 3.

Findings on Research Question Three

This study sought to answer Research Question Three: Do the following factors—herding, prospect (loss aversion, regret aversion, and escalating the commitment), heuristic (availability bias and overconfidence), and market factors (public information and expert information)—significantly differ by the demographic and psychographic characteristics of individual investors in the NSE? This section presents the inferential statistics results of measuring differences in all behavioural factors: herding, prospect, heuristic, and market factors in terms of their demographic and psychographic characteristics. The summary of differences is presented in Appendices C and D.

Demographic Differences on Herding Behaviour

This section was to determine the differences in herding behaviour between the demographic characteristics. Therefore, the findings of the differences in herding behaviour by the demographic characteristics are presented. The demographic characteristics included: gender, age, education, occupation, income, trading experience, and trading frequency.

By Gender. The study sought to determine whether the herding behaviour of individual investors differed by gender. The descriptive statistics are shown in Table 25. The findings (see Table 26) show that the level of herding significantly differs between males and females, t (109.288) = -9.102, p = .000.

	Demographic-Gender	**N**	**Mean**	**Std. Deviation**	**Std. Error Mean**
Herding	Male	452	3.9196	.87494	.04115
	Female	46	4.5362	.36500	.05382

Table 18: Descriptive Statistics of Herding Behaviour Comparison by Gender

Levene's Test for Equality of Variances						
		F	**Sig.**	**t**	**df**	**Sig. (2-tailed)**
Herding	Equal variances assumed	18.547	.000	-4.735	496	.000
	Equal variances not assumed			-9.102	109.288	.000

Table 19: The t-test of Herding Behaviour Comparison by Gender

The individual investors who are female (M = 4.536, SD = .365) reported significantly higher levels of herding than the males (M = 3.920, SD = .875). Therefore, the females among the individual investors of the NSE exhibited more herding behavior than the males. This could be because females tend to share information more than males, which may lead to higher herding. In addition, women in Kenya often form groups for economic and social empowerment, which may further encourage herding behavior more than among males. These findings are supported by other studies (Alrabadi, Al-abdallah, Ibrahim, & Aljarayesh, 2018; Nyamute, 2016), which also found significant differences in herding behavior between males and females. However, other studies have found no significant gender differences in herding behavior (Prosad, Kapoor, & Sengupta, 2015; Velumoni, 2017).

By Age

The study sought to determine differences in herding among individual investors of the NSE by age. The descriptive comparison of herding by age is shown in Table 19. The age groups 18–35 years (M = 3.887, SD = .729) and 36–52 years (M = 3.992, SD = .879) did not differ significantly in their levels of herding, $t(496) = -.961$, $p = .337$ (Table 27). This indicates that individual investors in the NSE exhibited similar levels of herding across the age groups. It suggests that both age groups are exposed to the same set of information, which leads them to herd. This is because individual investors are likely to trade in the same direction when they receive and interpret stock information similarly. The findings of this study concur with those of Prosad et al. (2015). However, Nyamute (2016) found a significant difference in herding among individual investors when compared by age.

Levene's Test for Equality of Variances						
		F	**Sig.**	**t**	**df**	**Sig. (2-tailed)**
Herding	Equal variances assumed	1.486	.223	-.961	496	.337
	Equal variances not assumed			-1.097	109.144	.275

Table 20: The t-test of Herding Behaviour Comparison by Age

By marital status. Table 28 shows that herding behaviour of the individual investors does not significantly differ by the marital status ($F [2,495] = 2.402$, $p = .092$). This means that the individual investors were not affected by their marital status on herding behaviour. Therefore, their level of herding is similar across the marital status. This implies that individual investors of NSE are not influenced by their marital status because the investors may make investment decisions without consulting their spouses. As such, they make individual decisions which are not affected by their marital status.

By Occupation. This section attempted to compare herding behaviour by occupation of the individual investors of NSE. Table 29 presents the descriptive statistics of herding comparison by occupation. The results show that comparison of herding by the occupation was significantly different, $t\,(110.329) = -3.511$, $p = .001$ (Table 30).

	Sum of Squares	df	Mean Square	F	Sig.
Between Groups	3.528	2	1.764	2.402	0.092
Within Groups	363.588	495	0.735		
Total	367.116	497			

Table 21: ANOVA-Herding Behaviour Comparison by Marital Status

	Demographic-Occupation	N	Mean	Std. Deviation	Std. Error Mean
Herding	Employed	87	3.6418	1.01173	0.10847
	Business	411	4.0474	0.80739	0.03983

Table 22: Descriptive Statistics of Herding Behaviour Comparison by Occupation

Levene's Test for Equality of Variances						
		F	Sig.	t	df	Sig. (2-tailed)
Herding	Equal variances assumed	26.118	.000	-4.062	496	.000
	Equal variances not assumed			-3.511	110.329	.001

Table 23: The t-test of Herding Behaviour Comparison by Occupation

The individual investors with businesses (M = 4.047, SD = .807) and those who are employed (M = 3.642, SD = 1.012) significantly differed on herding (see Table 29). This means that the individual investors in the NSE who are businesspeople have a higher level of herding than those who are employed. This may indicate that the businesspeople may be herding more because they are investing in stocks as part of their business portfolio. Therefore, they follow the decisions other investors in the stock market are making, hoping that they are the best decisions that will produce more earnings. The findings of this study contradict the findings of Prosad et al. (2015), who found that individual investors do not significantly differ when compared by occupation.

By education: The study sought to compare levels of herding behaviour by the levels of education of the individual investors. One-way ANOVA was used to compare the herding by the level of education (Table 31). The findings showed that there was a significant difference in herding behaviour when the individual investors were compared by their level of education ($F(2, 495) = 5.599$, $p = .004$). Table 32 shows the descriptive statistics of herding by level of education.

This indicated that the individual investors of NSE were affected by their level of education. A Games-Howell test was conducted since the homogeneity test was not achieved (see Table 33). The findings show that the herding level is higher among the individual investors with a high school level of education (M = 4.152, SD = .676) when compared with individual investors with a college education (M = 3.886, SD = .952), with p = .001. In addition, there was no statistically significant difference between individual investors with high school education and those with postgraduate education (M = 3.854, SD = .584), with p = .071. The individual investors with a high school level of education are likely to herd more because of the belief that other investors may have better information for investment decision-making.

	Sum of Squares	**df**	**Mean Square**	**F**	**Sig.**
Between Groups	8.121	2	4.061	5.599	.004
Within Groups	358.994	495	.725		
Total	367.116	497			

Table 24: ANOVA-Herding Behaviour Comparison by Level of Education

Demographic-Highest level of education	**N**	**Mean**	**Std. Deviation**	**Std. Error**
High school	172	4.1521	.67607	.05155
College	302	3.8863	.95233	.05480
Post graduate	24	3.8542	.58424	.11926
Total	498	3.9766	.85946	.03851

Table 25: Descriptive Statistics of Herding Behaviour Comparison by Level of Education

(I) Demographic-Highest level of education	**(J) Demographic-Highest level of education**	**Mean Difference (I-J)**	**Std. Error**	**Sig.**
High school	College	.26582*	.07524	.001
	Post graduate	.29797	.12992	.071
College	High school	-.26582*	.07524	.001
	Post graduate	.03215	.13125	.968
Post graduate	High school	-.29797	.12992	.071
	College	-.03215	.13125	.968

Table 26: Group Comparison of Herding Behaviour by Level of Education

There was no significant difference between the individual investors with college education and those with postgraduate education (*p* = .968). This means that the individual investors with college education may have the same ability to interact with investment information at the same level with those who have postgraduate level of education. Investors with the same set of information and ability may herd in the same direction.

By income. This section presents the results of comparison of herding by the income of the individual investors. One-way ANOVA was used to compare the herding behaviour by income (Table 34). The findings show that there was a statistically significant difference on herding when compared by income (F [2,495] = 5.566), *P* = .004). Therefore, herding of the individual investors is affected by their income.

	Sum of Squares	df	Mean Square	F	Sig.
Between Groups	8.075	2	4.037	5.566	.004
Within Groups	359.041	495	.725		
Total	367.116	497			

Table 27: ANOVA-Herding Behaviour Comparison by Income

Table 35 shows the descriptive of the herding comparison by income. Games-Howell test (Table 36) was conducted since homogeneity of variance test was not achieved. The level of herding between the individual investors with income of less than kshs. 50,000 (M = 4.161, SD = .660) and with income of kshs. 50,001-100,000 (M = 3.886, SD = .937) was significantly different (p = .002). This shows that those with earning of less than kshs. 50,000 and those earning more than kshs.100,000 were herding more than those earning income of kshs. 50,001-100,000. On the other hand, those with income of less than kshs. 50,000 when compared with those with income of over kshs. 100,000 (M = 4.141, SD = .611) were found to have no significant difference (p = .981).

Demographic-Monthly income	N	Mean	Std. Deviation	Std. Error
Less than Kshs. 50,000	122	4.1612	.65972	.05973
Kshs. 50,001 - 100,000	331	3.8862	.93733	.05152
Over Kshs. 100,000	45	4.1407	.61129	.09113
Total	498	3.9766	.85946	.03851

Table 28: Descriptive Statistics of Herding Behaviour Comparison by Income

(I) Demographic-Monthly income	(J) Demographic-Monthly income	Mean Difference (I-J)	Std. Error	Sig.
Less than Kshs. 50,000	Kshs. 50,001 - 100,000	.27500*	.07888	.002
	Over Kshs. 100,000	.02046	.10896	.981
Kshs. 50,001 - 100,000	Less than Kshs. 50,000	-.27500*	.07888	.002
	Over Kshs. 100,000	-.25454*	.10468	.045
Over Kshs. 100,000	Less than Kshs. 50,000	-.02046	.10896	.981
	Kshs. 50,001 - 100,000	.25454*	.10468	.045

Table 29: Group Comparison of Herding Behaviour by Income

The individual investors of the NSE who earn Kshs. 50,000–100,000 may be more cautious in following the investment decisions of others because they want to safeguard their investments in the stock market. Therefore, they will herd less to avoid the prospect of losing their hard-earned cash. On the other hand, those investors earning more than Kshs. 100,000 may have extra income, which they may care less about losing in an investment, so they will herd more. Additionally, individual investors earning Kshs. 50,001–100,000 exhibited significantly lower levels of herding when compared with those earning over Kshs. 100,000, with p = 0.045. The findings of this study are not consistent with the findings of Prosad et al. (2015), who found that individual investors do not significantly differ in herding when compared by income.

By investing experience. This section aimed to determine whether individual investors significantly differ by investing experience. The findings of the comparison on herding behavior between individual investors (see Table 37) showed that there was no significant difference in herding behavior when compared among different years of investing experience (F [2,495] = 0.386, p = 0.680).

	Sum of Squares	df	Mean Square	F	Sig.
Between Groups	.572	2	.286	.386	.680
Within Groups	366.544	495	.740		
Total	367.116	497			

Table 30: ANOVA-Herding Behaviour Comparison by Investing Experience

The findings point to the fact that individual investors of the NSE, across different years of investing experience, have the same level of herding because they do not do their own analysis when herding, and hence, investing experience would not affect their level of herding. This is supported by Aduda et al. (2012), who noted that a majority of NSE investors do not have sufficient investment knowledge. Therefore, investing experience would not influence their level of herding behaviour.

Demographic Differences in Prospect Behaviour

Independent sample t-tests and ANOVA were performed to determine the differences in prospect behaviour based on demographic characteristics. This section presents the findings regarding differences in prospect behaviour by demographic characteristics. The demographic characteristics included gender, age, education, occupation, income, trading experience, and trading frequency.

By Gender. Descriptive statistics of prospect behaviour by gender are shown in Table 38. The findings (see Table 39) showed that male and female individual investors differed significantly when compared on loss aversion by gender: t(80.798) = -9.294, p = .000. Females (M = 4.667, SD = .471) exhibited a higher level of loss aversion compared to males (M = 3.917, SD = .872). Regarding regret aversion and escalating commitment, individual investors differed significantly with t(131.764) = -5.492, p = .000 and t(76.768) = -9.093, p = .000, respectively. On regret aversion, females (M = 3.791, SD = .283) showed a higher level compared to males (M = 3.487, SD = .772).

	Demographic - Gender	N	Mean	Std. Deviation	Std. Error Mean
Loss aversion	Male	452	3.9167	.87177	.04100
	Female	46	4.6667	.47140	.06950
Regret aversion	Male	452	3.4876	.77243	.03633
	Female	46	3.7913	.28271	.04168
Escalating com	Male	452	3.8123	.86377	.02473
	Female	46	4.7267	.47740	.07543

Table 31: Descriptive Statistics of Prospect Behaviour Comparison by Gender

Levene's Test for Equality of Variances						
		F	Sig.	t	df	Sig. (2-tailed)
Loss aversion	Equal variances assumed	4.097	.043	-5.746	496	.000
	Equal variances not assumed			-9.294	80.798	.000
Regret aversion	Equal variances assumed	27.202	.000	-2.647	496	.008
	Equal variances not assumed			-5.492	131.764	.000
Escalating com	Equal variances assumed	3.897	.033	-5.546	496	.000
	Equal variances not assumed			-9.093	76.768	.000

Table 32: The t-test of Prospect Behaviour Comparison by Gender

In addition, females (M = 4.727, SD = .477) had a higher level of escalating commitment compared to males (M = 3.812, SD = .864). The findings show that females had higher levels on all prospect variables. This may indicate that females are more cautious when investing because they do not want to lose their investment, whereas males are more risk-taking and consider the prospects of losing their investment less when investing in the stock market. The findings on loss aversion being significantly different are supported by Alrabadi et al. (2018). On the other hand, the findings of this study are not supported by Velumoni (2017), who found that individual investors did not significantly differ in terms of loss aversion and regret aversion when compared by gender.

By age, the findings (Table 40) from the study indicate that individual investors aged 18-35 years did not differ significantly when compared with investors aged 36-52 years in terms of loss aversion, t(496) = -1.759, p = .079, regret aversion, t(496) = -.534, p = .594, and escalating commitment, t(496) = -2.256, p = .054. This means that individual investors on the NSE did not differ significantly in terms of loss aversion, regret aversion, and escalating commitment when compared by age. Therefore, their levels on the prospect variables were similar across the age groups. This is because individual investors aged 18-52 are in their prime years for accumulating wealth for retirement, and the thought of losing is undesirable and will be avoided by all investors. These findings are confirmed by Velumoni (2017), who found that individual investors did not significantly differ in terms of loss aversion and regret aversion when compared by age.

Levene's Test for Equality of Variances						
		F	Sig.	t	df	Sig. (2-tailed)
Loss aversion	Equal variances assumed	2.063	.152	-1.759	496	.079
	Equal variances not assumed			-2.002	108.682	.048
Regret aversion	Equal variances assumed	.755	.385	-.534	496	.594

	Equal variances not assumed			-.567	101.569	.572
Escalating com	Equal variances assumed	1.931	.152	-2.256	496	.054
	Equal variances not assumed			-1.782	102.682	.032

Table 33: The t-test of Prospect Behaviour Comparison by Age

By marital status. The findings (see Table 41) show that there was no statistically significant difference among the different marital status groups on their loss aversion (p = .088), regret aversion (.389), and escalating the commitment (p = .067). This means the individual investors of NSE had similar levels on loss aversion, regret aversion, and escalating the commitment. An indication that risk consideration in investing receives the same consideration while investing in the stock market since all the investors know that investment in the stock market is risky.

		Sum of Squares	**df**	**Mean Square**	**F**	**Sig.**
Loss aversion	Between Groups	3.685	2	1.842	2.448	.088
	Within Groups	372.550	495	.753		
	Total	376.235	497			
Regret aversion	Between Groups	1.054	2	.527	.947	.389
	Within Groups	275.484	495	.557		
	Total	276.538	497			
Escalating com	Between Groups	2.908	2	1.454	2.132	.067
	Within Groups	337.590	495	.682		
	Total	340.498	497			

Table 41: ANOVA-Prospect Behaviour Comparison by Marital Status

These findings are supported by Velumoni (2017) who found that the individual investors did not significantly differ on loss aversion and regret aversion when they were compared by marital status.

By occupation. Table 42 shows the descriptive statistics of prospect behaviour by occupation. The findings showed that the individual investors who are employed differed in loss aversion, regret aversion, and escalating commitment (see Table 43). The employed individual investors (M = 3.644, SD = 1.088) had significantly lower levels of loss aversion when compared to business people (M = 4.058, SD = .800), t (106.513) = -3.369, p = .001. Also, business people (M = 3.559, SD = .738) reported significantly higher levels of regret aversion than the employed (M = 3.313, SD = .756), t (123.152) = -2.770, p = .006.

	Demographic-Occupation	N	Mean	Std. Deviation	Std. Error Mean
Loss aversion	Employed	87	3.6437	1.08762	.11661
	Business	411	4.0584	.79963	.03944
Regret aversion	Employed	87	3.3126	.75557	.08101
	Business	411	3.5586	.73766	.03639
Escalating com	Employed	87	3.4235	.94361	.03221
	Business	411	3.9221	.67342	.02214

Table 42: The t-test of Prospect Behaviour Comparison by Occupation

Levene's Test for Equality of Variances						
		F	Sig.	t	df	Sig. (2-tailed)
Loss aversion	Equal variances assumed	19.759	.000	-4.103	496	.000
	Equal variances not assumed			-3.369	106.513	.001
Regret aversion	Equal variances assumed	7.670	.006	-2.814	496	.005
	Equal variances not assumed			-2.770	123.152	.006
Escalating com	Equal variances assumed	16.478	.000	-3.215	496	.000
	Equal variances not assumed			-3.831	98.424	.001

Table 43: The t-test of Prospect Behaviour Comparison by Occupation

Regarding escalating commitment, individual investors who are business people (M = 3.922, SD = .673) had significantly higher levels compared to the employed (M = 3.424, SD = .944), t (98.424) = -3.831, p = .001. This means that business people had significantly higher levels of loss aversion, regret aversion, and escalating commitment. Business people give much more thought to risk in investment because of their background in business, which is fraught with a lot of risk. On the other hand, the employed may give less thought to risk because they are employed and, hence, not exposed to a lot of risk in losing their investment. The findings of this study contradict the findings of Velumoni (2017), who found that individual investors did not significantly differ in loss aversion and regret aversion when compared by occupation.

By education: The findings (see Table 44) show that there was a significant difference among the different levels of education groups in their loss aversion (p = .022), regret aversion (p = .000), and escalating commitment (p = .018). This means that the behaviour of individual investors on the NSE significantly differed in loss aversion, regret aversion, and escalating commitment. See Table 45 for the descriptive statistics.

A post hoc Games-Howell test was conducted to determine the differences between the different levels of education. When individual investors were compared on loss aversion (see Table 46) by level of education, those with a high school education (M = 4.134, SD =

.693) significantly differed from those with a college education (M = 3.905, SD = .973) with a p-value of p = .009. However, when those with a high school education were compared with those with postgraduate education (M = 3.944, SD = .363), they did not differ significantly (p = .105). Additionally, those with a college education, when compared with those with postgraduate education, were found not to differ statistically (p = .906).

		Sum of Squares	df	Mean Square	F	Sig.
Loss aversion	Between Groups	5.772	2	2.886	3.856	.022
	Within Groups	370.463	495	.748		
	Total	376.235	497			
Regret aversion	Between Groups	11.634	2	5.817	10.870	.000
	Within Groups	264.903	495	.535		
	Total	276.538	497			
Escalating com	Between Groups	4.518	2	2.259	3.342	.018
	Within Groups	334.620	495	.676		
	Total	339.138	497			

Table 44: ANOVA-Prospect Behaviour Comparison by Education

		N	Mean	Std. Deviation	Std. Error
Loss aversion	High school	172	4.1337	.69310	.05285
	College	302	3.9051	.97353	.05602
	Post graduate	24	3.9444	.36338	.07417
	Total	498	3.9859	.87006	.03899
Regret aversion	High school	172	3.7256	.65144	.04967
	College	302	3.4086	.78121	.04495
	Post graduate	24	3.3583	.61285	.12510
	Total	498	3.5157	.74593	.03343
Escalating com	High school	172	3.9182	.64520	.06341
	College	302	3.8422	.87693	.04328
	Post graduate	24	3.8104	.45324	.07643
	Total	498	3.8922	.98763	.04536

Table 45: Descriptive Statistics of Prospect Behaviour by Level of Education

The findings show that when individual investors are compared on regret aversion by level of education, those with a high school level of education (M = 3.726, SD = .651) significantly differed from those with a college education (M = 3.409, SD = .781), with p = .000. On the other hand, those with a high school education (M = 3.726, SD = .651) also significantly differed from those with postgraduate education (M = 3.358, SD = .613), with a p-value of .027. However, when those with a college education were compared with those with postgraduate education, they were found not to differ significantly (p = .924).

On escalating the commitment, those investors with a high school education (M = 3.918, SD = .645), when compared with those with a college education (M = 3.842, SD = .877), differed significantly, with a p-value of .001. Likewise, those who had a high school education, when compared with those with postgraduate education (M = 3.810, SD = .453), did not differ significantly (p = .084). Also, the individual investors with a college education, when compared with those who have postgraduate qualifications, were found not to differ statistically (p = .734).

Dependent Variable			Mean Difference (I-J)	Std. Error	Sig.
Loss aversion	High school	College	.22864*	.07701	.009
		Post graduate	.18928	.09108	.105
	College	High school	-.22864*	.07701	.009
		Post graduate	-.03937	.09295	.906
	Post graduate	High school	-.18928	.09108	.105
		College	.03937	.09295	.906
Regret aversion	High school	College	.31697*	.06699	.000
		Post graduate	.36725*	.13460	.027
	College	High school	-.31697*	.06699	.000
		Post graduate	.05028	.13293	.924
	Post graduate	High school	-.36725*	.13460	.027
		College	-.05028	.13293	.924
Escalating com	High school	College	.22864*	.07701	.001
		Post graduate	.18928	.09108	.084
	College	High school	-.22864*	.07701	.001
		Post graduate	-.03937	.09295	.734
	Post graduate	High school	-.18928	.09108	.084
		College	.03937	.09295	.734
*. The mean difference is significant at the 0.05 level.					

Table 46: Group Comparison of Prospect Behaviour by Level of Education
**. The mean difference is significant at the 0.05 level.*

The major finding is that individual investors on the NSE with a high school education had a higher level of loss aversion, regret aversion, and escalation of commitment when compared with those who had a college education. This is because those with a college education may possess skills in minimising investment risks and therefore think less about avoiding risks. However, those with a high school education may have fewer skills in managing risks and hence, make decisions to avoid investment risks. These findings are not supported by Velumoni (2017), who found that individual investors do not significantly differ in terms of loss aversion and regret aversion when compared by their level of qualification.

By income: The findings (see Table 47) show that there was a significant difference among the different income groups regarding their regret aversion (p = .000), but there was no significant difference on loss aversion (p = .107) or escalation of commitment (p = .093). This means that individual investors on the NSE significantly differed in terms of regret aversion when compared by income, but did not differ on the other prospect dimensions. Table 48 shows the descriptive statistics of prospect behaviour by income.

		Sum of Squares	df	Mean Square	F	Sig.
Lossaversion	Between Groups	3.383	2	1.692	2.246	.107
	Within Groups	372.852	495	.753		
	Total	376.235	497			
Regretaversion	Between Groups	12.157	2	6.078	11.380	.000
	Within Groups	264.381	495	.534		
	Total	276.538	497			
Escalatingcom	Between Groups	2.754	2	1.377	1.987	.093
	Within Groups	343.035	495	.693		
	Total	345.789	497			

Table 47: ANOVA-Prospect Behaviour Comparison by Income

A post hoc Games-Howell test was conducted (see Table 49). The individual investors in the income group of less than Kshs. 50,000 (M = 3.766, SD = .660) had a higher level of regret aversion when compared to those in the income group of between Kshs. 50,001-100,000 (M = 3.407, SD = .780) with p = .000. The individual investors in the income group of Kshs. 50,001-100,000 (M = 3.407, SD = .780) had a lower level of regret aversion compared to those in the income group of over Kshs. 100,000 (M = 3.636, SD = .499) with p = .026. This means that individual investors with a lower income had a higher level of regret when compared with those with a higher income. This could be because individual investors with a lower income level experience a higher level of regret, as any small loss in an investment represents a significant percentage loss relative to their modest income.

However, there was no significant difference between individual investors in the income groups of less than Kshs. 50,000 and those with an income over Kshs. 100,000 in terms of their regret aversion. These findings are supported by Velumoni (2017), who found that individual investors did not significantly differ in terms of loss aversion when compared by income. However, the findings of this study contradict Velumoni (2017), who found a significant difference in regret aversion.

		N	Mean	Std. Deviation	Std. Error
Loss aversion	Less than Kshs. 50,000	122	4.0464	.73270	.06634
	Kshs. 50,001 - 100,000	331	3.9345	.94784	.05210
	Over Kshs. 100,000	45	4.2000	.50951	.07595
	Total	498	3.9859	.87006	.03899
Regret aversion	Less than Kshs. 50,000	122	3.7656	.66042	.05979
	Kshs. 50,001 - 100,000	331	3.4073	.77971	.04286
	Over Kshs. 100,000	45	3.6356	.49962	.07448
	Total	498	3.5157	.74593	.03343
Escalating com	Less than Kshs. 50,000	122	3.9834	.46531	.07254
	Kshs. 50,001 - 100,000	331	3.8435	.83242	.04533
	Over Kshs. 100,000	45	4.1435	.62345	.04322
	Total	498	3.9367	.67456	.04536

Table 48: Descriptive Statistics of Prospect Behaviour Comparison by Income

Dependent Variable			Mean Difference (I-J)	Std. Error	Sig.
Loss aversion	Less than Kshs. 50,000	Kshs. 50,001 - 100,000	.11191	.08435	.382
		Over Kshs. 100,000	-.15355	.10084	.284
	Kshs. 50,001 - 100,000	Less than Kshs. 50,000	-.11191	.08435	.382
		Over Kshs. 100,000	-.26546*	.09210	.013
	Over Kshs. 100,000	Less than Kshs. 50,000	.15355	.10084	.284
		Kshs. 50,001 - 100,000	.26546*	.09210	.013
Regret aversion	Less than Kshs. 50,000	Kshs. 50,001 - 100,000	.35832*	.07356	.000
		Over Kshs. 100,000	.13002	.09551	.365
	Kshs. 50,001 - 100,000	Less than Kshs. 50,000	-.35832*	.07356	.000
		Over Kshs. 100,000	-.22830*	.08593	.026
	Over Kshs. 100,000	Less than Kshs. 50,000	-.13002	.09551	.365
		Kshs. 50,001 - 100,000	.22830*	.08593	.026
Escalating Com	Less than Kshs. 50,000	Kshs. 50,001 - 100,000	.11191	.08435	.264
		Over Kshs. 100,000	-.15355	.10084	.232
	Kshs. 50,001 - 100,000	Less than Kshs. 50,000	-.11191	.08435	.264
		Over Kshs. 100,000	-.26546*	.09210	.009
	Over Kshs. 100,000	Less than Kshs. 50,000	.15355	.10084	.232
		Kshs. 50,001 - 100,000	.26546*	.09210	.009
*. The mean difference is significant at the 0.05 level.					

Table 49: Group Comparison of Prospect Behavior by Income

When the individual investors were compared on loss aversion, those with an income of Kshs. 50,001-100,000 (M = 3.935, SD = .948), when compared with those who had an income over Kshs. 100,000 (M = 4.200, SD = .510), were found to be significantly different (p = .013). This means that the individual investors with higher income had a lower level of loss aversion compared to those with lower income, indicating that individual investors with lower income do everything possible to avoid losses. This is because the losses would comprise a large percentage of their income, hence the high propensity to avoid losses.

By investing experience, the findings (see Table 50) show that there was a statistically significant difference among the different income groups on their regret aversion (p = .049), but there was no statistically significant difference on loss aversion (p = .638) or escalating the commitment (p = .453). This means that the individual investors' levels were not significantly different when compared on loss aversion and escalating the commitment by their investing experience. However, when they were compared on regret aversion, there was a significant difference between the individual investors when compared by their income.

		Sum of Squares	df	Mean Square	F	Sig.
Loss aversion	Between Groups	.682	2	.341	.449	.638
	Within Groups	375.553	495	.759		
	Total	376.235	497			
Regret aversion	Between Groups	3.350	2	1.675	3.035	.049
	Within Groups	273.188	495	.552		
	Total	276.538	497			
Escalating com	Between Groups	.466	2	.233	.367	.453
	Within Groups	314.325	495	.635		
	Total	314.791	497			

Table 50: ANOVA-Prospect Behaviour Comparison by Investing Experience

Table 51 shows the descriptive statistics of prospect behaviour by investing experience. A post hoc Games-Howell test was conducted (see Table 52) to determine the difference within the groups on regret aversion. When the individual investors were compared on regret aversion by their investing experience, only those with investing experience of between 6-10 years (M = 3.498, SD = .747) significantly differed from those with more than 11 years of experience (M = 4.000, SD = .374) with p = .001. Therefore, individuals with more than 11 years of investing experience had a higher level of regret aversion than those with 6-10 years of investing experience. These people, with more experience, could be older and would regret more because they consider themselves to have less time to recover from losses before retirement. The individual investors with investment experience of up to 5 years (M = 3.600, SD = .809), when compared with those with more than 11 years' experience, were significantly different with p = .021.

On escalating the commitment, the individual investors with experience of up to 5 years (M = 3.645, SD = .345) were significantly different when compared with investors with over 10 years of experience (M = 4.056, SD = .345). Also, the individual investors with 6-10 years of experience (M = 3.822, SD = .754) were significantly different when compared with investors with up to 5 years of experience. These findings show that individual investors have the mindset of continuing to invest in stocks that are currently underperforming in the stock market, hoping that they will increase in value in the future and thus reap more benefits.

		N	Mean	Std. Deviation	Std. Error
Loss aversion	Upto 5 years	22	3.8485	.43312	.09234
	6-10 years	463	3.9885	.89618	.04165
	11 years and above	13	4.1282	.21681	.06013
	Total	498	3.9859	.87006	.03899
Regret aversion	Upto 5 years	22	3.6000	.80947	.17258
	6-10 years	463	3.4981	.74692	.03471
	11 years and above	13	4.0000	.37417	.10377
	Total	498	3.5157	.74593	.03343

Escalatin gcom	Upto 5 years	22	3.6453	.34527	.07654
	6-10 years	463	3.8223	.75432	.06548
	11 years and above	13	4.0564	.34526	.07786
	Total	498	3.8764	.76874	.03421

Table 34: Descriptive Statistics of Prospect Behaviour Comparison by Investing Experience

When the individual investors were compared on loss aversion by investing experience, those with up to 5 years of experience (M = 3.849, SD = .433) were significantly different from those with 11 years and above of experience (M = 4.128, SD = .217), with a p-value of .042. Likewise, those with 6-10 years of investing experience (M = 3.989) were compared with investors with up to 5 years of experience and were significantly different with a p-value of .042. These findings suggest that individual investors with more experience are more concerned with avoiding losses when making investment decisions. This may be because they have experienced losses in the past and are therefore less willing to encounter similar losses.

Dependent Variable	(I) Demographic-Experience in investing in stock	(J) Demographic-Experience in investing in stock	Mean Difference (I-J)	Std. Error	Sig.
Loss aversion	Upto 5 years	6-10 years	-.14000	.10130	.363
		11 years and above	-.27972*	.11019	.042
	6-10 years	Upto 5 years	.14000	.10130	.363
		11 years and above	-.13972	.07315	.156
	11 years and above	Upto 5 years	.27972*	.11019	.042
		6-10 years	.13972	.07315	.156
Regret aversion	Upto 5 years	6-10 years	.10194	.17604	.833
		11 years and above	-.40000	.20138	.132
	6-10 years	Upto 5 years	-.10194	.17604	.833
		11 years and above	-.50194*	.10943	.001
	11 years and above	Upto 5 years	.40000	.20138	.132
		6-10 years	.50194*	.10943	.001
Escalating com	Upto 5 years	6-10 years	-.14000	.10130	.312
		11 years and above	-.27972*	.11019	.021
	6-10 years	Upto 5 years	.14000	.10130	.312
		11 years and above	-.13972	.07315	.212
	11 years and above	Upto 5 years	.27972*	.11019	.021
		6-10 years	.13972	.07315	.212

Table 52: Group Comparison of Prospect Behaviour by Investing Experience

Demographic Differences on Heuristic Behaviour

This section presents the findings on the differences in heuristic (availability bias and overconfidence) by the demographic characteristics. The demographic characteristics included: gender, age, marital status, occupation, education, income, and experience investing in stocks. Each demographic characteristic will now be discussed.

By gender, Table 53 shows the descriptive statistics on heuristics by gender. The findings (see Table 54) show that females (M = 4.522, SD = .354) had higher levels of availability bias than males (M = 3.938, SD = .834), t (106.778) = -8.948, p = .000. Likewise, females (M = 4.409, SD = .152) had higher levels of overconfidence than males (M = 3.993, SD = 1.080), t (466.485) = -7.509, p = .000. This means that the individual investors of the NSE statistically differed when compared on availability bias and overconfidence by gender.Individual investors who are female are likely to have higher levels of availability bias and overconfidence. This is because females may trade more on available information about stocks, as they might share more investment opportunities among themselves than males. Additionally, they are likely to be more overconfident than males due to the sharing of information. Interestingly, this is different from what most studies have found, that males are more overconfident than females (Prosad et al., 2015). However, a study (Alrabadi et al., 2018) found no significant difference between males and females when compared on overconfidence. On the other hand, the findings of this study are supported by Alrabadi et al. (2018), who established that males and females significantly differ when compared on availability bias.

	Demographic-Gender	**N**	**Mean**	**Std. Deviation**	**Std. Error Mean**
Availability bias	Male	452	3.9376	.83382	.03922
	Female	46	4.5217	.35397	.05219
Overconfidence	Male	452	3.9926	1.07958	.05078
	Female	46	4.4094	.15197	.02241

Table 53: Descriptive Statistics of Heuristic Behaviour Comparison by Gender

Levene's Test for Equality of Variances						
		F	Sig.	t	df	Sig. (2-tailed)
Availability bias	Equal variances assumed	29.612	.000	-4.705	496	.000
	Equal variances not assumed			-8.948	106.778	.000
Overconfidence	Equal variances assumed	41.750	.000	-2.614	496	.009
	Equal variances not assumed			-7.509	466.485	.000

Table 54: The t-tests of Heuristic Behaviour Comparison by Gender

By age. The findings (see Table 55) show that individual investors aged between 18-35 years (M = 3.967, SD = .891) did not differ from those aged between 36-52 years (M = 3.996, SD = .807) in terms of levels of availability bias, t (496) = -0.279, p = .781. Similarly, individual investors aged between 18-35 years (M = 4.127, SD = 1.042) did not differ from those aged between 36-52 years (M = 4.015, SD = 1.036) in terms of levels of overconfidence, t (496) = 0.851, p = .395.

Levene's Test for Equality of Variances						
		F	Sig.	t	df	Sig. (2-tailed)
Availability bias	Equal variances assumed	.551	.458	-.279	496	.781
	Equal variances not assumed			-.260	91.762	.796
Overconfidence	Equal variances assumed	.373	.542	.851	496	.395
	Equal variances not assumed			.848	96.255	.399

Table 55: The t-test of Heuristic Behaviour Comparison by Age

This suggests that individual investors did not differ significantly when compared on heuristics by age groups. The findings indicate that individual investors of the NSE exhibited similar levels of availability bias and overconfidence when compared by age. This could be because both groups of individual investors are highly active in the stock market, accumulating wealth. The findings of this study do not support Prosad et al. (2015), who established that individual investors exhibited significant differences when compared by age.

By marital status: The findings (see Table 56) show that there was a significant difference in heuristics when individual investors were compared by marital status: availability bias (F [2,495] = 4.722, p = .009) and overconfidence (F [2,495] = 4.006, p = .019). This indicates that the heuristic behaviour of individual investors was statistically different when compared by marital status. Therefore, individual investors had different levels of availability bias and overconfidence when compared by marital status.

		Sum of Squares	df	Mean Square	F	Sig.
Availability bias	Between Groups	6.243	2	3.122	4.722	.009
	Within Groups	327.201	495	.661		
	Total	333.445	497			
Overconfidence	Between Groups	8.504	2	4.252	4.006	.019
	Within Groups	525.430	495	1.061		
	Total	533.934	497			

Table 56: ANOVA-Heuristic Behaviour Comparison by Marital Status

Descriptive statistics for heuristic behaviour by marital status are shown in Table 57. A Games-Howell post hoc test (see Table 58) was performed to determine the group differences. The individual investors who are single (M = 4.283, SD = .300) differed from the married (M = 3.977, SD = .835) with p = .000, when compared on availability bias. This is because singles can make investment decisions without consulting others, unlike the married, who must consult their spouses, as they consider money to be a family resource that can only be committed once both partners have given their consent. On the other hand, individual investors who are single (M = 4.283, SD = .300) differed from the divorced (M = 3.678, SD = 1.066) with p = .035. This suggests that the divorced have a lower level of availability bias, perhaps due to having to process available information alone. However, the difference between the married and the divorced was not significantly different.

		N	Mean	Std. Deviation	Std. Error
Availability bias	Single	46	4.2826	.29986	.04421
	Married	429	3.9772	.83461	.04030
	Divorced	23	3.6783	1.06641	.22236
	Total	498	3.9916	.81909	.03670
Overconfidence	Single	46	4.3478	.42864	.06320
	Married	429	4.0190	1.06473	.05141
	Divorced	23	3.6232	1.20523	.25131
	Total	498	4.0311	1.03649	.04645

Table 57: Descriptive Statistics of Heuristic Behaviour Comparison by Marital Status

Dependent Variable	(I) Demographic-Marital status	(J) Demographic-Marital status	Mean Difference (I-J)	Std. Error	Sig.
Availability bias	Single	Married	.30545*	.05982	.000
		Divorced	.60435*	.22671	.035
	Married	Single	-.30545*	.05982	.000
		Divorced	.29890	.22598	.397
	Divorced	Single	-.60435*	.22671	.035
		Married	-.29890	.22598	.397
Overconfidence	Single	Married	.32879*	.08147	.000
		Divorced	.72464*	.25913	.026
	Married	Single	-.32879*	.08147	.000
		Divorced	.39585	.25651	.289
	Divorced	Single	-.72464*	.25913	.026
		Married	-.39585	.25651	.289

Table 58: Group Comparison of Heuristic Behaviour by Marital Status

On overconfidence, individual investors who are single (M = 4.348, SD = .429) were found to differ significantly from those who are married (M = 4.019, SD = 1.065) with p = .000. Similarly, individual investors who are single had a higher level of overconfidence than those who are divorced (M = 3.623, SD = 1.036). Single individual investors appear to have higher levels of overconfidence because they make decisions alone, without depending on a spouse.

By occupation. Table 59 shows the descriptive statistics of heuristics by occupation. The results (Table 60) showed that business people (M = 4.040, SD = .788) reported significantly higher levels of availability bias than those who are employed (M = 3.761, SD = .922), t (114.095) = -2.631, p = .010. This suggests that individual investors in the NSE who are business people have a higher level of availability bias. The reason for this could be that business people may be considering the available stocks to buy regularly, especially if stocks are part of their business portfolio.

Individual investors who are business people (M = 4.030, SD = 1.033) and those who are employed (M = 4.035, SD = 1.058) did not differ significantly on levels of overconfidence, t (496) = 0.033, p = .974. This indicates that individual investors in the NSE who are business people and those who are employed have similar levels of overconfidence when compared by occupation. Their occupation did not affect them because they consider investment in stocks to be separate from their occupations. Therefore, decisions regarding stock investments are made independently of their primary occupation. The findings of this study contradict Prosad et al. (2015), who determined that individual investors were significantly different in terms of overconfidence when compared by profession.

	Demographic-Occupation	N	Mean	Std. Deviation	Std. Error Mean
Availability bias	Employed	87	3.7609	.92200	.09885
	Business	411	4.0404	.78822	.03888
Overconfidence	Employed	87	4.0345	1.05811	.11344
	Business	411	4.0304	1.03317	.05096

Table 59: Descriptive Statistics of Heuristic Behaviour Comparison by Occupation

Levene's Test for Equality of Variances						
		F	Sig.	t	df	Sig. (2-tailed)
Availability bias	Equal variances assumed	6.093	.014	-2.913	496	.004
	Equal variances not assumed			-2.631	114.095	.010
Overconfidence	Equal variances assumed	.021	.884	.033	496	.974

Table 60: The t-test of Heuristic Behaviour Comparison by Occupation

By education: The findings (see Table 61) show that when individual investors were compared on heuristics by education, there was a significant difference in overconfidence (F [2,495] = 15.405, p = .000), while they did not differ in availability bias (F [2,495] = 1.142, p = .320). This indicates that individual investors of the NSE significantly differed in terms of overconfidence. However, they did not significantly differ in terms of availability bias. This may be because available shares are in the public domain, and thus education is not necessary to determine which shares are available for purchase.

Table 62 shows the descriptive statistics of heuristics by level of education. A post hoc test (see Table 63) was conducted to show the differences in overconfidence. The post hoc test revealed that for availability bias, individual investors with a college education (M = 3.985, SD = .762) had a higher level when compared to those with postgraduate education (M = 3.767, SD = 1.041), with a p-value of .000.

		Sum of Squares	df	Mean Square	F	Sig.
Availability bias	Between Groups	1.531	2	.765	1.142	.320
	Within Groups	331.914	495	.671		
	Total	333.445	497			
Overconfidence	Between Groups	30.810	2	15.405	15.156	.000

	Within Groups	503.124	495	1.016		
	Total	533.934	497			

Table 61: ANOVA-Heuristic Behaviour Comparison by Level of Education

		N	Mean	Std. Deviation	Std. Error
Availability bias	High school	172	4.0337	.87967	.06707
	College	302	3.9854	.76174	.04383
	Post graduate	24	3.7667	1.04118	.21253
	Total	498	3.9916	.81909	.03670
Overconfidence	High school	172	3.7151	1.19286	.09095
	College	302	4.2312	.86542	.04980
	Post graduate	24	3.7778	1.22244	.24953
	Total	498	4.0311	1.03649	.04645

Table 62: Descriptive Statistics of Heuristic Behaviour Comparison by Level of Education

Post hoc test (see Table 63) showed that individual investors who had a college education (M = 4.231, SD = .865) were more confident than those with high school level of education (M = 3.715, SD = 1.193), with *p* = .000. This means that those with college education are able to evaluate investment opportunities more confidently because of their level of education.

Dependent Variable	(I) Demographic-Highest level of education	(J) Demographic-Highest level of education	Mean Difference (I-J)	Std. Error	Sig.
Availability bias	High school	College	.04829	.08013	.819
		Post graduate	.26705	.22286	.464
	College	High school	-.04829	.08013	.819
		Post graduate	.21876	.21700	.579
	Post graduate	High school	-.26705	.22286	.464
		College	-.21876	.21700	.579
Overconfidence	High school	College	-.51612*	.10370	.000
		Post graduate	-.06266	.26559	.970
	College	High school	.51612*	.10370	.000
		Post graduate	.45346	.25445	.196
	Post graduate	High school	.06266	.26559	.970
		College	-.45346	.25445	.196

Table 63: Group Comparison of Heuristic Behaviour by Level of Education

By Income: The findings (see Table 64) show that individual investors had a significant difference in availability bias (F [2,495] = 4.519, p = .011) when compared by income. However, individual investors did not show a statistically significant difference in overconfidence (F [2,495] = .541, p = .583). Therefore, individual investors of the NSE significantly differed in availability bias but did not significantly differ in overconfidence. The finding on overconfidence is contradicted by Prosad et al. (2015), who found that individual investors significantly differed when they were compared by income.

		Sum of Squares	Df	Mean Square	F	Sig.
Availability bias	Between Groups	5.979	2	2.989	4.519	.011
	Within Groups	327.466	495	.662		
	Total	333.445	497			
Overconfidence	Between Groups	1.164	2	.582	.541	.583
	Within Groups	532.770	495	1.076		
	Total	533.934	497			

Table 64: ANOVA-Heuristic Behaviour Comparison by Income

Table 65 shows the descriptive statistics of the individual heuristic factors. It enabled the researcher to identify which factors had higher levels of availability bias when compared by income. A post hoc test was done to compare the group statistics (see Table 66).

		N	Mean	Std. Deviation	Std. Error
Availabilitybias	Less than Kshs. 50,000	122	4.1574	.71315	.06457
	Kshs. 50,001 - 100,000	331	3.9142	.83362	.04582
	Over Kshs. 100,000	45	4.1111	.91210	.13597
	Total	498	3.9916	.81909	.03670
Overconfidence	Less than Kshs. 50,000	122	3.9645	1.06691	.09659
	Kshs. 50,001 - 100,000	331	4.0655	1.01781	.05594
	Over Kshs. 100,000	45	3.9593	1.09933	.16388
	Total	498	4.0311	1.03649	.04645

Table 65: Descriptive Statistics of Heuristic Behaviour Comparison by Income

Dependent Variable	(I) Demographic-Monthly income	(J) Demographic-Monthly income	Mean Difference (I-J)	Std. Error	Sig.
Availability bias	Less than Kshs. 50,000	Kshs. 50,001 - 100,000	.24318*	.07917	.007
		Over Kshs. 100,000	.04627	.15052	.949
	Kshs. 50,001 - 100,000	Less than Kshs. 50,000	-.24318*	.07917	.007
		Over Kshs. 100,000	-.19691	.14348	.362

	Over Kshs. 100,000	Less than Kshs. 50,000	-.04627	.15052	.949
		Kshs. 50,001 - 100,000	.19691	.14348	.362
Overconfidence	Less than Kshs. 50,000	Kshs. 50,001 - 100,000	-.10098	.11162	.638
		Over Kshs. 100,000	.00522	.19023	.768
	Kshs. 50,001 - 100,000	Less than Kshs. 50,000	.10098	.11162	.638
		Over Kshs. 100,000	.10620	.17316	.813
	Over Kshs. 100,000	Less than Kshs. 50,000	-.00522	.19023	.563
		Kshs. 50,001 - 100,000	-.10620	.17316	.813

Table 66: Group Comparison of Heuristic Behaviour by Income

The post hoc test (see Table 66) showed that individual investors who had an income of less than Kshs. 50,000 (M = 4.157, SD = .713) had a higher level of availability bias than those with an income between Kshs. 50,001 and Kshs. 100,000 (M = 3.914, SD = .834), with p = .007. This is because their income is smaller, and hence, when they get spare income to invest, they will consider the available shares for purchase. All other combinations of groups had no significant differences.

By Investing Experience: The findings of the comparison of heuristic variables by investing experience are shown in Table 67. There was no significant difference in availability bias (F [2,495] =.941, p =.391) when individual investors were compared by investing experience. However, when individual investors were compared on overconfidence, they significantly differed (F [2,495] = 6.919, p = .001). This finding is confirmed by Prosad et al. (2015), who determined that individual investors significantly differed when they were compared on overconfidence by investing experience.

Although ANOVA indicated a significant difference on overconfidence when individual investors were compared by their investing experience, the post hoc test (see Table 68) showed that the individual investors perceived there were no significant differences. This could be because of the small sample size in some categories.

		Sum of Squares	df	Mean Square	F	Sig.
Availability bias	Between Groups	1.263	2	.631	.941	.391
	Within Groups	332.182	495	.671		
	Total	333.445	497			
Overconfidence	Between Groups	14.521	2	7.260	6.919	.001
	Within Groups	519.414	495	1.049		
	Total	533.934	497			

Table 67: ANOVA-Heuristic Behaviour Comparison by Investing Experience

Dependent Variable	(I) Demographic-Experience in investing in stock	(J) Demographic-Experience in investing in stock	Mean Difference (I-J)	Std. Error	Sig.
Availability bias	Upto 5 years	6-10 years	-.05671	.23256	.968
		11 years and above	.25315	.30325	.684
	6-10 years	Upto 5 years	.05671	.23256	.968
		11 years and above	.30985	.20174	.307
	11 years and above	Upto 5 years	-.25315	.30325	.684
		6-10 years	-.30985	.20174	.307
Overconfidence	Upto 5 years	6-10 years	-.12504	.26783	.887
		11 years and above	.93939	.48052	.147
	6-10 years	Upto 5 years	.12504	.26783	.887
		11 years and above	1.06443	.40433	.052
	11 years and above	Upto 5 years	-.93939	.48052	.147
		6-10 years	-1.06443	.40433	.052

Table 68: Group Comparison of Heuristic Behaviour by Investment Experience

Demographic Differences on Market Factors

The t-tests and ANOVA were used to determine the difference in market factors when compared by the demographic characteristics. This section presents the findings of the differences in market factors (public information and expert information) by demographic characteristics. The demographic characteristics included: gender, age, marital status, occupation, education, income, and experience investing in stocks.

By Gender: The descriptive statistics are shown in Table 69. The findings (Table 70) show the comparison of market factors (public information and expert information) by gender. The males (M = 2.120, SD = 1.234) reported higher levels of public information than females (M = 1.478, SD = .246), t (344.538) = 9.365, p = .000. This means that public information for individual investors of the NSE is influenced by gender.

	Demographic-Gender	N	Mean	Std. Deviation	Std. Error Mean
Public inform	Male	452	2.1195	1.23414	.05805
	Female	46	1.4783	.24623	.03630
Expert inform	Male	452	2.1836	1.06454	.05007
	Female	46	1.7681	.18418	.02716

Table 69: Descriptive Statistics of Market Factors Comparison by Gender

Likewise, the males (M = 2.184, SD = 1.065) reported higher levels of expert information than females (M = 1.768, SD = .184), t (404.584) = 7.295, p = .000. This indicated that expert information for individual investors of the NSE is influenced by gender. Although the levels of market factors are low generally, the males had higher levels of public information because they tend to watch and read news, thus gaining more stock market information.

		Levene's Test for Equality of Variances				
		F	Sig.	T	df	Sig. (2-tailed)
Public inform	Equal variances assumed	37.365	.000	3.514	496	.000
	Equal variances not assumed			9.365	344.538	.000
Expert inform	Equal variances assumed	35.336	.000	2.641	496	.009
	Equal variances not assumed			7.295	404.544	.000

Table 70: The t-test of Market Factors Comparison by Gender

By Age: The individual investors of the NSE were compared on market factors (public information and expert information) by age. Table 71 shows the descriptive statistics of market factors comparison by age. The findings (see Table 72) show that individual investors aged 36-52 years (M = 2.189, SD = 1.027) reported higher levels of expert information when compared to those aged 18-35 years (M = 1.889, SD = .964), t (496) = -2.310, p = .021. This means that age influences expert information for individual investors of the NSE. This may indicate that older individual investors tend to use expert information and find it more reliable, using it more than younger ones.

	Demographic-Age bracket	N	Mean	Std. Deviation	Std. Error Mean
Public inform	18-35 years	72	1.8194	1.12840	.13298
	36-52 years	426	2.1009	1.19954	.05812
Expert inform	18-35 years	72	1.8889	.96415	.11363
	36-52 years	426	2.1886	1.02704	.04976

Table 71: Descriptive Statistics of Market Factors Comparison by Age

		Levene's Test for Equality of Variances				
		F	Sig.	T	df	Sig. (2-tailed)
Public inform	Equal variances assumed	1.455	.228	-1.857	496	.064
	Equal variances not assumed			-1.940	100.102	.055
Expert inform	Equal variances assumed	.383	.536	-2.310	496	.021
	Equal variances not assumed			-2.416	100.229	.018

Table 72: The t-test of Market Factors Comparison by Age

On the other hand, individual investors aged 18-35 years (M = 1.819, SD = 1.128) and those aged 36-52 years (M = 2.101, SD = 1.200) did not significantly differ on public information, t (496) = -1.857, p = .064. Therefore, it can be deduced that individual investors of the NSE had similar levels of public information. This is because public information is available to everybody, making it not a source of difference in individual investors' behaviour.

By Marital Status: The findings (Table 73) show that there was a significant difference in both market factors: public information and expert information, as determined by one-way ANOVA, ($F[2,495] = 7.497$, $p = .001$) and ($F[2,495] = 6.298$, $p = .002$) respectively. Table 74 shows the descriptive statistics on market factors by marital status. A post hoc test (Table 75) was conducted to determine the group differences when compared on market factors by their marital status.

When compared on public information, the individual investors who were single (M = 1.424, SD = .603) were statistically different from those who were married (M = 2.120, SD = 1.210) with p = .000 and those who were divorced (M = 2.228, SD = 1.396) with a p value of .035. This is perhaps because married individuals have partners with whom they share investment information, which increases their usage of public information. Interestingly, there was no statistically significant difference between the married and the divorced (p = .929). This may be due to the difference in sample sizes of the groups and should be interpreted with caution.

		Sum of Squares	df	Mean Square	F	Sig.
Public inform	Between Groups	20.780	2	10.390	7.497	.001
	Within Groups	686.038	495	1.386		
	Total	706.818	497			
Expert inform	Between Groups	12.899	2	6.450	6.298	.002
	Within Groups	506.928	495	1.024		
	Total	519.827	497			

Table 73: ANOVA-Market Factors Comparison by Marital Status

		N	Mean	Std. Deviation	Std. Error
Public inform	Single	46	1.4239	.60293	.08890
	Married	429	2.1195	1.21017	.05843
	Divorced	23	2.2283	1.39584	.29105
	Total	498	2.0602	1.19255	.05344
Expert inform	Single	46	1.6449	.66445	.09797
	Married	429	2.1911	1.04033	.05023
	Divorced	23	2.2899	1.04110	.21708
	Total	498	2.1452	1.02271	.04583

Table 74: Descriptive Statistics of Market Factors Comparison by Marital Status

On expert information, the individual investors who were single (M = 1.645, SD = .664) were statistically different from those who were married (M = 2.191, SD = 1.040) with a p value of .000 and those who were divorced (M = 2.290, SD = 1.041) with a p value of .029. However, there was no significant difference in expert information between the married and the divorced (p = .898). This may be due to the difference in sample sizes of the groups and should be interpreted with caution.

Dependent Variable			Mean Difference (I-J)	Std. Error	Sig.
Public inform	Single	Married	-.69555*	.10638	.000
		Divorced	-.80435*	.30433	.035
	Married	Single	.69555*	.10638	.000
		Divorced	-.10880	.29686	.929
	Divorced	Single	.80435*	.30433	.035
		Married	.10880	.29686	.929
Expert inform	Single	Married	-.54621*	.11009	.000
		Divorced	-.64493*	.23817	.029
	Married	Single	.54621*	.11009	.000
		Divorced	-.09871	.22282	.898
	Divorced	Single	.64493*	.23817	.029
		Married	.09871	.22282	.898
*. The mean difference is significant at the 0.05 level.					

Table 75: Group Comparison of Market Factors by Marital Status

By Occupation: Table 76 shows the descriptive statistics of the comparison by occupation. The findings showed that the employed (M = 1.980, SD = 1.140) and the businesspeople (M = 2.077, SD = 1.204) did not differ significantly on public information, t (496) = -.691, p = .490 (see Table 77). This means that the individual investors of the NSE had similar levels of market factors when compared by occupation.

	Demographic-Occupation	N	Mean	Std. Deviation	Std. Error Mean
Public inform	Employed	87	1.9799	1.14006	.12223
	Business	411	2.0773	1.20402	.05939
Expert inform	Employed	87	2.0613	.87682	.09400
	Business	411	2.1630	1.05109	.05185

Table 76: Descriptive Statistics of Market Factors Comparison by Occupation

Levene's Test for Equality of Variances						
		F	Sig.	t	df	Sig. (2-tailed)
Public inform	Equal variances assumed	.407	.524	-.691	496	.490
	Equal variances not assumed			-.716	129.884	.475
Expert inform	Equal variances assumed	2.157	.143	-.843	496	.400
	Equal variances not assumed			-.947	143.493	.345

Table 77: The t-test of Market Factors Comparison by Occupation

In addition, the employed (M = 2.061, SD = .877) and the businesspeople (M = 2.163, SD = 1.051) did not differ significantly on expert information, t (496) = -.843, p = .400. This means that the behaviour of individual investors of the NSE is not affected by the market factors (public information and expert information). This is because individual investors in both professions may be exposed to both market factors and hence, there would not be a source of difference.

By Education: The findings (see Table 78) show that there was a significant difference among the individual investors on both market factors, as determined by one-way ANOVA. The individual investors differed significantly on the public information factor (F [2,495] = 13.304, p = .000). Also, the individual investors significantly differed on expert information (F [2,495] = 11.854, p = .000). All the p values were < .05.

		Sum of Squares	df	Mean Square	F	Sig.
Publicinform	Between Groups	36.056	2	18.028	13.304	.000
	Within Groups	670.762	495	1.355		
	Total	706.818	497			
Expertinform	Between Groups	23.758	2	11.879	11.854	.000
	Within Groups	496.069	495	1.002		
	Total	519.827	497			

Table 78: ANOVA-Market Factors Comparison by Level of Education

Table 79 tabulates the descriptive statistics on market factors by level of education. The Games-Howell post hoc test (see Table 80) was conducted to determine the group differences. When compared on public information, individual investors with a high school level of education (M = 2.398, SD = 1.442) were significantly different from those with a college level of education (M = 1.844, SD = .952) with p = .000. On the other hand, on expert information, individual investors with a high school level of education (M = 2.440, SD = 1.266) were significantly different from those with a college level of education (M = 1.975, SD = .791) with p = .000.

		N	Mean	Std. Deviation	Std. Error
Publicinform	High school	172	2.3983	1.44205	.10996
	College	302	1.8435	.95221	.05479
	Post graduate	24	2.3646	1.35530	.27665
	Total	498	2.0602	1.19255	.05344
Expertinform	High school	172	2.4399	1.26568	.09651
	College	302	1.9746	.79060	.04549
	Post graduate	24	2.1806	1.21575	.24816
	Total	498	2.1452	1.02271	.04583

Table 79: Descriptive Statistics of Market Factors Comparison by Level of Education

Dependent Variable			Mean Difference (I-J)	Std. Error	Sig.
Public inform	High school	College	.55471*	.12285	.000
		Post graduate	.03367	.29770	.993
	College	High school	-.55471*	.12285	.000
		Post graduate	-.52104	.28202	.175

	Post graduate	High school	-.03367	.29770	.993
		College	.52104	.28202	.175
Expert inform	High school	College	.46531*	.10669	.000
		Post graduate	.25937	.26627	.599
	College	High school	-.46531*	.10669	.000
		Post graduate	-.20594	.25230	.697
	Post graduate	High school	-.25937	.26627	.599
		College	.20594	.25230	.697
*. The mean difference is significant at the 0.05 level.					

Table 80: Group Comparison of Market Factors by Level of Education

The individual investors who are high school graduates seek more public and expert information than their counterparts who are college graduates because they possess less education. However, those individual investors who are college graduates assume that, because they have attended college, they are able to make investment decisions without seeking public or expert information.

By Income: The findings (see Table 81) show that there was no significant difference for the individual investors of the NSE on both market factors when they were compared by income; public information and expert information, as determined by one-way ANOVA, (F [2,495] = 1.232, p = .293) and (F [2,495] = 1.820, p = .163), where all the p values were > .05. This may be because public information is easily available without cost. The reason why there is no difference in expert information when compared by income is that few individual investors seek to get this information.

		Sum of Squares	df	Mean Square	F	Sig.
Public inform	Between Groups	3.501	2	1.751	1.232	.293
	Within Groups	703.316	495	1.421		
	Total	706.818	497			
Expert inform	Between Groups	3.794	2	1.897	1.820	.163
	Within Groups	516.033	495	1.042		
	Total	519.827	497			

Table 81: ANOVA-Market Factors Comparison by Income

By Investing Experience: The findings (Table 82) show that there was a significant difference in both market factors—public information and expert information—when compared by the investing experience of individual investors, as determined by one-way ANOVA, (F [2,495] = 8.507, p = .000) and (F [2,495] = 8.350, p = .000), where all the p-values were < .05. However, the Games-Howell test revealed that there was no significant difference between the different groups when compared by investing experience.

		Sum of Squares	df	Mean Square	F	Sig.
Public inform	Between Groups	23.487	2	11.744	8.507	.000
	Within Groups	683.331	495	1.380		
	Total	706.818	497			
Expert inform	Between Groups	16.966	2	8.483	8.350	.000
	Within Groups	502.861	495	1.016		
	Total	519.827	497			

Table 82: ANOVA-Market Factors Comparison by Investing Experience

Psychographic Differences on Herding Behaviour

This section sought to determine the differences in herding behaviour between psychographic characteristics. Therefore, this section presents the findings on herding according to psychographic characteristics. The psychographic characteristics included: investment objective, frequency of investments, investment size, sector of investment, and type of stock.

By Investment Objective: This section presents the results of herding comparison by investment objectives. The findings (see Table 83) show that there was a statistically significant difference in individual investors' herding behaviour when compared by investment objective, as determined by one-way ANOVA, (F [2,495] = 18.474, p = .000), the p-values being less than .05. This means that the individual investors did not exhibit similar levels of herding. Table 84 shows the descriptive statistics.

The Games-Howell post hoc test was conducted (see Table 85) to establish the actual differences in herding when individual investors were compared by investment objective. Individual investors with a medium-term investment objective (M = 4.654, SD = .159) exhibited a higher level of herding compared to individual investors with a long-term objective (M = 3.979, SD = .844), with p = .000.

	Sum of Squares	df	Mean Square	F	Sig.
Between Groups	25.500	2	12.750	18.474	.000
Within Groups	341.616	495	.690		
Total	367.116	497			

Table 83: ANOVA-Herding Behaviour Comparison by Investment Objective

This may be because medium-term investors are more likely to review their investment portfolios regularly, hence giving them the opportunity to herd. In contrast, investors with a long-term objective do not change their portfolios regularly, thereby reducing their chances of herding. Interestingly, individuals with a short-term investment objective exhibited the lowest level of herding (M = 2.000, SD = .000), with p = .000. This may be because short-term investments are available elsewhere and not in the stock market. The short-term individual investors may depict a low level of herding due to their small sample size in this study.

Psychographic-Investment objective	N	Mean	Std. Deviation	Std. Error
Short term	5	2.0000	.00000	.00000
Medium term	13	4.6538	.15901	.04410
Long term	480	3.9788	.84413	.03853
Total	498	3.9766	.85946	.03851

Table 84: Descriptive Statistics of Herding Behaviour Comparison by Investment Objectives

(I) Psychographic-Investment objective		Mean Difference (I-J)	Std. Error	Sig.
Short term	Medium term	-2.65385*	.04410	.000
	Long term	-1.97882*	.03853	.000
Medium term	Short term	2.65385*	.04410	.000
	Long term	.67503*	.05856	.000
Long term	Short term	1.97882*	.03853	.000
	Medium term	-.67503*	.05856	.000
*. The mean difference is significant at the 0.05 level.				

Table 85: Group Comparison of Herding Behaviour by Investment Objective

By Frequency of Investments. This section presents the results of comparison of herding by the frequency of investment of individual investors on the NSE. The findings (see Table 86) show that there was a statistically significant difference in herding when individual investors were compared by frequency of investment, as determined by one-way ANOVA, (F [2,495] = 8.894, p = .000), the p-value being less than .05. Table 87 presents the descriptive statistics of herding by frequency of investment.

The Games-Howell post hoc test was conducted (see Table 88). The level of herding according to frequency of investment was significantly different between daily individual investors (M = 2.691, SD = 1.204) and weekly individual investors (M = 4.157, SD = .538), with a p-value of .041.

	Sum of Squares	df	Mean Square	F	Sig.
Between Groups	12.735	2	6.368	8.894	.000
Within Groups	354.380	495	.716		
Total	367.116	497			

Table 86: ANOVA-Herding Behaviour Comparison by Frequency of Investment

The weekly individual investors are shown as herding more than the daily investors. This is probably because daily investors had a smaller sample size compared to weekly investors.

However, the difference between daily and monthly individual investors was not significant (p = .066). The results could be due to the small sample size of daily investors. On the other hand, the difference between weekly and monthly investors was also not significant (p = .195). The sample size of weekly investors could have influenced the results of the significant difference. The findings of this study are supported by Prosad et al. (2015), who established that individual investors significantly differed in herding when compared by trading frequency.

Psychographic-Frequency of investment	N	Mean	Std. Deviation	Std. Error
Daily	7	2.6905	1.20350	.45488
Weekly	35	4.1571	.53770	.09089
Monthly	456	3.9825	.85916	.04023
Total	498	3.9766	.85946	.03851

Table 87: Descriptive Statistics of Herding Behaviour Comparison by Frequency of Investment

(I) Psychographic-Frequency of investment		Mean Difference (I-J)	Std. Error	Sig.
Daily	Weekly	-1.46667*	.46387	.041
	Monthly	-1.29198	.45666	.066
Weekly	Daily	1.46667*	.46387	.041
	Monthly	.17469	.09940	.195
Monthly	Daily	1.29198	.45666	.066
	Weekly	-.17469	.09940	.195
*. The mean difference is significant at the 0.05 level.				

Table 88: Group Comparison of Herding Behaviour by the Frequency of Investment

By investment size. Herding behaviour was studied to determine whether individual investors significantly differed based on their investment size. The results (see Table 89) demonstrate no significant difference between investment sizes of 100–200 shares (M = 3.965, SD = .860) and 201–1000 shares (M = 4.080, SD = .852), t (496) = -.918, p = .359. This means that individual investors on the NSE who invest between 100–200 shares and 201–1000 shares exhibited similar levels of herding. Investment size does not influence herding, as herding depends on the influence of other investors, not the investment size.

By Sector of Investment: The findings (see Table 90) show that there was a significant difference in individual investors' herding when compared by sector of investment, as determined by one-way ANOVA, (F [2,495] = 6.619, p = .001), with all p-values being less than .05. This indicates that individual investors on the NSE did not exhibit similar levels of herding. A post hoc test was conducted to reveal the differences in herding levels by sector of investment.

Levene's Test for Equality of Variances						
		F	Sig.	t	df	Sig. (2-tailed)
Herding	Equal variances assumed	.201	.654	-.918	496	.359
	Equal variances not assumed			-.925	63.745	.358

Table 89: The t-test of Herding Behaviour Comparison by Investment Size

	Sum of Squares	df	Mean Square	F	Sig.
Between Groups	9.563	2	4.781	6.619	.001
Within Groups	357.553	495	.722		
Total	367.116	497			

Table 90: ANOVA-Herding Behaviour Comparison by Sector of Investment

Table 91 shows the descriptive statistics of herding behaviour comparison by sector of investment. A post hoc test (see Table 92) revealed that herding among individual investors in the banking sector (M = 4.113, SD = .860) was lower than among individual investors in the other sectors (M = 4.667, SD = .234), with p = .000. This may be because the banking sector reports higher profits than other sectors, and hence, fewer individual investors may be inclined to change their investment in this sector.

On the other hand, individual investors in the commercial sector (M = 3.921, SD = .861) were significantly different from those in the "other" category, with p = .000. However, the difference between individual investors in the commercial sector and the banking sector was not significant, p = .140. This may be because both of these sectors have well-performing firms, which reduces the opportunity for herding among individual investors.

Psychographic-Sector of investment	N	Mean	Std. Deviation	Std. Error
Banking	90	4.1130	.86036	.09069
Commercial	394	3.9209	.86149	.04340
Other	14	4.6667	.23421	.03734
Total	498	3.9766	.85946	.03851

Table 91: Descriptive Statistics of Herding Behaviour Comparison by Sector of Investment

(I) Psychographic -Sector of investment	(J) Psychographic-Sector of investment	Mean Difference (I-J)	Std. Error	Sig.
Banking	Commercial	.19207	.10054	.140
	Other	-.55370*	.09069	.000
Commercial	Banking	-.19207	.10054	.140
	Other	-.74577*	.04340	.000
Other	Banking	.55370*	.09069	.000
	Commercial	.74577*	.04340	.000

Table 92: Group Comparison of Herding Behaviour by Sector of Investment

By Type of Stock

This section presents the results of the comparison of individual investors of NSE on herding by the type of stock. The findings (see Table 93) show that there is a statistically significant difference in herding among individual investors when compared by the type of stock, as determined by one-way ANOVA ($F [2,495] = 14.968$, $p = .000$), the p-value being $< .05$. This indicates that individual investors of the NSE did not exhibit similar levels of herding. Table 94 shows the descriptive statistics of herding by type of stock.

A post hoc test was conducted to determine the group differences in herding (see Table 95). Individual investors of blue-chip stocks (M = 3.748, SD = 1.037) exhibited significantly lower herding compared to investors in income stocks (M = 4.222, SD = .159) and actively traded stocks (M = 4.148, SD = .681).

	Sum of Squares	df	Mean Square	F	Sig.
Between Groups	20.936	2	10.468	14.968	.000
Within Groups	346.179	495	.699		
Total	367.116	497			

Table 93: ANOVA-Herding Behaviour Comparison by Type of Stock

Psychographic-Type of stock bought	N	Mean	Std. Deviation	Std. Error
Blue Chip	221	3.7481	1.03726	.06977
Income stock	42	4.2222	.15904	.02454
Actively traded	235	4.1475	.68075	.04441
Total	498	3.9766	.85946	.03851

Table 94: Descriptive Statistics of Herding Behaviour Comparison by Type of Stock

(I) Psychographic-Type of stock bought		Mean Difference (I-J)	Std. Error	Sig.
Blue Chip	Income stock	-.47411*	.07396	.000
	Actively traded	-.39940*	.08271	.000
Income stock	Blue Chip	.47411*	.07396	.000
	Actively traded	.07470	.05074	.306
Actively traded	Blue Chip	.39940*	.08271	.000
	Income stock	-.07470	.05074	.306

Table 95: Group Comparison of Herding Behaviour by Type of Stock

**. The mean difference is significant at the 0.05 level*

Individual investors are likely to herd less in blue-chip companies because these are well-performing, offering fewer opportunities for herding. Actively traded stocks provide an avenue for herding since their trade volume is high. However, the difference between individual investors of income stock and actively traded stock was not significant (p = .306), possibly due to the small sample size of income stock investors. These findings are supported by Prosad et al. (2015), who found significant herding differences among investors based on investment type.

Psychographic Differences in Prospect Behaviour

T-tests and ANOVA were used to determine the differences in prospect behaviour by psychographic characteristics. This section examines individual investor differences in prospect behaviours (loss aversion, regret aversion, and escalating commitment) by psychographic characteristics.

By Investment Objective

The findings (see Table 96) indicated significant differences among individual investors in loss aversion (F [2,495] = 28.061, p = .000) and escalating commitment (F [2,495] = 18.752, p = .023), with all p-values < .05. However, no significant differences were found in regret aversion (F [2,495] = 2.626, p = .073), as the p-value was > .05. This suggests that investors varied in levels of loss aversion and escalating commitment, but not in regret aversion.

		Sum of Squares	df	Mean Square	F	Sig.
Loss aversion	Between Groups	38.313	2	19.156	28.061	.000
	Within Groups	337.922	495	.683		
	Total	376.235	497			
Regret aversion	Between Groups	2.904	2	1.452	2.626	.073
	Within Groups	273.634	495	.553		
	Total	276.538	497			
Escalating com	Between Groups	17.102	2	8.551	18.752	.023
	Within Groups	225.720	495	.456		
	Total	242.822	497			

Table 96: ANOVA-Prospect Behaviour Comparison by Investment Objective

Table 97 shows the descriptive statistics of prospect behaviour by investment objectives. A post hoc test was conducted to determine the individual group differences in loss aversion and escalating commitment. The findings (Table 98) revealed that, for the loss aversion variable, individual investors differed significantly across short-term, medium-term, and long-term investors with means and standard deviations of (M = 1.667, SD = .000), (M = 4.923, SD = .277), and (M = 3.985, SD = .839), respectively, with all p-values being less than .05. Those individual investors who invest in the medium term are more concerned about potential losses, as they prioritise current income over share appreciation.

In addition, for the escalating commitment variable, individual investors also showed significant differences among short-term, medium-term, and long-term investors, with (M = 1.543, SD = .235), (M = 3.897, SD = .435), and (M = 2.868, SD = .454), respectively, with p-values less than .05. On the other hand, long-term investors may continue investing in a stock even if it is underperforming, in the hope that it will recover and appreciate in the long run. However, there was no statistically significant difference in regret aversion when individual investors were compared by investment objective, p = .073.

		N	Mean	Std. Deviation	Std. Error
Loss aversion	Short term	5	1.6667	.00000	.00000
	Medium term	13	4.9231	.27735	.07692
	Long term	480	3.9847	.83878	.03828
	Total	498	3.9859	.87006	.03899
Regret aversion	Short term	5	2.8000	.00000	.00000
	Medium term	13	3.6769	.17394	.04824
	Long term	480	3.5188	.75532	.03448
	Total	498	3.5157	.74593	.03343
Escalating com	Short term	5	1.5432	.23451	.07212

	Medium term	13	3.8974	.43532	.06984
	Long term	480	2.8684	.45362	.05784
	Total	498	2.9172	.76543	.06754

Table 97: Descriptive Statistics of Prospect Behaviour Comparison by Investment Objective

Dependent Variable			Mean Difference (I-J)	Std. Error	Sig.
Loss aversion	Short term	Medium term	-3.25641*	.07692	.000
		Long term	-2.31806*	.03828	.000
	Medium term	Short term	3.25641*	.07692	.000
		Long term	.93835*	.08592	.000
	Long term	Short term	2.31806*	.03828	.000
		Medium term	-.93835*	.08592	.000
Regret aversion	Short term	Medium term	-.87692*	.04824	.000
		Long term	-.71875*	.03448	.000
	Medium term	Short term	.87692*	.04824	.000
		Long term	.15817*	.05930	.033
	Long term	Short term	.71875*	.03448	.000
		Medium term	-.15817*	.05930	.033
Escalating com	Short term	Medium term	-3.25641*	.07692	.000
		Long term	-2.31806*	.03828	.000
	Medium term	Short term	3.25641*	.07692	.000
		Long term	.93835*	.08592	.000
	Long term	Short term	2.31806*	.03828	.000
		Medium term	-.93835*	.08592	.000
*. The mean difference is significant at the 0.05 level.					

Table 98: Group Comparison of Prospect Behaviour by Investment Objective

By Frequency of Investment: The findings of the comparison of prospect variables among individual investors are presented in Table 99. The results indicated significant differences in loss aversion (F [2,495] = 14.783, p = .000) and escalating commitment (F [2,495] = 12.654, p = .012), with all p-values less than .05. However, individual investors showed no significant difference in regret aversion (F [2,495] = 1.238, p = .291), as the p-value was greater than .05.

		Sum of Squares	df	Mean Square	F	Sig.
Loss aversion	Between Groups	21.205	2	10.603	14.783	.000
	Within Groups	355.030	495	.717		
	Total	376.235	497			
Regret aversion	Between Groups	1.377	2	.688	1.238	.291
	Within Groups	275.161	495	.556		
	Total	276.538	497			
Escalatin gcom	Between Groups	21.107	2	10.553	12.654	.012
	Within Groups	412.830	495	.834		
	Total	433.937	497			

Table 99: ANOVA-Prospect Behaviour Comparison by Frequency of Investments

Table 100 presents the descriptive statistics of prospect behaviour by frequency of investment. A post hoc test (Table 101) was conducted to determine individual group differences in loss aversion and escalating commitment. The findings revealed that, for the loss aversion variable, individual investors differed significantly among the daily (M = 2.429, SD = 1.315) and weekly (M = 4.333, SD = .536) investors with p = .019. Daily and monthly investors (M = 3.983, SD = .857) also differed with p = .046. Weekly and monthly investors also differed significantly with p = .003. The sample sizes of the daily and weekly investor groups were small; therefore, these results should be interpreted with caution.

		N	M	SD	Std. Error
Loss aversion	Daily	7	2.4286	1.31535	.49716
	Weekly	35	4.3333	.53627	.09065
	Monthly	456	3.9832	.85789	.04017
	Total	498	3.9859	.87006	.03899
Regret aversion	Daily	7	3.1143	.56400	.21317
	Weekly	35	3.6000	.42565	.07195
	Monthly	456	3.5154	.76617	.03588
	Total	498	3.5157	.74593	.03343
Escalating com	Daily	7	2.5643	.12653	.54673
	Weekly	35	4.1234	.46537	.07865
	Monthly	456	3.8764	.54678	.04352
	Total	498	3.8777	.78645	.03765

Table 100: Descriptive Statistics of Prospect Behaviour Comparison by Frequency of Investments

Dependent Variable			Mean Difference (I-J)	Std. Error	Sig.
Loss aversion	Daily	Weekly	-1.90476*	.50535	.019
		Monthly	-1.55462*	.49878	.046
	Weekly	Daily	1.90476*	.50535	.019
		Monthly	.35015*	.09915	.003
	Monthly	Daily	1.55462*	.49878	.046
		Weekly	-.35015*	.09915	.003
Regret aversion	Daily	Weekly	-.48571	.22499	.143
		Monthly	-.40107	.21617	.227
	Weekly	Daily	.48571	.22499	.143
		Monthly	.08465	.08040	.547
	Monthly	Daily	.40107	.21617	.227
		Weekly	-.08465	.08040	.547
Escalating com	Daily	Weekly	-1.90476*	.50535	.015
		Monthly	-1.55462*	.49878	.024
	Weekly	Daily	1.90476*	.50535	.009
		Monthly	.35015*	.09915	.008
	Monthly	Daily	1.55462*	.49878	.024

Table 101: Group Comparison of Prospect Behaviour by Frequency of Investments

By Investment Size: The findings (see Table 102) indicate that there were no significant differences among individual investors in loss aversion, t (496) = -.853, p = .394. There were also no significant differences in regret aversion, t (496) = -.940, p = .348. The comparison on escalating commitment also showed no significant differences, t (496) = -.817, p = .296.

This implies that individual investors in the NSE had similar levels of loss aversion, regret aversion, and escalating commitment, regardless of investment size. This may be because the difference in investment amounts between the two groups was not substantial enough to influence behaviour.

By Sector of Investment: This section presents the results of a comparison of prospect behaviour by sector. The findings (see Table 103) showed significant differences in prospect variables among individual investors: loss aversion (F [2,495] = 5.609, p = .004), regret aversion (F [2,495] = 8.060, p = .000), and escalating commitment (F [2,495] = 4.996, p = .028), with all p-values less than .05. This means that individual investors in the NSE exhibited different levels of prospect behaviour depending on their investment sector. Table 104 presents the descriptive statistics of prospect behaviour by investment sector.

Levene's Test for Equality of Variances							
		F	Sig.	t	df	Sig. (2-tailed)	Upper
Loss aversion	Equal variances assumed	.885	.347	-.853	496	.394	.14182
	Equal variances not assumed			-.761	60.267	.449	.17694
Regret aversion	Equal variances assumed	1.118	.291	-.940	496	.348	.11203
	Equal variances not assumed			-.981	64.979	.330	.10645
Escalating com	Equal variances assumed	.746	.325	-.817	496	.296	.14182
	Equal variances not assumed			-.731	87.765	.476	.17694

Table 102: The t-test of Prospect Behaviour Comparison by Investment Size

		Sum of Squares	**df**	**Mean Square**	**F**	**Sig.**
Loss aversion	Between Groups	8.338	2	4.169	5.609	.004
	Within Groups	367.897	495	.743		
	Total	376.235	497			
Regret aversion	Between Groups	8.722	2	4.361	8.060	.000
	Within Groups	267.816	495	.541		
	Total	276.538	497			
Escalating com	Between Groups	8.123	2	4.062	4.996	.028

	Within Groups	402.435	495	.813		
	Total	410.558	497			

Table 103: ANOVA-Prospect Behaviour Comparison by Sector of Investment

A Games-Howell post hoc test was conducted (see Table 105). The results showed that loss aversion among individual investors in the banking sector (M = 4.089, SD = 1.012) differed significantly from those in other sectors (M = 4.667, SD = .000), with p = .000. This suggests that investors in the banking sector were less concerned about potential losses than those in the commercial sector. The small sample size in the "other" category warrants cautious interpretation. Moreover, investors categorised as "other" (M = 4.667, SD = .000) exhibited higher loss aversion compared to those in the banking sector, which may again be influenced by the small sample size.

		N	M	SD	Std. Error
Loss aversion	Banking	90	4.0889	1.01154	.10663
	Commercial	394	3.9382	.83929	.04228
	Other	14	4.6667	.00000	.00000
	Total	498	3.9859	.87006	.03899
Regret aversion	Banking	90	3.7689	.67435	.07108
	Commercial	394	3.4477	.76058	.03832
	Other	14	3.8000	.00000	.00000
	Total	498	3.5157	.74593	.03343
Escalating com	Banking	90	3.9345	.97653	.12456
	Commercial	394	3.8756	.76493	.05674
	Other	14	4.4673	.16451	.07854
	Total	498	3.8675	.86785	.06754

Table 104: Descriptive Statistics of Prospect Behaviour Comparison by Sector of Investment

Dependent Variable			Mean Difference (I-J)	Std. Error	Sig.
Loss aversion	Banking	Commercial	.15065	.11470	.391
		Other	-.57778*	.10663	.000
	Commercial	Banking	-.15065	.11470	.391
		Other	-.72843*	.04228	.000
	Other	Banking	.57778*	.10663	.000
		Commercial	.72843*	.04228	.000
Regret aversion	Banking	Commercial	.32117*	.08075	.000
		Other	-.03111	.07108	.900
	Commercial	Banking	-.32117*	.08075	.000
		Other	-.35228*	.03832	.000
	Other	Banking	.03111	.07108	.900
		Commercial	.35228*	.03832	.000

Escalating com	Banking	Commercial	.15065	.11470	.413
		Other	-.57778*	.10663	.016
	Commercial	Banking	-.15065	.11470	.413
		Other	-.72843*	.04228	.016
	Other	Banking	.57778*	.10663	.016
		Commercial	.72843*	.04228	.016
*. The mean difference is significant at the 0.05 level.					

Table 105: Group Comparison of Prospect Behaviour by Sector of Investment

The regret aversion was also significantly different for the individual investors in the banking sector (M = 3.769, SD = .674) when they were compared with those in the commercial sector (M = 3.448, SD = .761) with *p* = .000. The individual investors in the others (M = 3.800, SD = .000) differed significantly when compared with the commercial sector (*p* = .000). On escalating the commitment, the individual investors had a significant difference when those in the banking sector (M = 3.935, SD = .977) were compared with those in the commercial sector (M = 3.876, SD = .765) with *p* = .016. Likewise, those individual investors in the other sectors (M = 4.467, SD = .165) differed significantly when they were compared with those in the commercial sector. The results should be interpreted cautiously because of the small sample size of the investors in the others sector.

By Type of Stock: The findings (see Table 106) indicated a significant difference among individual investors for all the prospect dimensions. The results showed that loss aversion was significant with (F [2,495] = 8.148, p = .000), regret aversion (F [2,495] = 19.736, p = .000), and escalating commitment (F [2,495] = 6.978, p = .031), all p-values being less than (.05). This indicated that the individual investors of NSE had different levels of prospect behaviour when compared by type of stock.

		Sum of Squares	df	Mean Square	F	Sig.
Loss aversion	Between Groups	11.991	2	5.995	8.148	.000
	Within Groups	364.244	495	.736		
	Total	376.235	497			
Regret aversion	Between Groups	20.423	2	10.211	19.736	.000
	Within Groups	256.115	495	.517		
	Total	276.538	497			

Escalating com	Between Groups	9.754	2	4.877	6.987	.031
	Within Groups	345.510	495	.698		
	Total	355.264	497			

Table 106: ANOVA-Prospect Behaviour Comparison by Type of Stock

The descriptive statistics are presented in Table 107. The Games-Howell post hoc test (Table 108) was conducted to show the differences between the groups. With respect to loss aversion, individual investors in the blue chip stocks (M = 4.000, SD = .275) were significantly different when compared with those in actively traded stocks (M = 4.142, SD = .742), with p = .000. The investors in the actively traded stocks had a higher level of loss aversion, as they do not want to lose their investment in stocks that are actively traded. This is because such stocks may sometimes report substantial changes in prices.

		N	Mean	Std. Deviation	Std. Error
Loss aversion	Blue Chip	221	3.8175	1.02759	.06912
	Income stock	42	4.0000	.27546	.04251
	Actively traded	235	4.1418	.74199	.04840
	Total	498	3.9859	.87006	.03899
Regret aversion	Blue Chip	221	3.2977	.90466	.06085
	Income stock	42	3.8667	.38169	.05890
	Actively traded	235	3.6579	.54730	.03570
	Total	498	3.5157	.74593	.03343
Escalating com	Blue Chip	221	3.6453	.7643	.05647
	Income stock	42	3.8987	.54637	.06745
	Actively traded	235	3.9546	.76453	.04534
	Total	498	3.8756	.76854	.04342

Table 107: Descriptive Statistics of Prospect Behaviour Comparison by Type of Stock

Dependent Variable			Mean Difference (I-J)	Std. Error	Sig.
Loss aversion	Blue Chip	Income stock	-.18250	.08115	.065
		Actively traded	-.32435*	.08438	.000
	Income stock	Blue Chip	.18250	.08115	.065
		Actively traded	-.14184	.06442	.074
	Actively traded	Blue Chip	.32435*	.08438	.000
		Income stock	.14184	.06442	.074

Regret aversion	Blue Chip	Income stock	-.56893*	.08469	.000
		Actively traded	-.36013*	.07055	.000
	Income stock	Blue Chip	.56893*	.08469	.000
		Actively traded	.20879*	.06887	.009
	Actively traded	Blue Chip	.36013*	.07055	.000
		Income stock	-.20879*	.06887	.009
Escalatingcom	Blue Chip	Income stock	-.18250	.08115	.043
		Actively traded	-.32435*	.08438	.008
	Income stock	Blue Chip	.18250	.08115	.043
		Actively traded	-.14184	.06442	.052
	Actively traded	Blue Chip	.32435*	.08438	.008
		Income stock	.14184	.06442	.052

Table 108: Group Comparison of Prospect Behaviour by Type of Stock
**. The mean difference is significant at the 0.05 level*

On regret aversion, individual investors in the blue chip stocks (M = 3.298, SD = .905) were significantly different when compared with those in income stocks (M = 3.867, SD = .382), with p = .000. Individual investors in actively traded stocks (M = 3.657, SD = .547) also significantly differed from those in blue chip stocks (p = .000). Similarly, investors in income stocks significantly differed from those in actively traded stocks.

With respect to escalating commitment, individual investors in blue chip stocks (M = 3.645, SD = .764) were significantly different from those in actively traded stocks (M = 3.955, SD = .765), with p = .008. The individual investors in actively traded stocks may have a higher level of escalating commitment, since they hope that even if a stock's price has declined, it will recover in a short time. On the other hand, investors in blue chip companies reported lower levels of escalating commitment when compared with those who invest in income stocks (M = 3.899, SD = .546).

Psychographic Differences on Heuristic Behaviour

This section was intended to establish individual investor differences in heuristic behaviour (availability bias and overconfidence) when compared by psychographic characteristics. Therefore, this section presents the findings of differences in heuristic behaviour (availability bias and overconfidence) by psychographic characteristics.

By investment objective: This section presents the results of comparison on heuristic behaviour by investment objective. The findings (see Table 109) indicated that there was a significant difference in heuristic behaviour when compared by investment objective, as indicated by the availability bias (F [2,495] = 16.098, p = .000) and overconfidence (F [2,495] = 13.857, p = .000), all p-values being less than (.05). This showed that the individual investors of NSE had different levels of heuristic behaviour.

		Sum of Squares	df	Mean Square	F	Sig.
Availability bias	Between Groups	20.364	2	10.182	16.098	.000
	Within Groups	313.081	495	.632		
	Total	333.445	497			
Overconfidence	Between Groups	28.308	2	14.154	13.857	.000
	Within Groups	505.626	495	1.021		
	Total	533.934	497			

Table 109: ANOVA-Heuristic Behaviour Comparison by Investment Objective

Table 110 presents the descriptive statistics of heuristic behaviour by investment objective. Post hoc test findings on availability bias (see Table 111) revealed that individual investors with a short-term objective (M = 2.000, SD = .000) were significantly different from those with a medium-term objective (M = 4.169, SD = .243). This result may be due to the small sample size of the short-term and medium-term investor groups.

The short-term investors were also different from those with a long-term investment objective (M = 4.008, SD = .808). On the other hand, regarding overconfidence, the findings indicated that individual investors with a short-term objective (M = 1.667, SD = .000) were significantly different from those with a medium-term objective (M = 4.128, SD = .642). The short-term investors were also significantly different from those with a long-term investment objective (M = 4.053, SD = 1.022). Investors with a long-term objective exhibit a lower level of herding compared to those with a medium-term objective. This may be because individuals with medium-term objectives review their investments regularly and hence have more opportunities to exhibit overconfident behaviour.

		N	Mean	Std. Deviation	Std. Error
Availability bias	Short term	5	2.0000	.00000	.00000
	Medium term	13	4.1692	.24285	.06735
	Long term	480	4.0075	.80755	.03686
	Total	498	3.9916	.81909	.03670
Overconfidence	Short term	5	1.6667	.00000	.00000
	Medium term	13	4.1282	.64246	.17819
	Long term	480	4.0531	1.02237	.04666
	Total	498	4.0311	1.03649	.04645

Table 110: Descriptive Statistics of Heuristic Behaviour Comparison by Investment Objective

Dependent Variable			Mean Difference (I-J)	Std. Error	Sig.
Availability bias	Short term	Medium term	-2.16923*	.06735	.000
		Long term	-2.00750*	.03686	.000
	Medium term	Short term	2.16923*	.06735	.000
		Long term	.16173	.07678	.114
	Long term	Short term	2.00750*	.03686	.000
		Medium term	-.16173	.07678	.114
Overconfidence	Short term	Medium term	-2.46154*	.17819	.000
		Long term	-2.38646*	.04666	.000
	Medium term	Short term	2.46154*	.17819	.000
		Long term	.07508	.18419	.913
	Long term	Short term	2.38646*	.04666	.000
		Medium term	-.07508	.18419	.913

Table 111: Group Comparison of Heuristic Behaviour by Investment Objective

By Frequency of Investments: The findings (see Table 112) indicated that there was a significant difference in heuristics when compared by frequency of investment; availability bias (F [2,495] = 10.929, p = .000) and overconfidence (F [2,495] = 13.142, p = .000), all the p-values being less than (.05). This showed that the individual investors of NSE did not have similar levels of heuristics when compared by the frequency of investment. Table 113 shows the descriptive statistics of heuristics by frequency of investment. A post hoc Games-Howell test was performed (see Table 114) to show the differences.

		Sum of Squares	Df	Mean Square	F	Sig.
Availabilitybias	Between Groups	14.101	2	7.050	10.929	.000
	Within Groups	319.344	495	.645		
	Total	333.445	497			
Overconfidence	Between Groups	26.922	2	13.461	13.142	.000
	Within Groups	507.012	495	1.024		
	Total	533.934	497			

Table 112: ANOVA-Heuristic Behaviour Comparison by Frequency of Investments

The findings of the post hoc test showed that only individual investors who invested on a weekly basis (M = 3.703, SD = .712) and those who invested on a monthly basis (M = 4.033, SD = .800) were significantly different when compared on availability bias by frequency of investment. Those investors who invested on a monthly basis had a higher level of availability bias because their earnings may be received at the end of the month and, hence, they buy the shares that are available.

		N	Mean	Std. Deviation	Std. Error
Availabilitybias	Daily	7	2.7714	1.32880	.50224
	Weekly	35	3.7029	.71187	.12033
	Monthly	456	4.0325	.80044	.03748
	Total	498	3.9916	.81909	.03670
Overconfidence	Daily	7	2.5476	1.51142	.57126
	Weekly	35	3.5048	1.31450	.22219
	Monthly	456	4.0943	.97728	.04577
	Total	498	4.0311	1.03649	.04645

Table 113: Descriptive Statistics of Heuristic Behaviour Comparison by Frequency of Investment

Dependent Variable			Mean Difference (I-J)	Std. Error	Sig.
Availabilitybias	Daily	Weekly	-.93143	.51645	.239
		Monthly	-1.26103	.50364	.101
	Weekly	Daily	.93143	.51645	.239
		Monthly	-.32960*	.12603	.033
	Monthly	Daily	1.26103	.50364	.101
		Weekly	.32960*	.12603	.033
Overconfidence	Daily	Weekly	-.95714	.61295	.316
		Monthly	-1.54668	.57309	.078
	Weekly	Daily	.95714	.61295	.316
		Monthly	-.58954*	.22686	.035
	Monthly	Daily	1.54668	.57309	.078
		Weekly	.58954*	.22686	.035
*. The mean difference is significant at the 0.05 level.					

Table 114: Group Comparison of Heuristic Behaviour by Frequency of Investment

Regarding overconfidence, only the individual investors who invested on a weekly basis (M = 3.505, SD = 1.316) and those who invested on a monthly basis (M = 4.943, SD = .977) were significantly different when compared by the frequency of investment. Those who invested monthly had a higher level of overconfidence since the period from the last investment to the end of the month is long enough to gather stock information and, hence, feel they are in a position to make better decisions. The findings of this study are supported by Prosad et al. (2015), who determined that individual investors significantly differed in overconfidence when compared by trading frequency.

By Investment Size: Table 115 shows the descriptive statistics. The findings (see Table 116) show that individual investors whose investment size is between 100–200 stocks (M = 4.01, SD = .840) and those with investment size between 201–1000 stocks (M = 3.839, SD = .599) did not differ significantly on availability bias, t (496) = 1.426, p = .155. However, those individual investors whose investment size is 100–200 stocks (M = 4.082, SD = 1.00) had a higher level of overconfidence than those with investment size of 201–1000 stocks (M

= 3.599, SD = 1.223), t (59.260) = 2.738, p = .008. This showed that the individual investors of NSE had similar levels of availability bias, while they did not have similar levels of overconfidence.

	Psychographic -Investment size (No. of shares)	N	Mean	Std. Deviation	Std. Error Mean
Availability bias	100-200	446	4.0094	.83969	.03976
	201-1000	52	3.8385	.59940	.08312
Overconfidence	100-200	446	4.0815	1.00210	.04745
	201-1000	52	3.5994	1.22263	.16955

Table 115: Descriptive Statistics of Heuristic Behaviour Comparison by Investment Size

Levene's Test for Equality of Variances						
		F	Sig.	t	df	Sig. (2-tailed)
Availability bias	Equal variances assumed	1.922	.166	1.426	496	.155
	Equal variances not assumed			1.855	76.550	.067
Overconfidence	Equal variances assumed	16.213	.000	3.204	496	.001
	Equal variances not assumed			2.738	59.260	.008

Table 116: The t-test of Heuristic Behaviour Comparison by Investment Size

The individual investors of NSE who buy investment sizes of 100–200 stocks are more overconfident than those who buy larger sizes when trading stocks. This may be because when they buy 100–200 stocks, they may feel more capable of selecting appropriate stocks than those who buy 201–1000 stocks.

By Sector of Investment: The findings shown in Table 117 reported that the individual investors were significantly different on both dimensions of heuristics: availability bias (F [2,495] = 8.888, p = .000) and overconfidence (F [2,495] = 19.454, p = .000). This indicated that the individual investors of NSE did not have similar levels of heuristic behaviour when compared by sector of investment. Table 118 presents the descriptive statistics of heuristics by sector. A post hoc test was conducted (Table 119) to determine the differences in heuristic variables when compared by sector of investment.

The findings of the post hoc test showed that the availability bias of individual investors purchasing stock from the banking sector (M = 3.829, SD = .717) was significantly different from those investing in other sectors (M = 4.800, SD = .000). The level of availability bias in other sectors was higher because individuals consider them easier to buy as they are cheaper compared to the banking sector, which is quite expensive. The individual investors investing in the commercial sector (M = 4.000, SD = .838) were also significantly different when compared to those in other sectors. Investors in other sectors had a higher level of availability bias because those sectors are more easily accessible compared to the commercial sector.

		Sum of Squares	df	Mean Square	F	Sig.
Availability bias	Between Groups	11.560	2	5.780	8.888	.000
	Within Groups	321.885	495	.650		
	Total	333.445	497			
Overconfidence	Between Groups	38.910	2	19.455	19.454	.000
	Within Groups	495.025	495	1.000		
	Total	533.934	497			

Table 117: ANOVA-Heuristic Behaviour Comparison by Sector of Investment

		N	Mean	Std. Deviation	Std. Error
Availability bias	Banking	90	3.8289	.71740	.07562
	Commercial	394	4.0000	.83815	.04223
	Other	14	4.8000	.00000	.00000
	Total	498	3.9916	.81909	.03670
Overconfidence	Banking	90	3.4389	1.31600	.13872
	Commercial	394	4.1675	.93134	.04692
	Other	14	4.0000	.00000	.00000
	Total	498	4.0311	1.03649	.04645

Table 118: Descriptive Statistics of Heuristic Behaviour Comparison by Sector of Investment

Dependent Variable			Mean Difference (I-J)	Std. Error	Sig.
Availability bias	Banking	Commercial	-.17111	.08661	.122
		Other	-.97111*	.07562	.000
	Commercial	Banking	.17111	.08661	.122
		Other	-.80000*	.04223	.000
	Other	Banking	.97111*	.07562	.000
		Commercial	.80000*	.04223	.000
Overconfidence	Banking	Commercial	-.72862*	.14644	.000
		Other	-.56111*	.13872	.000
	Commercial	Banking	.72862*	.14644	.000
		Other	.16751*	.04692	.001
	Other	Banking	.56111*	.13872	.000
		Commercial	-.16751*	.04692	.001
*. The mean difference is significant at the 0.05 level.					

Table 119: Group Comparison of Heuristic Behaviour by Sector of Investment

On the other hand, regarding overconfidence, all combinations of individual investors were significantly different; all the p-values were less than .05. The individual investors in the banking sector (M = 3.439, SD = 1.316) reported significantly lower levels of overconfidence compared to those who invested in the commercial sector (M = 4.167, SD = .931), with p = .000. Also, the individual investors who invested in the banking sector were significantly different from those who invested in the other sectors (M = 4.000, SD = .000), with p = .000. In addition, those individual investors who invested in the commercial sector, when compared with those investing in the other sectors, were found to be significantly different (p = .001).

By Type of Stock: The findings (see Table 120) showed that the individual investors were significantly different in heuristic behaviour when compared by the type of stock: availability bias (F [2,495] = 22.700, p = .000) and overconfidence (F [2,495] = 7.602, p = .001). This indicated that the individual investors of NSE exhibited different levels of heuristic behaviour. The descriptive statistics of heuristic behaviour comparison by type of stock are presented in Table 121. A post hoc test (see Table 122) was conducted to determine the differences among the types of stock purchased.

		Sum of Squares	df	Mean Square	F	Sig.
Availability bias	Between Groups	28.013	2	14.007	22.700	.000
	Within Groups	305.431	495	.617		
	Total	333.445	497			
Overconfidence	Between Groups	15.911	2	7.956	7.602	.001
	Within Groups	518.023	495	1.047		
	Total	533.934	497			

Table 120: ANOVA-Heuristic Behaviour Comparison by Type of Stock

The findings of the post hoc test showed that when the individual investors were compared on availability bias by the type of stock they purchased, all the combinations were found to be significantly different, and all the p-values were less than .05.

		N	Mean	Std. Deviation	Std. Error
Availability bias	Blue Chip	221	3.7575	.86666	.05830
	Income stock	42	4.5333	.34406	.05309
	Actively traded	235	4.1149	.76050	.04961
	Total	498	3.9916	.81909	.03670
Overconfidence	Blue Chip	221	3.9442	1.10172	.07411
	Income stock	42	4.6111	.28671	.04424
	Actively traded	235	4.0092	1.02869	.06710
	Total	498	4.0311	1.03649	.04645

Table 121: Descriptive Statistics of Heuristic Behaviour Comparison by Type of Stock

On the other hand, when the individual investors were compared on overconfidence by the type of stock purchased, those who purchased blue chip stocks (M = 3.944, SD = 1.102) and income stocks (M = 4.611, SD = .287) were found to be significantly different. Likewise, individual investors purchasing income stocks were found to be significantly different from those buying actively traded stocks (M = 4.009, SD = 1.029). The findings of this study are supported by Prosad et al. (2015), who determined that individual investors significantly differed on overconfidence when compared by investment type.

Dependent Variable			Mean Difference (I-J)	Std. Error	Sig.
Availability bias	Blue Chip	Income stock	-.77587*	.07885	.000
		Actively traded	-.35743*	.07655	.000
	Income stock	Blue Chip	.77587*	.07885	.000
		Actively traded	.41844*	.07266	.000
	Actively traded	Blue Chip	.35743*	.07655	.000
		Income stock	-.41844*	.07266	.000
Overconfidence	Blue Chip	Income stock	-.66692*	.08631	.000
		Actively traded	-.06503	.09998	.792
	Income stock	Blue Chip	.66692*	.08631	.000
		Actively traded	.60189*	.08038	.000
	Actively traded	Blue Chip	.06503	.09998	.792
		Income stock	-.60189*	.08038	.000
*. The mean difference is significant at the 0.05 level.					

Table 122: Group Comparison of Heuristic Behaviour by Type of Stock

On the other hand, when the individual investors were compared on overconfidence by the type of stock purchased, those who purchased blue chip stocks (M = 3.944, SD = 1.102) and income stocks (M = 4.611, SD = .287) were found to be significantly different. Likewise, individual investors purchasing income stocks were found to be significantly different from those buying actively traded stocks (M = 4.009, SD = 1.029). The findings of this study are supported by Prosad et al. (2015), who determined that individual investors significantly differed on overconfidence when compared by investment type.

Psychographic Differences on Market Factors

This section was intended to establish the differences in individual investors' responses to market factors (public information and expert information) when compared by psychographic characteristics. Therefore, it presents the findings of the differences in market factors by psychographic characteristics. The psychographic characteristics included: investment objective, frequency of investments, investment size, sector of investment, and type of stock.

By investment objective. This section presents the results of the comparison on market factors by investment objective. The findings (see Table 123) show that the individual investors of NSE were significantly different in market factors: public information ($F [2,495] = 11.027$, $p = .000$) and expert information ($F [2,495] = 8.578$, $p = .000$), with p-values less than 0.05. This means that the individual investors did not share similar levels on market factors.

		Sum of Squares	df	Mean Square	F	Sig.
Public inform	Between Groups	30.149	2	15.075	11.027	.000
	Within Groups	676.669	495	1.367		
	Total	706.818	497			
Expert inform	Between Groups	17.413	2	8.706	8.578	.000
	Within Groups	502.415	495	1.015		
	Total	519.827	497			

Table 123: ANOVA-Market Factors Comparison by Investment Objective

The descriptive statistics of market factors comparison by investment objective are presented in Table 124. A post hoc test (see Table 125) was conducted to determine the differences among individual investors when compared on market factors by investment objective. The findings show that individual investors who invested in the short term (M = 4.500, SD = .000) reported significantly higher levels of public information usage compared to those who invested in the medium term (M = 2.115, SD = .911) and long term (M = 2.033, SD = 1.180). This may be because short-term investors need to analyse more information to support their decisions, and therefore seek more information.

On the other hand, when individual investors were compared on expert information, those who invested in the short term (M = 4.000, SD = .000) were significantly higher compared to those who invested in the medium term (M = 2.180, SD = .857) and long term (M = 2.125, SD = 1.015). Short-term investors may require more information for evaluating their investments, as they are regularly engaged in investment activities.

		N	Mean	Std. Deviation	Std. Error
Public inform	Short term	5	4.5000	.00000	.00000
	Medium term	13	2.1154	.91067	.25258
	Long term	480	2.0333	1.17979	.05385
	Total	498	2.0602	1.19255	.05344
Expert inform	Short term	5	4.0000	.00000	.00000
	Medium term	13	2.1795	.85652	.23755
	Long term	480	2.1250	1.01514	.04633
	Total	498	2.1452	1.02271	.04583

Table 124: Descriptive Statistics of Market Factors Comparison by Investment Objective

Dependent Variable			Mean Difference (I-J)	Std. Error	Sig.
Public inform	Short term	Medium term	2.38462*	.25258	.000
		Long term	2.46667*	.05385	.000
	Medium term	Short term	-2.38462*	.25258	.000
		Long term	.08205	.25825	.946
	Long term	Short term	-2.46667*	.05385	.000
		Medium term	-.08205	.25825	.946
Expert inform	Short term	Medium term	1.82051*	.23755	.000
		Long term	1.87500*	.04633	.000
	Medium term	Short term	-1.82051*	.23755	.000
		Long term	.05449	.24203	.973
	Long term	Short term	-1.87500*	.04633	.000
		Medium term	-.05449	.24203	.973
*. The mean difference is significant at the 0.05 level.					

Table 125: Group Comparison of Market Factors by Investment Objective

By Frequency of Investments. The study sought to determine whether individual investors exhibited any significant differences in heuristics when compared by frequency of investments. The findings (see Table 126) reported that both variables of heuristics were significantly different: availability bias ($F [2,495] = 16.244$, $p = .000$) and overconfidence ($F [2,495] = 17.410$, $p = .000$). A discussion on the significant differences will follow.

		Sum of Squares	df	Mean Square	F	Sig.
Public inform	Between Groups	43.533	2	21.767	16.244	.000
	Within Groups	663.285	495	1.340		
	Total	706.818	497			
Expert inform	Between Groups	34.162	2	17.081	17.410	.000
	Within Groups	485.665	495	.981		
	Total	519.827	497			

Table 126: ANOVA-Market Factors Comparison by Frequency of Investment

The descriptive statistics of the market factors comparison by frequency of investment are shown in Table 127. A post hoc test was conducted to determine the differences among the types of stock purchased, as indicated in Table 128. When the groups are compared on public information by the frequency of investment, individual investors with weekly frequency ($M = 2.864$, $SD = 1.493$) had a higher uptake of public information than those with monthly frequency ($M = 1.974$, $SD = 1.124$).

		N	M	SD	Std. Error
Public inform	Daily	7	3.6429	1.47095	.55597
	Weekly	35	2.8643	1.49305	.25237
	Monthly	456	1.9742	1.12368	.05262
	Total	498	2.0602	1.19255	.05344
Expert inform	Daily	7	3.3810	1.06160	.40125
	Weekly	35	2.9143	1.28425	.21708
	Monthly	456	2.0673	.96400	.04514
	Total	498	2.1452	1.02271	.04583

Table 127: Descriptive Statistics of Market Factors Comparison by Frequency of Investment

Dependent Variable			Mean Difference (I-J)	Std. Error	Sig.
Public inform	Daily	Weekly	.77857	.61057	.444
		Monthly	1.66862	.55845	.054
	Weekly	Daily	-.77857	.61057	.444
		Monthly	.89005*	.25780	.004
	Monthly	Daily	-1.66862	.55845	.054
		Weekly	-.89005*	.25780	.004
Expert inform	Daily	Weekly	.46667	.45620	.580
		Monthly	1.31370*	.40378	.039
	Weekly	Daily	-.46667	.45620	.580
		Monthly	.84703*	.22172	.001
	Monthly	Daily	-1.31370*	.40378	.039
		Weekly	-.84703*	.22172	.001

*. The mean difference is significant at the 0.05 level.

Table 128: Group Comparison of Market Factors by Frequency of Investment

On expert information, individual investors with a daily frequency (M = 3.381, SD = 1.062) had a higher uptake of expert information when compared with those with monthly frequency (M = 1.974, SD = 1.124). Likewise, when individual investors were compared on expert information by frequency of investment, those with monthly frequency (M = 2.067, SD = .964) were statistically different from those with weekly investments (M = 2.914, SD = 1.284). Individual investors with daily investments may require more public and expert information because their daily investments need frequent tracking to inform decisions on where to invest.

By Investment Size: T-tests and ANOVA were used to determine the significant differences. Table 129 presents the descriptive statistics of market factors comparison by investment size. The findings (Table 130) show that individual investors who buy investment sizes of 201–1000 stocks (M = 2.639, SD = 1.3489) had significantly higher levels of public information than those who buy 100–200 stocks (M = 1.993, SD = 1.156), t (60.055) = -3.318, p = .002.

Individual investors who buy 201–1000 stocks (M = 2.639, SD = 1.349) had higher levels of public information compared to those who buy 100–200 stocks (M = 1.993, SD = 1.156). This indicates that the behaviour of individual investors at the NSE is influenced by investment size. Although the levels of public and expert information are low overall, but the results show that the larger the investment size, the higher the levels of public and expert information. This is due to the greater analysis required to make appropriate decisions when buying or selling larger quantities of stocks.

	Psychographic-Investment size (No. of shares)	N	Mean	Std. Deviation	Std. Error Mean
Public inform	100-200	446	1.9927	1.15587	.05473
	201-1000	52	2.6394	1.34894	.18706
Expert inform	100-200	446	2.0852	.99598	.04716
	201-1000	52	2.6603	1.11142	.15413

Table 129: Descriptive Statistics of Market Factors Comparison by Investment size

Levene's Test for Equality of Variances						
		F	Sig.	t	df	Sig. (2-tailed)
Public inform	Equal variances assumed	11.924	.001	-3.749	496	.000
	Equal variances not assumed			-3.318	60.055	.002
Expert inform	Equal variances assumed	9.186	.003	-3.891	496	.000
	Equal variances not assumed			-3.568	60.936	.001

Table 130: The t-test of Market Factors Comparison by Investment Size

By Sector of Investment. This section determined the significant difference in heuristics for individual investors when compared by sector of investment. The findings (see Table 131) reported that both dimensions of heuristics were significantly different: availability bias (F [2,495] = 14.921, p = .000) and overconfidence (F [2,495] = 18.915, p = .000). A discussion of each is provided.

Table 132 presents the descriptive statistics of market factors comparison by sector of investment. A post hoc test (see Table 133) was conducted to determine the differences among individual investors when grouped by sector of investment. The findings show that all comparisons were significantly different, with all p-values being less than .05. When individual investors were compared on public information by sector of investment, they differed significantly between all sectors: banking (M = 2.644, SD = 1.518), commercial (M = 1.947), and others (M = 1.500, SD = .000), with p = .000 in all cases. Surprisingly, this usage of public information is very low, which needs to be addressed.

		Sum of Squares	df	Mean Square	F	Sig.
Public inform	Between Groups	40.190	2	20.095	14.921	.000
	Within Groups	666.628	495	1.347		
	Total	706.818	497			
Expert inform	Between Groups	36.907	2	18.454	18.915	.000
	Within Groups	482.920	495	.976		
	Total	519.827	497			

Table 131: ANOVA-Market Factors Comparison by Sector of Investment

Individual investors were also compared on expert information by sector of investment. Findings showed significant differences: banking (M = 2.667, SD = 1.220), commercial (M = 2.055, SD = .944), and others (M = 1.333, SD = .000), all with p = .000. The low usage of expert information for investment decision-making is a source of concern.

By Type of Stock: This study sought to establish significant differences in market factors when individual investors were compared by type of stock. The findings (see Table 134) indicate statistically significant differences in market factors when compared by type of stock: public information (F [2,495] = 8.774, p = .000) and expert information (F [2,495] = 7.394, p = .001), with all p-values being less than .05. Therefore, NSE individual investors demonstrated different levels of market factor usage.

		N	Mean	Std. Deviation	Std. Error
Public inform	Banking	90	2.6444	1.51814	.16003
	Commercial	394	1.9467	1.08366	.05459
	Other	14	1.5000	.00000	.00000
	Total	498	2.0602	1.19255	.05344
Expert inform	Banking	90	2.6667	1.21989	.12859
	Commercial	394	2.0550	.94435	.04758
	Other	14	1.3333	.00000	.00000
	Total	498	2.1452	1.02271	.04583

Table 132: Descriptive Statistics of Market Factors Comparison by Sector of Investment

Dependent Variable	Mean Difference	Std. Error	Sig.

			(I-J)		
Public inform	Banking	Commercial	.69774*	.16908	.000
		Other	1.14444*	.16003	.000
	Commercial	Banking	-.69774*	.16908	.000
		Other	.44670*	.05459	.000
	Other	Banking	-1.14444*	.16003	.000
		Commercial	-.44670*	.05459	.000
Expert inform	Banking	Commercial	.61168*	.13711	.000
		Other	1.33333*	.12859	.000
	Commercial	Banking	-.61168*	.13711	.000
		Other	.72166*	.04758	.000
	Other	Banking	-1.33333*	.12859	.000
		Commercial	-.72166*	.04758	.000

Table 133: Group Comparison of Market Factors by Sector of Investment

**. The mean difference is significant at the 0.05 level*

		Sum of Squares	df	Mean Square	F	Sig.
Public inform	Between Groups	24.198	2	12.099	8.774	.000
	Within Groups	682.619	495	1.379		
	Total	706.818	497			
Expert inform	Between Groups	15.080	2	7.540	7.394	.001
	Within Groups	504.747	495	1.020		
	Total	519.827	497			

Table 134: ANOVA-Market Factors Comparison by Type of Stock

The descriptive statistics are presented in Table 135. A post hoc Games-Howell test was conducted (see Table 136) to determine the differences among the groups when compared by the type of stock purchased. When they were compared on public information, those individual investors who purchased blue chip stocks (M = 2.230, SD = 1.120) were significantly higher than those who purchased income stocks (M = 1.417, SD = .316). However, those who bought income stocks were significantly lower than those who bought actively traded stocks (M = 2.016, SD = 1.156).

		N	Mean	Std. Deviation	Std. Error
Public inform	Blue Chip	221	2.2296	1.28944	.08674
	Income stock	42	1.4167	.31558	.04870
	Actively traded	235	2.0160	1.15609	.07542
	Total	498	2.0602	1.19255	.05344
Expert inform	Blue Chip	221	2.2926	1.12045	.07537
	Income stock	42	1.6667	.47712	.07362
	Actively traded	235	2.0922	.96791	.06314
	Total	498	2.1452	1.02271	.04583

Table 135: Descriptive Statistics of Market Factors Comparison by Type of Stock

Dependent Variable			Mean Difference (I-J)	Std. Error	Sig.
Public inform	Blue Chip	Income stock	.81297*	.09947	.000
		Actively traded	.21368	.11494	.152
	Income	Blue Chip	-.81297*	.09947	.000

	stock	Actively traded	-.59929*	.08977	.000
	Actively traded	Blue Chip	-.21368	.11494	.152
		Income stock	.59929*	.08977	.000
Expert inform	Blue Chip	Income stock	.62594*	.10536	.000
		Actively traded	.20041	.09832	.104
	Income stock	Blue Chip	-.62594*	.10536	.000
		Actively traded	-.42553*	.09699	.000
	Actively traded	Blue Chip	-.20041	.09832	.104
		Income stock	.42553*	.09699	.000

Table 136: Group Comparison of Market Factors by Type of Stock
**. The mean difference is significant at the 0.05 level*

When they were compared on expert information, those individual investors who purchased blue chip stocks (M = 2.293, SD = 1.120) were significantly higher than those who purchased income stocks (M = 1.667, SD = .477). However, those who bought income stocks were significantly lower than those who bought actively traded stocks (M = 2.092, SD = .968). The individual investors in blue chip stocks sought and used more public and expert information. This is because they need to be sure that the blue chip companies will retain their status in order to continue investing in them. The section that follows presents the findings on research question 4.

Findings on Research Question Four

This section attempts to answer research question four: Are the following factors—herding, prospect (loss aversion, regret aversion, and escalating the commitment), heuristic (availability bias and overconfidence), market factors (public information and expert information), and investment decisions—significantly correlated with each other in the NSE? To answer this question, correlation analysis was conducted to determine the relationships and the strength of relationships among herding (HE), loss aversion (LA), regret aversion (RA), escalating the commitment (EC), availability bias (AB), overconfidence (OV), public information (PI), expert information (EI), and investment decisions (ID), with the dependent variable being investment performance (IP).Correlation Analysis

The correlation was computed using SPSS among six behavioural variables, two market variables, and one control variable that influence investment performance (see Table 137). There is a significant strong positive correlation between investment decisions and investment performance

	HE	LA	RA	EC	AB	OV	PI	EI	ID	IP
HE	1									
LA	.934**	1								
RA	.894**	.706**	1							
EC	.874**	.906**	.706**	1						
AB	.767**	.589**	.731**	.589**	1					
OV	.185**	.094*	.097*	.094*	.688**	1				
PI	-.250**	-.163**	-.116**	-.163**	-.692**	-.795**	1			
EI	-.196**	-.123**	-.046	-.123**	-.641**	-.675**	.923**	1		
ID	.141**	.054	.046	.054	.666**	.922**	-.906**	-.905**	1	
IP	.155**	.116**	.019	.116**	.589**	.850**	-.841**	-.818**	.828**	1

Table 137: Correlations for the Independent Variables with the Dependent Variable
***. Correlation is significant at the 0.01 level (2-tailed)*

(r = .828, N = 498, p < .01, two-tailed). This means that for every increase in investment decisions, there is a positive increase in investment performance. There is also a significant strong negative correlation between expert information and investment performance (r = -.818, N = 498, p < .01, two-tailed). This indicates that for every increase in expert information, there is a decrease in investment performance.

There is a significant strong negative correlation between public information and investment performance (r = - .841, N = 498, p < .01, two-tailed). There is a strong positive correlation between overconfidence and investment performance (r = .850, N = 498, p < .01, two-tailed). This means that 85% of the variation in investment performance can be attributed to overconfident behaviour. There is also a strong positive correlation between availability bias and investment performance (r = .589, N = 498, p < .01, two-tailed). This shows that for every increase in availability bias, there is a corresponding increase in investment performance.

There is a weak positive correlation between herding and investment performance (r = .155, N = 498, p < .01, two-tailed). This means that only 15.5% of the variation in investment performance is attributed to herding behaviour. There is a weak positive relationship between regret aversion and investment performance which is not significant (r = .019, N = 498, p > .01, two-tailed). There is a weak positive correlation between escalating commitment and investment performance (r = .116, N = 498, p < .01, two-tailed). Therefore, 11.6% of the significant variation in investment performance can be accounted for by escalating commitment.

The correlations of some independent variables among themselves are higher than .80, which should be addressed when developing a predictive model for investment performance. Where two predictors are highly correlated, one should be removed from the model. This is why correlation analysis is important—it helps identify highly correlated variables so they can be excluded to produce a more robust predictive model.

The herding variable was highly correlated with loss aversion (r = .934, N = 498, p < .01), regret aversion (r = .894, N = 498, p < .01), and escalating the commitment (r = .874, N = 498, p < .01). These variables were scrutinised to establish their contribution to the overall model, so that those contributing less could be omitted. Loss aversion and escalating the commitment were also highly correlated (r = .906), meaning they too should be considered for removal from the predictive model. However, the high correlation of the independent variables with the dependent variable does not affect the model. This is desirable, as it indicates that the independent variables are good predictors of the dependent variable.

Following the presentation of findings on correlation, the next section presents findings on research question five.

Findings on Research Question Five

This section attempted to answer research question five: Do the following behavioural factors—herding; prospect (loss aversion, regret aversion, and escalating the commitment); heuristic (availability bias and overconfidence); and market factors (public information and expert information)—combined together significantly influence investment performance in the NSE? To answer this research question, multiple regression analysis was conducted using SPSS. The multiple regression analysis was carried out using the stepwise method.

In the first step, the variables that did not have multiple correlations were entered: availability bias, overconfidence, public information, and expert information. The model was significant, producing an R^2 of 74.9%. In the second step, loss aversion was entered, which produced an R^2 of 75.1%—the same as for escalating the commitment. Both were retained even though they exhibited multicollinearity. In the third step, herding was added to the model, which produced an R^2 of 77.8%. However, when regret aversion was added, the model reduced to 76.9%. Therefore, it was decided to remove regret aversion and retain herding in the model. The variables that remained for model regression were herding, escalating the commitment, loss aversion, availability bias, overconfidence, public information, and expert information. These indicators were used in the regression to arrive at the model dimensions, which were then used to determine their individual contribution to the final model.

Dimensions Regression Model

The findings of the multiple regression (see Table 138) show that herding, escalating the commitment, availability bias, overconfidence, and public information collectively predict investment performance (R^2 = 77.8%), with all values being $p < .05$.

Model	R	R Square	Adjusted R Square	Std. Error of the Estimate
1	.882[a]	.778	.776	.32035

Table 138: Model Summary of Investment Performance

Expert information was not a significant contributor to the prediction model, with p = .247. The model was statistically significant (F [6, 491] = 287.587, p = .000) and, therefore, a good model for predicting investment performance (see Table 139). The regression equation was derived from the unstandardised beta coefficients (see Table 140).

IP = 3.102 + (- .952 x HE) + (.603 x EC) + (.540 x AB) + (.129 x OV) + (-.282 x PI)

Where IP = Investment Performance

HE = Herding

EC = Escalating the Commitment

AB = Availability Bias

OV = Overconfidence
PI = Public Information
Investment Performance Predictive Model
$IP = \propto + \beta_1 HE + \beta_2 EC + \beta_3 AB + \beta_4 OV + \beta_5 PI + \varepsilon$

Model		Sum of Squares	df	Mean Square	F	Sig.
1	Regression	177.076	6	29.513	287.587	.000[b]
	Residual	50.387	491	.103		
	Total	227.463	497			

Table 139: ANOVA Regression Results
a. Dependent Variable: Investment perform
b. Predictors: (Constant), Expert inform, Escalating com, Availability bias, Overconfidence, Public inform, Herding

Model		Unstandardized Coefficients		Standardized Coefficients	t	Sig.
		B	Std. Error	Beta		
1	(Constant)	3.102	.223		13.914	.000
	Herding	-.952	.121	-1.210	-7.843	.000
	Escalating com	.603	.075	.776	8.053	.000
	Availability bias	.540	.086	.654	6.260	.000
	Overconfidence	.129	.049	.197	2.637	.009
	Public inform	-.282	.068	-.497	-4.155	.000
	Expert inform	.076	.066	.116	1.160	.247

Table 140: Coefficients of Market Efficiencies Impact on Investment Performance Model

The diagram below (Figure 3) shows the relationship established between herding, escalating the commitment, availability bias, overconfidence, and public information as predictors of investment performance. The model showed that the predictors explained 77.8% of the variance in investment performance. This means that performance will vary by 77.8% when investors use these predictors in investment decision-making.

Herding behaviour was conceptualised to have a positive relationship with investment performance. However, the model indicated a negative relationship between herding and investment performance. This relationship is supported by the herding theory, which notes that there are two types of herding: spurious and intentional herding (Bikhchandani & Sharma, 2000). Spurious herding occurs when individual investors have the same set of information and, as a result, conduct similar analyses and arrive at the same conclusions. This may make them appear to be herding, potentially leading to a positive relationship between herding and investment performance. On the other hand, intentional herding may lead to a negative relationship, as investors do not perform their own analyses before making investment decisions. This kind of herding is more likely to result in poor investment performance.

Escalating the commitment was postulated to have a negative relationship with investment performance. However, the model showed a positive relationship. Escalating the commitment may negatively impact performance when investors do so for a short period (Lin et al., 2014). However, if they escalate commitment and hold stocks for a longer period, they are likely to earn a positive return as stock prices may increase over time.

Availability bias positively influences investment performance. This means that as availability bias increases, investment performance also increases. Availability bias occurs when individual investors rely on available information when making investment decisions (Tversky & Kahneman, 1974). This information could include companies currently performing well in the stock market. Therefore, if individual investors increasingly use such information to invest in well-performing companies, their investment performance is also likely to improve.

Overconfidence had a positive influence on investment performance. Therefore, an increase in overconfidence leads to an increase in investment performance. Overconfidence refers to individual investors overestimating their private information. Their belief that they possess superior information leads to increased trading (Barberis & Thaler, 2003). While increased trading can yield positive returns, it often results in returns lower than the market average due to trading costs.

The model indicated that public information had a negative relationship with investment performance. This was contrary to the hypothesised positive relationship. Information theory suggests that more information helps people make better decisions (Morris & Shin, 2002; Satti et al., 2013). A study by Patrick, Tavershima, and Eje (2017) also showed that financial statements indicate expected returns if an investment is made in a firm. Therefore, if such statements project losses, investors might associate public information with negative investment performance. Additionally, according to the signalling theory of information content, public information signals the future prospects of a company (Patrick, Tavershima, & Eje, 2017). This signalling enables individual investors to project investment performance in stock markets.

Expert information did not have a significant influence on investment performance. Compared to public information, expert information often incurs access costs. Therefore, individual investors in the NSE may prefer public information as it is relatively inexpensive to access. This may explain why public information remained in the model, despite its negative influence on investment performance.

The Final Model

The R results in Table 141 shows the strength of the independent variables and the dependent variables. Herding has an influence on investment performance of about (R = .155).

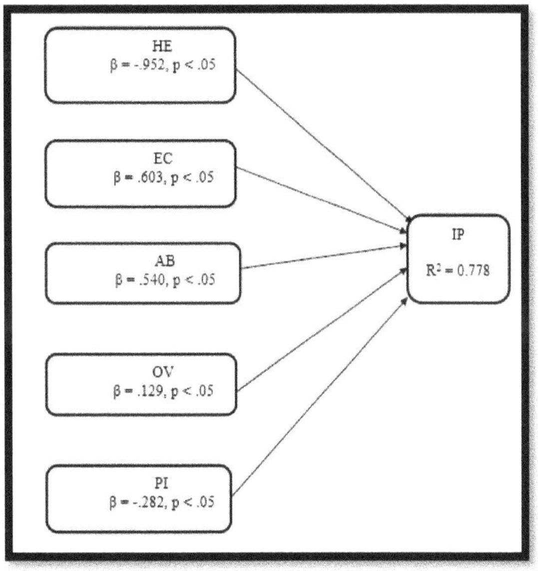

Figure 3: Dimensions Investment Performance Predictive Model

When the herding factor is combined with prospect factor, the strength increases to (R = .175). The strength of the association increases to (.869) when the herding, prospect, and heuristic factors are combined. When all the four factors are combined (herding, prospect, heuristic, and market factor) the strength of association increases to (R = .880). The model summary shows that around 77.4% of investment performance of the individual investors of NSE is determined by herding, prospect, heuristic, and market factors.

Regression results for the final integrated model. The coefficients (Table 142) were used to determine whether the model is a good fit for investment performance. The results show that the independent variables: herding F (1, 496) = 12.200, p < .05; prospect F (2, 495) = 7.811, p < .05; heuristic F (3, 494) = 506.805; and market F (4, 493) = 421.079 are a good fit for investment performance. Therefore, it is useful in predicting investment performance given the predictor variables.

Model	R	R Square	Adjusted R Square	Std. Error of the Estimate
1	.155[a]	.024	.022	.66902
2	.175[b]	.031	.027	.66743
3	.869[c]	.755	.753	.33603
4	.880[d]	.774	.772	.32322

a. Predictors: (Constant), Herding
b. Predictors: (Constant), Herding, Prospect
c. Predictors: (Constant), Herding, Prospect, Heuristic
d. Predictors: (Constant), Herding, Prospect, Heuristic, Market
e. Dependent Variable: Investmentperform

Table 141: Final Model Summary

Model		Sum of Squares	df	Mean Square	F	Sig.
1	Regression	5.460	1	5.460	12.200	.001[a]
	Residual	222.003	496	.448		
	Total	227.463	497			
2	Regression	6.959	2	3.480	7.811	.000[b]
	Residual	220.504	495	.445		
	Total	227.463	497			
3	Regression	171.682	3	57.227	506.805	.000[c]
	Residual	55.781	494	.113		
	Total	227.463	497			
4	Regression	175.960	4	43.990	421.079	.000[d]
	Residual	51.503	493	.104		
	Total	227.463	497			

Table 142: ANOVA Regression Results

To generate the unstandardised coefficients, the enter method of multiple regression analysis was used. The coefficients indicate the variance of the dependent variable with an independent variable when others are held constant. From the coefficients table, β1 for herding behaviour is -.602. This means that for every increase in herding, there is a decrease in the market efficiency's impact on investment performance. There was also an influence of prospect behaviour on the market efficiency's impact on investment performance of β2 = .424. Heuristic behaviour also had an influence on the market efficiency's impact on investment performance of β3 = .536. Market factors had a negative influence on the market efficiency's impact on investment performance of β4 = -.195. The p-values for all the coefficients were less than .05 and hence, significant (see Table 143)..

Model		Unstandardized Coefficients		Standardized Coefficients	t	Sig.
		B	Std. Error	Beta		
1	(Constant)	2.936	.219		13.404	.000
	Herding	-.602	.059	-.765	-10.151	.000
	Prospect	.424	.052	.545	8.163	.000
	Heuristic	.536	.049	.676	10.915	.000
	Market	-.195	.030	-.344	-6.399	.000
a. Dependent Variable: Investmentperform						

Table 143: Coefficients

Discussion of the final integrated model. The general form of the predictive equation from herding, prospect, heuristic and market for investment performance is a follows.

$IP = \propto + \beta_1 HF + \beta_2 PF + \beta_3 HUF + \beta_4 MF + \varepsilon$

Where IP = Investment Performance

HF = Herding Factors

PF = Prospect Factors

HUF = Heuristic Factors

MF = Market Factors

The general equation model was made up of the following components. The herding factors was made up of:

1. Herding (HE)

The prospect factor was made of the following indicator:

2. Escalating the commitment (EC)

Heuristic factors comprised of the following indicators:

3. Availability Bias (AB)
4. Overconfidence (OV)

Finally, the market factor had only one indicator:

5. Public Information (PI)

The beta values for the final model was:

$IP = 2.936 - .602\ HF + .424\ PF + .536\ HUF - .195\ MF + \varepsilon$

Where IP = Investment Performance
HF = Herding Factors
PF = Prospect Factors
HUF = Heuristic Factors
MF = Market Factors

The predictive final model was derived from five independent variables. All four factors were significant predictors of investment performance. The model was significant with $F(4, 493) = 421.079$, $p < .05$. The model (see Table 144) explains 77.4% of the variance in investment performance ($R^2 = .774$). The remaining 22.6% of the variance in investment performance could be explained by rational factors or a combination of both rational and irrational factors. Future studies should consider combining both irrational and rational factors in one study to explicitly show the contribution of each to the variance in investment performance. Herding and market had a negative relationship with the market efficiency's impact on investment performance, while prospect and heuristic had a positive relationship. Therefore, the overall integrated final model comprised the following:

$IP = 2.936 - \beta_1\ HF + \beta_2\ PF + \beta_3\ HUF - \beta_4\ MF + \varepsilon$

Where IP = Investment Performance
HF = Herding Factors
PF = Prospect Factors
HUF = Heuristic Factors
MF = Market Factors

The conceptual framework for the study (see Figure 1) was tested using multiple regression. The findings show that herding, prospect, heuristic and market factors influences investment performance (see Figure 4).

Model	R	R Square	Adjusted R Square	Std. Error of the Estimate
1	.880[a]	.774	.772	.32322
a. Predictors: (Constant), Herding, Prospect, Heuristic, Market				
b. Dependent Variable: Investment perform				

Table 144: Regression Model Summary

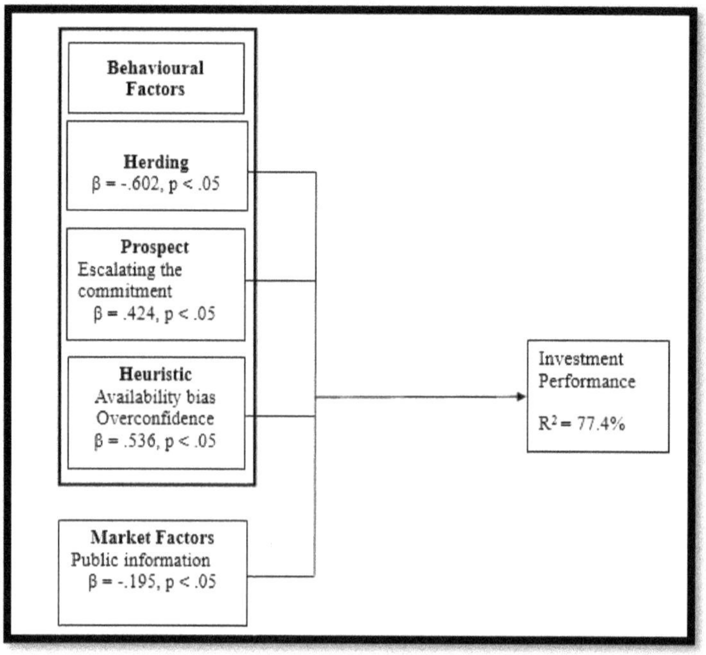

Figure 4: Final Investment Performance Predictive Model

Findings on Research Question Six

The following section attempts to answer research question six: Do the following behavioural factors—herding, prospect (loss aversion, regret aversion, and escalating the commitment), heuristic (availability bias and overconfidence), and market factors (public information and expert information)—combined together significantly influence investment performance, with investment decisions as a control variable in the NSE?

To answer the research question, a multiple regression was conducted including all the variables (herding, regret aversion, escalating the commitment, availability bias, overconfidence, public information, expert information), with investment decisions included as a control variable. The control variable was input in the same manner as an additional independent variable, and then a multiple regression was run.

The findings (Table 145) show that investment decisions, as a control variable, do not have a significant effect on the model. The model remains the same even after including investment decisions. Therefore, the variable has no significant effect on investment performance. The findings also indicate that the beta coefficient for investment decisions is insignificant, with a p-value of .920 (see Table 146).

Model	R	R Square	Adjusted R Square	Std. Error of the Estimate
1	.880[a]	.774	.771	.32354
a. Predictors: (Constant), Investmentdecisions, Prospect, Market, Heuristic, Herding				
b. Dependent Variable: Investmentperform				

Table 145: Model Summary with Control Variable

Model		Unstandardized Coefficients		Standardized Coefficients	t	Sig.
		B	Std. Error	Beta		
1	(Constant)	2.920	.275		10.601	.000
	Herding	-.599	.066	-.761	-9.104	.000
	Prospect	.422	.053	.543	7.914	.000
	Heuristic	.531	.065	.670	8.176	.000
	Market	-.194	.033	-.342	-5.905	.000
	Investment decisions	.007	.066	.007	.100	.920

Table 146: Regression Coefficients

Chapter 5 | Summary of Findings and Discussions

Following the presentation of findings in Chapter 4, the focus now shifts to the discussion of the significant findings. This study aimed to establish the behavioural and market factors that influence investment performance. Therefore, this chapter presents the discussion under the following sections: the statement of the problem and the methodology used, significant findings, interpretations, conclusions, implications, recommendations, and suggestions of the study. This summary is based on the findings from the study.

Investors are expected to be guided by the Efficient Market Hypothesis (EMH) to facilitate rational investment decisions, which means they should not be influenced by their behavioural biases. Therefore, there should be no abnormal occurrences in the financial market, and as such, individual investors are expected to earn a return equivalent to the market performance. However, individual investors have often been found to be influenced by behavioural factors in their investment decisions (Aduda et al., 2012). Furthermore, anomalies have been reported in the securities market that the EMH could not explain (Latif et al., 2011). Therefore, this points to the fact that investment decisions may be influenced by factors other than the EMH.

This influence of behavioural factors on investors has resulted in anomalies in the securities market, leading to major losses on the investments made. The underperformance of individual investors, to a large extent, may be due to factors related to the individual investors' behaviour and not the performance of the securities market. Therefore, this study aimed to investigate the behavioural (herding, prospect, and heuristics) and market factors influencing investment decisions, with an additional indicator of prospect, namely, escalating commitment, and ultimately determining their influence on investment performance. Few studies have investigated escalating commitment as a behavioural factor that may be exhibited by investors and its influence on investment performance.

To answer the research questions of the study, descriptive statistics, t-tests, one-way ANOVA, correlation analysis, and multiple regression were employed. Descriptive statistics were used to analyse the demographic and psychographic characteristics of the individual investors and the levels of herding, loss aversion, regret aversion, escalating commitment, availability bias, overconfidence, public information, and expert information. Descriptive statistics were also used to determine the ranking of the behavioural factors. T-tests, Levene's tests, one-way ANOVA and post hoc tests were used to determine whether individual investors exhibit any significant differences in the behavioural factors when compared by demographic and psychographic characteristics. Multicollinearity was tested for the independent variables using correlation analysis. To determine the influence of behavioural and market factors on investment performance, multiple regression analysis was employed.

Discussion of Findings

This section starts with the findings on the descriptive statistics of the variables under study. This is followed by the extent of behavioural factors, the correlation of the behavioural factors, and the influence they have on investment performance. I will now discuss each finding. The discussion will be in the following order: the findings, interpretations, relationship to previous research, conclusions, implications, and recommendations.

Major Findings 1

These major findings were intended to answer Research Question 1: What behavioural factors such as herding, prospect (loss aversion, regret aversion, and escalating commitment), and heuristic (availability bias and overconfidence) are displayed by individual investors in the NSE? The findings are discussed in the following sections 1(a) to 1(f). Generally, the individual investors of the NSE displayed moderate to high levels of the behavioural factors.

Findings 1(a): The findings indicated a high level of herding among individual investors in the NSE (M = 3.98). This indicates that individual investors strongly displayed herding behaviour when making investment decisions in the NSE. The discussion of the finding is provided below.

Interpretation of Findings: The high level of herding displayed by individual investors in the NSE occurs when they follow the decisions of other investors in order to conform. In addition, investors may herd when they fail to carry out their own analysis before making investment decisions. On the other hand, individual investors may follow popular opinion in the stock market. This high level of herding is driven by the perception that others may be right or may possess information they themselves do not have. Investors who exhibit herding may be encouraged to do so when they lack the necessary knowledge and skills to evaluate investments for decision-making. Therefore, they rely on the decisions of other investors to guide their own.

Relationship to Previous Research: My findings are supported by Ngoc (2013), who found that individual investors are affected by herding with a mean score of M = 3.63. Likewise, Javed et al. (2017) established that individual investors are influenced by herding at a level of M = 3.10. In addition, another study by Alrabadi et al. (2018) determined that individual investors display herding when making investment decisions at a level of M = 4.94. This demonstrates that herding behaviour is prevalent among most individual investors.

Conclusion: These findings show that individual investors are influenced by herding behaviour. These high levels may affect their investment performance. This should be a source of concern for individual investors, the NSE management, and the Capital Markets Authority.

Implications: The NSE management, Capital Markets Authority, and policymakers should initiate training on stock market investment for individual investors. This is because a high level of herding may negatively affect investment performance. In addition, the economy could be impacted by this negative performance.

Recommendations: The findings showed that herding has a negative relationship with investment performance. This means that as herding increases, investment performance decreases. As such, there is a need to advise individual investors of the NSE to reduce their level of herding in order to improve their investment performance. Therefore, individual investors should conduct their own analysis before making investment decisions. They should avoid following popular opinion and instead trust their own analysis, even if it contradicts market sentiment.

Findings 1(b): The findings of the study showed that loss aversion behaviour was displayed by individual investors at a high level (M = 3.99). This means that individual investors were affected by loss aversion when making investment decisions. The interpretation of the finding is provided below.

Interpretation of Findings: The findings indicated that individual investors make investment decisions in order to avoid incurring losses. This occurs when a positive return in the past leads the investor to seek more risk. Consequently, when the return from past investments is positive, individual investors tend to invest in riskier assets, hoping for continued positive returns, thus exposing themselves to greater risk. On the other hand, if an individual investor has experienced a negative return in the past, they will become more risk-averse. This is because the thought of incurring another loss is more painful than the potential gain promised by the investment.

Relationship to Previous Research: The results of this study are confirmed by other studies that found loss aversion behaviour to be prevalent among individual investors: Ngoc (2013) with a level of M = 3.83, and Waweru et al. (2014) with a level of M = 3.02. Therefore, individual investors display loss aversion when making investment decisions. The thought of incurring a loss is more painful than the anticipated gain, even when the value is equivalent.

Conclusion: These findings show that individual investors display loss aversion, which may affect their investment performance. The NSE management and Capital Markets Authority should organise seminars for individual investors to sensitise them on the influence of loss aversion.

Implications: Individual investors should be sensitised to the effects of loss aversion. In addition, they should be encouraged to conduct their own analysis of investments before making decisions, to avoid loss aversion behaviour. Loss aversion may affect their investment performance.

Recommendations: Individual investors should be encouraged to avoid the influence of loss aversion. Instead, they should rely on fundamental analysis of stocks when making decisions. This will enable them to earn market returns, thereby avoiding the negative effects of loss aversion. In other words, individual investors should avoid seeking more risk when past returns have been positive, while at the same time avoiding being risk-averse simply because past returns were negative. Individual investors may end up losing if they rely on loss aversion without analysing the investment opportunities.

Findings 1(c): The findings indicate that individual investors are influenced by regret aversion at a moderate level (M = 3.516). This level is moderate, meaning that the individual investors of NSE are influenced by regret aversion. The interpretation of the findings is provided.

Interpretation of Findings: Individual investors' decisions are determined by regret aversion. They avoid losses by selling stocks whose prices have increased and delaying the sale of stocks whose prices have decreased. They sell the stocks whose prices have increased so that they can realise the gains immediately. This is to avoid regretting it if the prices were to drop before selling the stocks, thereby realising losses. On the other hand, individual investors do not sell stocks whose prices have decreased, to postpone realising the loss immediately, in the hope that the prices may increase in the future. This is because they want to postpone realising the losses, as they do not want to regret the decision, hoping that the prices will increase and offset the losses.

Relationship to Previous Research: The findings of this study are supported by Ngoc (2013), who found that regret aversion influences individual investors at a level of (M = 3.76). In addition, Waweru et al. (2014) established that regret aversion affects individual investors at a level of (M = 3.62). This indicates that individual investors are influenced by regret aversion when making investment decisions.

Conclusion: Individual investors of NSE display regret aversion behaviour when making investment decisions. Therefore, regret aversion should concern individual investors because it may influence their investment performance. As such, programmes should be initiated to sensitise individual investors to the dangers of regret aversion.

Implications: The dangers of regret aversion as a behavioural factor influencing individual investors may be significant if the effects are negative. This is because it leads investors to behave as noise traders in the stock market, thereby reducing the effectiveness of the efficient market hypothesis in determining the investment performance of the stock market. Therefore, there is an opportunity for NSE management and the Capital Markets Authority to hold seminars to sensitise individual investors on how to reduce regret aversion behaviour.

Recommendations: The study found that individual investors are influenced by regret aversion. Therefore, it is recommended that individual investors of NSE should be advised not to sell shares just because prices have increased, in order to avoid regret aversion. On the other hand, they need to avoid holding stocks simply to avoid regret if there are indications that those stocks should be sold.

Findings 1(d): The findings indicated that individual investors of NSE displayed escalating commitment at a high level (M = 3.79). This indicates that individual investors of NSE are influenced by escalating commitment. The interpretation of the findings is provided.

Interpretation of Findings: Individual investors of NSE escalate commitment because some stocks have regained their value after performing poorly for some time. Those who sold their stocks quickly to avoid further losses ended up losing. However, those who continued to buy the same stocks profited significantly when the prices of those shares bounced back, regaining their market value—for example, the initial public offering of Safaricom. The initial offer price was KShs. 5 per share, which immediately dropped to around KShs. 2.50 per share. Individual investors who took a long-term strategy and continued buying the stocks when the prices went down reaped significant gains when the prices rose to over KShs. 5 per share. This scenario may have encouraged NSE individual investors to escalate commitment in the hope that the prices of the stocks they bought were likely to bounce back.

Relationship to Previous Research: In a study by Lin et al. (2014), escalating commitment was found to affect mutual fund performance in investment decisions. Turino and Soetjipto (2012) also determined that escalating commitment influenced investors when making investment decisions. However, both studies did not indicate the level of escalating commitment among the respondents studied. The studies only established the effect it has on investment performance.

Conclusion: Individual investors of NSE displayed escalating commitment while making investment decisions. Since escalating commitment as a behavioural factor affects the efficient market hypothesis, it should be addressed. This is because the behavioural factor will affect stock market efficiency in determining investment performance. As such, individual investors may experience negative performance.

Implications: Individual investors affect the operations of the NSE, which in turn affects the economy. In addition, the NSE may not be efficient in allocating scarce resources due to the operations of individual investors displaying behavioural factors. Therefore, the NSE management, Capital Markets Authority, and policymakers should initiate training programmes on behavioural factors and their negative influence.

Recommendations: Individual investors should be encouraged to conduct thorough investment analysis before making investment decisions. This will help reduce the tendency towards escalating commitment. Individual investors should be advised to avoid continuing to invest in stocks even when they have experienced previous losses from those stocks. In addition, they should avoid persisting with investments that are performing poorly.

Findings 1(e): The results showed that availability bias among the individual investors of NSE had a high level (M = 3.99). This indicates that the individual investors of NSE are influenced by availability bias when making investment decisions. The interpretation of the finding is provided.

Interpretation of Findings: These results indicate that the individual investors of NSE were influenced by availability bias while making investment decisions. This means that the individual investors prefer to invest in stocks of local firms rather than foreign ones. In addition, they invest in stocks of companies whose names they can easily remember. Alternatively, they invest in stocks of well-performing firms. This is because local companies can easily be brought to mind when investment opportunities arise. The well-performing companies will also be remembered easily and, hence, individual investors will invest in them.

Relationship to Previous Research: The findings of this study are supported by Waweru et al. (2014), who determined that availability bias influences individual investors of NSE at a level of (M = 3.65). Also, Javed et al. (2017) and Alrabadi et al. (2018) found that availability bias influences individual investors at levels of (M = 2.84) and (M = 4.83) respectively. This shows that individual investors display availability bias when making investment decisions.

Conclusion: The individual investors of NSE are influenced by availability bias when making investment decisions. This may be detrimental to the performance of their investments. Therefore, it calls for the sensitisation of individual investors on the effect of availability bias so that they can avoid it. The reduction of availability bias may improve their investment performance.

Implications: This finding implies that individual investors should be enabled to make investment decisions by taking availability bias into consideration. The NSE management, Capital Markets Authority, and policymakers need to come up with programmes to sensitise individual investors on availability bias. This sensitisation provides an opportunity for individual investors to make better investment decisions.

Recommendations: This study recommends that individual investors should not simply prefer to invest in stocks of local firms rather than foreign ones, stocks of companies whose names they can easily remember, or stocks of well-performing firms. Rather, they should evaluate the investment opportunities for better decision-making. This is because investing in the stock market using only the available information may lead individual investors to achieve returns that are lower than the market return and, hence, underperform.

Findings 1(f): The findings indicated that the individual investors of NSE had an overconfidence level of (M = 4.03), which was high. This level means that the individual investors of NSE are influenced by overconfidence. The interpretation of the finding is provided.

Interpretation of Findings: These findings indicate that the individual investors of NSE are affected by overconfidence when making investment decisions. This overconfidence occurs when they trade more in terms of buying and selling stocks. Therefore, those individual investors who are more confident will trade more in the stock market than the less confident ones. In other words, overconfident individual investors think that they can beat the market. Overconfidence among individual investors occurs due to miscalibration and the better-than-average effect. Miscalibration occurs when individual investors overestimate their abilities and believe they are more accurate in their estimation of stock prices. Also, the better-than-average effect is where individual investors rate themselves as being better than other investors in the stock market.

Relationship to Previous Research: The findings of this study are confirmed by Ngoc (2013), who found that overconfidence influences individual investors at a level of (M = 3.66), and Waweru et al. (2014), with a level of (M = 3.44). In addition, Javed et al. (2017) and Alrabadi et al. (2018) established that individual investors display overconfidence at levels of (M = 2.87) and (M = 4.14) respectively. Therefore, overconfidence as a behavioural factor affects individual investors when they are making investment decisions.

Conclusion: The individual investors of NSE are influenced by overconfidence when making investment decisions. Studies have confirmed that it is not easy to beat the market. Therefore, individual investors should be enlightened on the effect of overconfidence so that they can avoid it. Reducing overconfidence may improve their investment performance.

Implications: The NSE management, Capital Markets Authority, and policymakers need to come up with programmes to inform individual investors about the possible effects of overconfidence on their investment performance. This is because beating the market is not easy. This finding implies that individual investors should be enabled to make investment decisions by taking overconfidence into consideration.

Recommendations: The study recommends that individual investors should avoid considering themselves overconfident. They should not be tempted to overestimate their abilities, nor should they rate themselves as better than other investors in the stock market. This is because they may be encouraged to trade more, which may negatively affect their investment performance.

Major Finding 2

This section provides a discussion on the ranking of the behavioural factors. They were ranked starting with the one having the highest mean and ending with the one having the lowest mean. The findings showed that the individual investors of the NSE displayed the behavioural factors under study in the following order of rank:

1. Overconfidence
2. Availability bias
3. Escalating the commitment
4. Loss aversion
5. Herding
6. Regret aversion

Interpretation of findings

There were six behavioural factors that were ranked among the individual investors of the NSE. Among these six factors, overconfidence was ranked highest (M = 4.031), while regret aversion was ranked lowest (M = 3.516). The other behavioural variables were ranked as follows: in second place was availability bias, third was escalating the commitment, fourth was loss aversion, and fifth was herding, with mean scores of (M = 3.992), (M = 3.986), (M = 3.986), and (M = 3.977) respectively. This shows that most individual investors sampled were overconfident when trading in the stock market. The mechanism that accounts for the high level of overconfidence in the NSE could be associated with the high trading activity of individual investors. This is because individual investors consider themselves to have better skills in trading in the stock market, which leads them to trade excessively.

Relationship to Previous Research

The findings of this study are supported by Ngoc (2013), who found that overconfidence influences individual investors at a level of (M = 3.66), and Waweru et al. (2014), at a level of (M = 3.44). In addition, Alrabadi et al. (2018) established that individual investors display overconfidence at a level of (M = 4.14). This indicates that overconfidence affects individual investors at high levels, although other studies did not rank the behavioural factors.

Conclusion

The high levels of behavioural factors among individual investors at the NSE could influence investment performance. In addition, these high levels may lead to underperformance of portfolio investments. Therefore, underperformance of the investment portfolio is an area of concern that should be addressed. The implications and recommendations are discussed in the following sections.

Implications

Investment advisers and policymakers need to initiate programmes to promote awareness among individual investors about the behavioural factors likely to influence their investment decisions and investment performance. The high levels of behavioural factors (especially overconfidence) among individual investors indicate the potential effect on investment performance. With high levels of behavioural influence, investment performance may be negatively affected. Additionally, individual investors do not earn returns equivalent to the market return, which may impact their wealth creation and the economy at large.

Recommendations

It is recommended that the NSE management and policymakers initiate awareness programmes to enlighten individual investors about the behavioural factors that may affect them when making investment decisions in the stock market. They should also be encouraged to seek investment advice whenever making investment decisions. Therefore, they should not be overconfident about their trading abilities in the stock market. In other words, individual investors should be advised not to overestimate their trading skills or assume they are better than other investors. This may reduce the high levels of behavioural bias and, hence, reduce its influence on investment performance.

Major Finding 3

This section presents a discussion of the findings of research question 3. The results are interpreted and discussed in relation to the differences in behavioural and market factors when compared by demographic and psychographic characteristics. The discussion begins with demographic characteristics, followed by psychographic characteristics.

Demographic Differences

The following section presents a discussion on behavioural and market factors that significantly differed across demographic categories. These categories included gender, age, education, occupation, income, trading experience, and trading frequency. The discussion is structured as follows: findings, conclusions, implications, and recommendations.

Herding

Regarding the herding variable, individual investors did not significantly differ across demographic categories such as age, marital status, and investing experience. However, they did significantly differ across gender, occupation, education, and income. The following section discusses the findings, conclusions, implications, and recommendations for each demographic category where herding behaviour differed significantly.

Gender

The findings show a statistically significant difference in herding behaviour between males and females. This means that females were more prone to herding than males. The NSE management, Capital Markets Authority, and policymakers should organise training for individual investors at the NSE. This study recommends that individual investors, especially females, should conduct their own analysis before making investment decisions.

Occupation

The results showed that individual investors who were businesspeople and those who were employed significantly differed in herding behaviour when compared by occupation. Businesspeople exhibited higher levels of herding compared to employed individuals. The NSE management and the Capital Markets Authority should develop programmes to sensitise individual investors, especially businesspeople, on the risks of high levels of herding. Businesspeople should be advised not to make investment decisions without conducting their own analysis.

Education

The findings showed a statistically significant difference in herding behaviour when investors were compared by level of education. Herding levels were higher among those with a high school level of education compared to those with a college education. The NSE management and the Capital Markets Authority should create programmes to sensitise individual investors—particularly those with only high school education—on the dangers of high levels of herding. These investors should be advised to carry out their own analysis before making investment decisions.

Income

The findings revealed a statistically significant difference in herding behaviour across income groups. Investors earning less than Kshs. 50,000 and those earning more than Kshs. 100,000 exhibited more herding than those earning between Kshs. 50,001 and 100,000. The NSE management and the Capital Markets Authority should develop targeted programmes for these income groups. These individual investors should be encouraged not to follow others' decisions blindly but to conduct their own analysis.

Loss Aversion

For the loss aversion variable, individual investors did not significantly differ across demographic categories such as age, marital status, income, and investing experience. However, significant differences were found across gender, occupation, and education. The following section discusses the findings, conclusions, implications, and recommendations for each demographic category where loss aversion behaviour differed significantly.

Gender

The findings show that male and female individual investors differed significantly when compared on loss aversion by gender. Females had higher levels of loss aversion when compared to males. The NSE management and the Capital Market Authority need to sensitise females on the pitfalls of loss aversion. Female individual investors should be advised not to become more risk-seeking without conducting investment analysis.

Occupation

The findings showed that individual investors who are employed differed on loss aversion when compared with those who were business people. Business people were more affected by loss aversion than employed individual investors. Therefore, the NSE management and the Capital Market Authority have an opportunity to develop training programmes for individual investors, tailored to business people. Business people should be cautioned against becoming more risk-seeking without conducting investment analysis.

Regret Aversion

Individual investors did not differ significantly on regret aversion across demographic categories such as age and marital status. However, they differed significantly across demographic categories such as gender, occupation, education, income, and investing experience. The sections that follow provide a discussion of the findings, conclusions, implications, and recommendations for each demographic category where regret aversion behaviour differed significantly.

Gender

Individual investors differed significantly on regret aversion. Females had a higher level of regret aversion when compared with males. This provides an opportunity for the NSE management and the Capital Market Authority to embark on sensitisation programmes for individual investors, especially females. In addition, females should be advised to avoid being more willing to sell stocks whose prices have increased or being less willing to sell those whose prices have decreased without conducting proper analysis.

Occupation

The findings showed that individual investors who are employed differed on regret aversion when compared with those who were business people. Business people had a higher level of regret aversion than the employed. Programmes should be tailored by the NSE management and the Capital Market Authority for business people on the effect of regret aversion on investment performance. Additionally, business people should be advised to avoid being more willing to sell stocks whose prices have increased or being less willing to sell those whose prices have decreased without proper analysis.

Education

The findings showed that there was a statistically significant difference among different education level groups in their regret aversion. Individual investors on the NSE with high school education had a higher level of regret aversion when compared with those who had college education. The NSE management and the Capital Market Authority should organise programmes for individual investors with high school education on the effect of regret aversion on investment performance. Furthermore, investors should be advised to avoid being more willing to sell stocks whose prices have increased or being less willing to sell those whose prices have decreased without proper analysis.

Income

The findings showed a statistically significant difference among different income groups in their regret aversion. Regret aversion decreases with increasing income. This suggests that the NSE management and the Capital Market Authority should introduce training programmes on regret aversion. Therefore, individual investors with lower incomes need to be educated about avoiding being overly willing to sell stocks whose prices have increased or being reluctant to sell those whose prices have decreased without conducting stock analysis.

Investing Experience

The findings showed a statistically significant difference among different groups based on investing experience. Individual investors with more than 11 years of experience had a higher level of regret aversion than those with 6–10 years of experience. This indicates the need for the NSE management and the Capital Market Authority to introduce training programmes on regret aversion. Therefore, investors with more than 11 years of experience should be educated about avoiding being overly willing to sell stocks whose prices have increased or being reluctant to sell those whose prices have decreased without stock analysis.

Escalating the Commitment

Regarding escalating the commitment, individual investors did not differ significantly across demographic categories such as age, marital status, income, and investing experience. However, they differed significantly across gender, occupation, and education. The sections that follow provide a discussion of the findings, conclusions, implications, and recommendations for each demographic category where escalating the commitment behaviour differed significantly.

Gender

Individual investors differed significantly on escalating the commitment. Females had higher levels of escalating the commitment when compared with males, and stakeholders in the stock market should be concerned. The NSE management and the Capital Market Authority should devise training programmes to educate females. Females should be educated on the dangers of continuing to invest in a failing course when analysis does not support continued investment.

Occupation

The findings showed that individual investors who are employed differed on escalating the commitment when compared with those who were business people. Business people had significantly higher levels compared with the employed, and this should be a cause for concern. The NSE management and the Capital Market Authority should devise training programmes for business people. They should be educated on the dangers of continuing to invest in a failing course when analysis does not support continued investment.

Education

The findings showed a statistically significant difference among education levels regarding escalating the commitment. Individual investors on the NSE with high school education had a higher level of escalating the commitment compared with those with college education. This should concern the NSE management and the Capital Market Authority, who should initiate educational programmes. These programmes should inform participants about the dangers of continuing to invest in a failing course when analysis does not support such investment.

Availability Bias

Regarding availability bias, individual investors did not differ significantly across demographic categories such as age, education, and investing experience. However, they differed significantly across gender, marital status, occupation, and income. The sections that follow provide a discussion of the findings, conclusions, implications, and recommendations for each demographic category where availability bias behaviour differed significantly.

Gender

The findings showed that females and males differed significantly on availability bias. Females displayed higher levels of availability bias than males. The NSE management and the Capital Market Authority need to organise training programmes to enlighten females on the dangers of higher availability bias. Females should be advised to invest in local companies and those that are performing well, supported by thorough stock investment analysis.

Marital Status

The findings showed a statistically significant difference in availability bias when individual investors were compared by marital status. Single investors had higher levels of availability bias than those who were married. The NSE management and the Capital Market Authority should develop training programmes to educate single investors about availability bias. In particular, they should be advised to invest in stocks of local companies and those that are performing well, after conducting stock investment analysis.

Occupation

The results showed that business people reported significantly higher levels of availability bias than the employed. This means that the individual investors who are business people were more influenced by availability bias when making investment decisions in the NSE. Therefore, this provided an opportunity for the NSE management and the Capital Markets Authority to start training programmes to educate individual investors who are business people. The training should focus on enlightening business people to invest in stocks of local companies and those that are performing well after conducting stock investment analysis.

Income

The findings showed that the individual investors had a statistically significant difference in availability bias when compared by income. The individual investors who had an income of less than Shs. 50,000 had a higher level of availability bias than those with an income between Shs. 50,001 and Shs. 100,000. The NSE management and the Capital Markets Authority should seize the opportunity and introduce training programmes for individual investors. These trainings should target individual investors who have an income of less than Shs. 50,000. Individual investors earning less than Shs. 50,000 need to be informed about investing in stocks of local companies and those that are performing well after conducting stock investment analysis.

Overconfidence

When individual investors were assessed on the overconfidence variable, they did not significantly differ for demographic categories such as age, occupation, and income. However, the individual investors significantly differed for demographic categories such as gender, marital status, education, and investing experience. The section that follows provides a discussion on the findings, conclusions, implications, and recommendations in each of the demographic categories where overconfidence behaviour significantly differed.

Gender

The findings showed that females and males significantly differed in overconfidence. Females displayed higher levels of overconfidence compared to males. Hence, there is a need for the NSE management and the Capital Markets Authority to create programmes aimed at educating individual investors, especially females, on the pitfalls of overconfidence. In addition, individual investors, especially females, should be advised to trust their trading skills in the stock market after conducting their own analysis.

Marital Status

The findings showed that there was a statistically significant difference in overconfidence when compared by marital status. Individual investors who are single had higher levels of overconfidence than those who are married. Therefore, the NSE management and the Capital Markets Authority should start programmes aimed at enlightening individual investors, especially singles, on the pitfalls of overconfidence. On the same note, individual investors, especially females, should be advised to trust their trading skills in the stock market after conducting their own analysis.

Education

The findings showed that when individual investors were compared on overconfidence by education, there was a statistically significant difference. Individual investors with a college education were more confident than those with a high school level of education. This calls for the NSE management and the Capital Markets Authority to start programmes to educate individual investors with a college level of education. In particular, they should be advised to trust their trading skills in the stock market after conducting their own analysis.

Public Information

On the public information variable, individual investors did not significantly differ for demographic categories such as age, occupation, and income. However, individual investors significantly differed for demographic categories such as gender, marital status, education, and investing experience. The section that follows provides a discussion on the findings, conclusions, implications, and recommendations in each of the demographic categories where public information differed significantly.

Gender

The findings showed that there was a significant difference in public information when individual investors were compared by gender. Although the levels were low, males reported higher levels of public information than females. This should provide an opportunity for the NSE management and the Capital Markets Authority to organise educative programmes for individual investors. These programmes should endeavour to highlight the importance of reading and analysing financial statements before investing in stocks of firms that promise good performance.

Marital Status

The results established that there was a significant difference in public information when individual investors were compared by their marital status. Individual investors who are married showed a higher level of using public information compared with singles. Therefore, the NSE management and the Capital Markets Authority should come up with training programmes on the use of public information. Individual investors should be encouraged to read financial statements in order to invest in stocks of companies promising good performance.

Education

The results established that there was a significant difference in public information when individual investors were compared by their level of education. Individual investors with a high school level of education displayed a higher level of using public information when compared to those with a college level of education. Individual investors, especially those with a high school level of education, should be encouraged to read financial statements in order to invest in stocks of companies promising good performance.

Expert Information

With the expert information variable, individual investors did not significantly differ for demographic categories such as occupation and income. However, individual investors significantly differed for demographic categories such as gender, age, marital status, education, and investing experience. The section that follows provides a discussion on the findings, conclusions, implications, and recommendations in each of the demographic categories where expert information differed significantly.

Gender

The findings showed that there was a significant difference in expert information when individual investors were compared by gender. Males had higher levels of expert information than females. This provided an opportunity for the NSE management and the Capital Markets Authority to have programmes to sensitise individual investors on expert information. These programmes need to highlight the importance of seeking expert advice before investing in stocks of firms.

Age

The findings established that individual investors significantly differed when compared on expert information by age. Individual investors aged 36–52 years reported higher levels of expert information compared to those aged 18–35 years. The NSE should endeavour to show individual investors the importance of expert information. In particular, they need to seek expert advice when making investment decisions.

Marital Status

The results established that there was a significant difference in expert information when individual investors were compared by their marital status. Individual investors who are married indicated using expert information more than those who are single. Therefore, the NSE management and the Capital Markets Authority should come up with training programmes on the use of expert information. Individual investors should be encouraged to seek expert information and use it to make investment decisions in stocks.

Education

The results established that there was a significant difference in expert information when individual investors were compared by their level of education. Individual investors with a high school level of education indicated using expert information more than those with a college level of education. Individual investors, especially those with a high school level of education, should be encouraged to seek expert advice before making investment decisions.

Psychographic Differences

The following section presents a discussion on those behavioural and market factors that significantly differed when compared by the psychographic categories. The psychographic categories included investment objective, frequency of investment, investment size, sector of investment, and type of stock. The discussion will follow the following order: the findings, conclusions, implications, and the recommendations.

Herding

On the herding variable, the individual investors did not significantly differ for the psychographic category of investment size. However, the individual investors significantly differed for psychographic categories such as investment objective, frequency of investment, sector of investment, and type of stock. The section that follows provides a discussion on the findings, conclusions, implications, and recommendations in each of the psychographic categories where herding differed significantly.

Investment objective

The findings indicated that there was a statistically significant difference in herding behaviour when the individual investors were compared by investment objective. The individual investors with a medium-term investment objective had a higher level of herding compared to individual investors with a long-term objective. The NSE management and the Capital Market Authority need to organise training programmes for the individual investors with a medium-term objective to sensitise them to the influence of herding on investment performance. In addition, the individual investors should be discouraged from following the decisions of other investors without conducting their own analysis.

Frequency of Investment

The findings show that there is a significant difference in herding when the individual investors are compared by the frequency of investment. The weekly individual investors are herding more than the daily investors. The NSE management and the Capital Market Authority should organise seminars to educate the weekly investors on the negative effect of herding on investment performance. These seminars need to discourage the weekly investors from making stock market investment decisions without conducting their own analysis.

Sector of Investment

The findings show that there was a statistically significant difference in herding among individual investors when compared by the sector of investment. Individual investors in other sectors were herding more than those in the banking sector. The NSE and the Capital Market Authority should develop sensitisation programmes for individual investors in other sectors to educate them on the pitfalls of herding. These programmes need to discourage the individual investors in other sectors from making stock market investment decisions without conducting their own analysis.

Type of Stock

The findings show that there was a statistically significant difference in herding among individual investors when compared by the type of stock. The individual investors of blue-chip stocks exhibited significantly lower levels of herding compared to individual investors in income stocks and actively traded stocks. Therefore, seminars should be organised for the individual investors of income stocks and actively traded stocks to enlighten them on the negative effects of herding. These seminars should discourage the individual investors of income stocks and actively traded stocks from following the decisions of other investors without conducting an analysis.

Loss Aversion

When the individual investors were compared on loss aversion, they did not significantly differ for the psychographic category of investment size. However, the individual investors significantly differed for psychographic categories such as investment objective, frequency of investment, sector of investment, and type of stock. The section that follows provides a discussion on the findings, conclusions, implications, and recommendations in each of the psychographic categories where loss aversion differed significantly.

Investment Objective

The findings indicated that there was a significant difference in loss aversion when the individual investors were compared by investment objective. The individual investors in medium-term stocks considered more of the losses they might incur because they valued current income more than future share appreciation. The NSE management and the Capital Market Authority should develop programmes aimed at individual investors in medium-term stocks to inform them of the possible negative effects of loss aversion. In addition, the individual investors who invest in medium-term stocks should be advised against being more risk-seeking without conducting an investment analysis.

Frequency of Investment

The findings indicated that there was a significant difference in loss aversion when the individual investors were compared by the frequency of investment. The individual investors who were investing on a weekly and monthly basis had a higher level of loss aversion, which should concern stock market stakeholders. Therefore, individual investors should receive training organised by the NSE management on the dangers of loss aversion. In particular, the weekly and monthly investors should be advised against being more risk-seeking without conducting an investment analysis.

Sector of Investment

The findings indicated that there was a significant difference in loss aversion among individual investors when compared by the sector of investment. The individual investors in other sectors displayed a higher level of loss aversion compared to those in the banking sector. The NSE management and the Capital Market Authority should organise training programmes on loss aversion for individual investors in other sectors. They should be advised against being more risk-seeking without conducting an investment analysis.

Type of Stock

The findings indicated that there was a significant difference in loss aversion among individual investors when compared by the type of stock. The individual investors in blue-chip stocks had lower levels of loss aversion compared to those in actively traded stocks. The NSE management and the Capital Market Authority should develop programmes to train individual investors, especially those in actively traded stocks, who should be advised against being more risk-seeking without conducting an investment analysis.

Regret Aversion

When the individual investors were compared on regret aversion, they did not significantly differ for the psychographic categories of investment objective, frequency of investment, and investment size. However, the individual investors significantly differed for psychographic categories such as sector of investment and type of stock. The section that follows provides a discussion on the findings, conclusions, implications, and recommendations in each of the psychographic categories where regret aversion differed significantly.

Sector of Investment

The findings indicated that there was a significant difference in regret aversion among individual investors when compared by the sector of investment. The individual investors who invested in the banking sector indicated a higher level of regret aversion compared to those who invested in the commercial sector. Therefore, the NSE management and the Capital Market Authority should develop training programmes for individual investors. In addition, the training should focus on informing investors in the banking sector to conduct analysis before being more willing to sell stocks whose prices have increased, or less willing to sell those stocks whose prices have decreased.

Type of Stock

The findings indicated that there was a significant difference in regret aversion among individual investors when compared by the type of stock. The individual investors in actively traded stocks had a higher level of regret aversion compared to those who invested in blue-chip stocks. Therefore, the NSE management and the Capital Market Authority should initiate training programmes for individual investors in actively traded stocks. These investors should be encouraged to conduct analysis before being more willing to sell stocks whose prices have increased, or less willing to sell those stocks whose prices have decreased.

Escalating the Commitment

On escalating the commitment variable, the individual investors did not significantly differ for the psychographic category of investment size. However, the individual investors significantly differed for psychographic categories such as investment objective, frequency of investment, sector of investment, and type of stock. The section that follows provides a discussion on the findings, conclusions, implications, and recommendations in each of the psychographic categories where escalating the commitment differed significantly.

Investment Objective

The findings indicated that there was a significant difference in escalating the commitment when the individual investors were compared by the investment objective. The medium-term and long-term individual investors were escalating the commitment more than the short-term investors. The NSE management and the Capital Market Authority should organise training on escalating the commitment targeting the medium-term and long-term individual investors. This training should focus on informing the medium-term and long-term individual investors to avoid escalating the commitment without conducting stock analysis.

Frequency of Investment

The findings indicated that there was a significant difference in escalating the commitment when the individual investors were compared by the frequency of investment. The individual investors who invested on a weekly and monthly basis reported a high level of escalating the commitment. This should form the basis for NSE management and the Capital Market Authority to initiate training programmes on escalating the commitment. The training should emphasise advising the weekly and monthly individual investors to invest after conducting stock analysis and not to rely only on continuing to invest in a failing course.

Sector of Investment

The findings indicated that there was a significant difference in escalating the commitment of individual investors when they were compared by the sector of investment. The individual investors in the banking sector indicated a higher level of escalating the commitment compared to those in the commercial sector. Hence, the need for the NSE management and the Capital Market Authority to organise training on escalating the commitment. These training sessions should inform the individual investors in the banking sector to continue investing in a failing course for the long term, but only after analysing the stock market.

Type of Stock

The findings indicated that there was a significant difference in escalating the commitment of individual investors when they were compared by the type of stock. The individual investors in the actively traded stocks had a higher level of escalating the commitment than the investors in blue-chip stocks. Therefore, the NSE management and the Capital Market Authority should organise training programmes to inform the investors in the actively traded stocks about escalating the commitment. Importantly, the investors should be encouraged to escalate the commitment if they are long-term investors.

Availability Bias

With the availability bias variable, the individual investors did not significantly differ for the psychographic category of investment size. However, the individual investors significantly differed for psychographic categories such as investment objective, frequency of investment, sector of investment, and type of stock. The section that follows provides a discussion on the findings, conclusions, implications, and recommendations in each of the psychographic categories where availability bias differed significantly.

Investment Objective

The findings indicated that there was a significant difference in availability bias when the individual investors were compared by the investment objective. The long-term individual investors had a higher level of availability bias when compared by the investment objective. Therefore, the NSE management and the Capital Market Authority should initiate training programmes on availability bias. The programmes should focus on informing the individual investors to invest in the stocks of local companies and those performing well.

Frequency of Investment

The findings indicated that there was a significant difference in availability bias when the individual investors were compared by the frequency of investment. The individual investors who invested on a monthly basis had a higher level of availability bias than those who invested on a weekly basis. The NSE management should organise training to inform the investors to invest in the stocks of local companies and those performing well.

Sector of Investment

The study determined that the individual investors significantly differed in availability bias when they were compared by the sector of investment. The individual investors who invested in the commercial sector had a higher level of availability bias compared to those who invested in the banking sector. The NSE management should initiate programmes to sensitise the individual investors in the commercial sector about availability bias. In particular, they should be sensitised to invest in stocks of local companies and good-performing companies after conducting their own analysis.

Type of Stock

The study established that the individual investors significantly differed in availability bias when they were compared by the type of stock. The individual investors in actively traded stocks had higher levels of availability bias when compared with those who invested in blue-chip stocks. The NSE management and the Capital Market Authority should initiate programmes to train the individual investors in actively traded stocks. This training should encourage the individual investors to invest in stocks of local companies and good-performing companies after conducting their own analysis.

Overconfidence

For the overconfidence variable, the individual investors significantly differed for all the psychographic categories. The section that follows provides a discussion on the findings, conclusions, implications, and recommendations in each of the psychographic categories.

Investment Objective

The findings indicated that there was a significant difference in overconfidence when the individual investors were compared by the investment objective. The individual investors with long-term and medium-term objectives were more confident than those with short-term objectives. Tailored programmes for the individual investors with long-term and medium-term objectives are required. The programmes need to focus on assisting the individual investors to avoid being overly willing to sell stocks whose prices have increased or being less willing to sell those stocks whose prices have reduced without conducting stock analysis.

Frequency of Investment

The findings indicated that there was a significant difference in overconfidence when the individual investors were compared by the frequency of investment. The individual investors who invested on a monthly basis had a higher level of overconfidence than the weekly investors. The NSE management should initiate programmes to enlighten the individual investors on overconfidence. Specifically, the individual investors should be encouraged to trust their trading skills in stocks without doing stock analysis.

Investment Size

The findings indicated that there was a significant difference in overconfidence when the individual investors were compared by the investment size. The individual investors of the NSE who buy investment sizes of 100–200 stocks are more overconfident than those who buy investment sizes of 201–1000 stocks. This provides an opportunity for the NSE management and the Capital Market Authority to sensitise the individual investors on overconfidence. In addition, the individual investors should be encouraged to trust their trading skills in stocks when they have conducted their own stock analysis.

Sector of Investment

The study determined that the individual investors significantly differed in overconfidence when they were compared by the sector of investment. The individual investors in the commercial sector displayed higher levels of overconfidence than those who invested in the banking sector. Therefore, investors in the commercial sector should be trained on overconfidence. This training should inform the individual investors about trusting their skills in trading in the stock market after conducting analysis.

Type of Stock

The study established that the individual investors significantly differed in overconfidence when they were compared by the type of stock. The individual investors in actively traded stocks showed higher levels of overconfidence than those who invested in blue-chip stocks. Therefore, the NSE management and the Capital Market Authority should initiate training programmes for the investors in actively traded stocks. This training is intended to advise the individual investors to trust their trading skills in the stock market after conducting stock market analysis.

Public information: On the public information variable, the individual investors significantly differed for all the psychographic categories. Therefore, there was no category in which the individual investors did not significantly differ. The section that follows provides a discussion on the findings, conclusions, implications, and recommendations in each of the psychographic categories.

Investment objective: The findings showed that the individual investors significantly differed on the public information when they were compared by investment objective. The individual investors who invested in the short term had higher levels of public information than those who invested in the medium term and long term. The NSE management and the Capital Market Authority need to initiate training programmes on public information. They should use public information and invest in companies that promise good performance.

Frequency of investment: The findings showed that the individual investors significantly differed on the public information when they were compared by the frequency of investment. The individual investors who invested weekly had higher levels of public information than the monthly individual investors. There is a need to train the individual investors on the use of public information and to invest in stocks of companies that promise good performance in the future.

Investment size: The results indicated that the individual investors significantly differed on the public information when they were compared by investment size. The investors who buy investment sizes of 201–1000 stocks had higher levels of public information than those who buy investment sizes of 100–200 stocks. The NSE management and the Capital Market Authority should organise training for individual investors to encourage them to read and use public information to determine the good performing companies to invest in.

Sector of investment: The findings indicated that the individual investors significantly differed on the public information when they were compared by sector of investment. The individual investors in the banking sector had higher levels of public information compared to those who invest in the commercial sector. The NSE management and the Capital Market Authority should sensitise the individual investors on the use of public information to determine companies that promise good performance, in order to make sound investment decisions.

Type of stock: The results showed that the individual investors significantly differed on the public information when they were compared by type of stock. The individual investors who bought blue chip stocks had higher levels of public information compared to those who invested in income stocks. There is a need to sensitise the individual investors on reading and using public information to identify good performing companies for investment.

Expert information: With the expert information variable, the individual investors significantly differed for all the psychographic categories. Therefore, there was no category in which the individual investors did not significantly differ. The section that follows provides a discussion on the findings, conclusions, implications, and recommendations in each of the psychographic categories.

Investment objective: The findings showed that the individual investors significantly differed on the expert information when they were compared by investment objective. The individual investors who invested in the short term had higher levels of expert information than those who had medium-term and long-term objectives. Therefore, there is importance in having training programmes for the individual investors with short-term objectives. The training should encourage individual investors to seek and utilise expert information for investment decision-making.

Frequency of investment: The findings showed that the individual investors significantly differed on the expert information when they were compared by the frequency of investment. The individual investors who invested weekly had higher levels of expert information compared to the monthly individual investors. There is a need to train the individual investors on seeking and using expert information in order to make good investment decisions.

Investment size: The results indicated that the individual investors significantly differed on the expert information when they were compared by investment size. The individual investors who buy investment sizes of 201–1000 stocks made greater use of expert information compared to those who buy stocks of between 100–200 stocks. Therefore, the NSE management and the Capital Market Authority need to embark on sensitisation programmes on seeking and using expert information for sound investment decision-making.

Sector of investment: The findings indicated that the individual investors significantly differed on the expert information when they were compared by sector of investment. The individual investors in the banking sector had higher levels of expert information compared to those who invest in the commercial sector. The NSE management and the Capital Market Authority should develop training programmes on seeking and using expert information. The individual investors should be exposed to seeking and using expert information for good decision-making.

Type of stock: The results showed that the individual investors significantly differed on the expert information when they were compared by type of stock. The individual investors who bought blue chip stocks had higher levels of expert information compared to those who bought income stocks. Therefore, there is a need to sensitise individual investors on seeking expert information for better decision-making. The section that follows presents a discussion on the findings of the correlation analysis.

Major Finding 4: Correlation Analysis

Interpretation of findings: The results showed that there is a significant strong positive correlation between investment decisions and investment performance ($r = .828$, $N = 498$, p

< .01, two-tailed). This means that investment decisions are a good predictor of investment performance. There is also a significant strong negative correlation between expert information and investment performance ($r = -.818$, $N = 498$, $p < .01$, two-tailed). This indicates that expert information is a good predictor of the degree of market efficiency's impact on investment performance, albeit negatively.

There is a significant strong negative correlation between public information and investment performance ($r = -.841$, $N = 498$, $p < .01$, two-tailed). This is a strong correlation between the variables and therefore a good predictor of investment performance. There is a strong positive correlation between overconfidence and investment performance ($r = .850$, $N = 498$, $p < .01$, two-tailed), which also makes it a good predictor of investment performance. There is a strong positive correlation between availability bias and investment performance ($r = .589$, $N = 498$, $p < .01$, two-tailed). This factor has a moderate predictive value for investment performance.

There is a weak positive correlation between herding and investment performance ($r = .155$, $N = 498$, $p < .01$, two-tailed). The herding factor is a weak predictor of the degree of market efficiency's impact on investment performance. There is a weak correlation between regret aversion and investment performance which was not significant ($r = .019$, $N = 498$, $p > .01$, two-tailed). There is a weak positive correlation between escalating commitment and investment performance ($r = .116$, $N = 498$, $p < .01$, two-tailed). The escalating commitment factor is a predictor of the degree of market efficiency's impact on investment performance, although a weak one.

The herding variable was highly correlated with loss aversion ($r = .934$, $N = 498$, $p < .01$), regret aversion ($r = .894$, $N = 498$, $p < .01$) and escalating commitment ($r = .874$, $N = 498$, $p < .01$). These variables will be scrutinised to establish their contribution to the overall model such that those contributing less can be omitted. Loss aversion and escalating commitment were also highly correlated ($r = .906$), meaning they should also be considered for elimination from the predictive model. However, the high correlation of the independent variables with the dependent variable does not affect the model.

Conclusion: These findings indicate that some independent variables are highly correlated. The development of the predictive model should be done with caution. This is because highly correlated independent variables reduce the effect of each independent variable on the overall model.

Implications: When developing the predictive model, some indicators of the independent variables were dropped in order to derive a good predictive model. There were eight factors in total, of which three were dropped. Therefore, the final model was composed of five factors which were grouped into four independent variables. The three factors that were dropped included: loss aversion, regret aversion, and expert information.

Major Finding 5: Regression Analysis

This section is presented in the following order: interpretation of the findings, conclusion, discussion, implications, and recommendation of the findings. This study was intended to determine the influence of behavioural and market factors on investment performance. The findings show that herding, escalating commitment, availability bias, overconfidence, and public information combined influence investment performance (R^2 = 77.8%). Hence, a model that determines investment performance was developed. Initially, a model comprising the factors of independent variables was formulated. Thereafter, a final predictive model was established.

Interpretation of Findings: The final model was established from three behavioural variables and the market variable, where all the variables significantly influenced investment performance. The results indicated a significant model ($F [4, 493] = 421.079, p < .05$). This model explains 77.4% of the variance in the degree of market efficiency's impact on investment performance. Herding, prospect, heuristic, and market factors are the significant influencers, with herding and market factors having a negative relationship, while prospect and heuristic factors have a positive relationship with investment performance, all with p-values of less than .05. The overall final model consisted of:

$IP = 2.936 - \beta_1 HF + \beta_2 PF + \beta_3 HUF - \beta_4 MF + \varepsilon$

Where:

IP = Investment Performance
HF = Herding Factors
PF = Prospect Factors
HUF = Heuristic Factors
MF = Market Factors

The model shows that herding is negatively correlated ($\beta = -0.952, p < .05$) with investment performance. Therefore, as herding increases, investment performance decreases. This shows that individual investors who follow popular opinion, follow other investors without conducting their own analysis, and have a desire to conform, experience negative performance. Therefore, individual investors are encouraged to conduct their own analysis before making investment decisions.

The finding of a positive relationship ($\beta = 0.603, p < .05$) between escalating commitment and investment performance was unexpected. Escalating commitment refers to individual investors continuing to invest in stocks that appear to be poor investments because prices are falling. Individual investors may have been encouraged to escalate commitment due to recent experiences in the NSE. For example, investors continued to buy Safaricom stock after its initial public offering, even after prices dropped drastically. Those who continued to buy the stocks when prices fell and waited for some time benefited significantly, as the stocks substantially regained their price.

Availability bias had a significant positive relationship ($\beta = 0.540, p < .05$) with investment performance. This suggests that when there is an increase in availability bias among individual investors in the NSE, their investment performance improves. This means individual investors perform better when they buy stocks of domestic companies or companies they are familiar with. This improved performance may be because they have followed the history of these firms and are better able to identify the strong performers and invest in their stocks.

Overconfidence among individual investors in the NSE had a significant positive relationship with investment performance (β = 0.129, $p \leq .05$). This indicates that as overconfidence increases, investment performance also improves. Overconfidence occurs when investors believe they possess superior skills compared to others. The investment performance of these individual investors may improve when they conduct their own analysis, which in turn boosts their confidence when trading stocks.

Public information was found to have a significant negative relationship (β = -0.282, $p \leq .05$) with the investment performance of individual investors in the NSE. The findings indicate that when public information increases, investment performance decreases. This occurs when individual investors access and read the financial statements of companies in which they have invested. The negative relationship may arise when financial statements reveal that the companies are incurring losses, leading investors to perceive the information as negatively affecting their investments. Data for this study were collected during a post-election period in Kenya, which was highly contested, resulting in reduced business activity and affecting the profitability of many companies.

Relationship to Previous Findings: The finding of this study (β = -0.952, $p < .05$) is supported by Bakar and Yi (2016), who also found herding to have a negative relationship with investment performance (β = -0.067, $p < .05$). However, it contradicts other studies that reported positive relationships between herding and investment performance: Kengatharan and Kengatharan (2014) with β = 0.113, $p \leq .05$; Ranjbar et al. (2014) with β = 0.21, $p \leq .05$; Nyamute et al. (2015) with β = 0.182, $p \leq .05$; Khan (2014) with β = 0.49, $p \leq .05$; Luong et al. (2011) with β = 0.11, $p \leq .05$; and Javed, Bagh, and Razzaq (2017) with β = 0.283, $p < .05$. These results suggest that herding may have a significant but varying level of impact on investment performance.

This study found that escalating commitment is positively correlated with investment performance (β = 0.603, $p < .05$). This finding is contradicted by Lin et al. (2014), who reported a significant negative relationship (β = -0.89, $p \leq .10$). Turino and Soetjipto (2012) found no significant relationship between escalating commitment and investment performance: t = -0.49, $p > .05$ during the bearish period, and t = 0.70, $p > .05$ during the bullish period.

This study also found availability bias to have a positive relationship (β = 0.540, $p < .05$) with investment performance. This finding is supported by Javed et al. (2017), who also reported a significant positive relationship (β = 0.285, $p \leq .05$). Similarly, Bakar and Yi (2016) found the relationship to be significantly positive (β = 0.466, $p \leq .05$).

Overconfidence had a significant positive relationship with investment performance (β = 0.129, $p \leq .05$). This finding is supported by Javed et al. (2017), who found a significant positive relationship between overconfidence and investment performance (β = 0.274, $p \leq .05$). Bakar and Yi (2016) also reported a significantly positive relationship (β = 0.466, $p \leq .05$).

However, these findings are contradicted by Kengatharan and Kengatharan (2014), who found a significantly negative relationship ($\beta = -0.356, p \leq .05$). Similarly, Nyamute et al. (2015) reported that overconfidence had a significantly negative relationship with portfolio performance ($\beta = -0.134, p \leq .05$).

This study established that public information had a significant negative relationship with investment performance ($\beta = -0.282, p \leq .05$). However, Kengatharan and Kengatharan (2014) found no significant relationship between public information and investment performance ($\beta = 0.087, p > .05$).

Conclusion

This section established that herding, escalating commitment, availability bias, overconfidence, and public information combined to influence investment performance. The final model showed that the three behavioural factors and the market factor significantly influenced investment performance. Herding and market factors (public information) had a negative relationship, while prospect (escalating commitment) and heuristic factors (availability bias and overconfidence) had a positive relationship with investment performance.

Implications

The findings align with the significance of the study. It is implied that the understanding of the performance of the NSE depends on the behaviour of individual investors in the stock market. This will guide individual investors in making investment decisions that improve their investment performance. The NSE management, Capital Market Authority, and policymakers should understand the behavioural and market factors influencing the investment performance of individual investors. This will enable the NSE management, Capital Market Authority, and policymakers to develop programmes aimed at helping individual investors reduce the effect of behavioural and market factors on their investment performance. Training for individual investors may be organised through media such as radio and television, while for the Capital Market Authority, publications in their monthly journal can be used to disseminate the findings of this study.

The use of both market factors (public and expert information) is very low. This means that individual investors are not seeking or using market information for investment decisions at the NSE. This should raise pertinent questions about the quality of decisions being made by individual investors. The NSE management, investment advisors, and the Capital Market Authority should develop sensitisation programmes for individual investors on the use of information available in the market for investment purposes.

Recommendations

The study noted that the investment performance of individual investors is negatively affected by herding. They should be advised not to follow the decisions of other investors without conducting their own analysis. In addition, they should not follow other investors simply to conform. They should be strongly encouraged to rely on their own analysis, even if it goes against the majority of investors.

Individual investors exhibited a positive relationship between escalating commitment and investment performance. They should invest in stocks that have decreased in price but be willing to wait longer to benefit from the appreciation in prices. This is because some stocks may recover from a price decrease, benefiting those investors who can wait patiently.

Availability bias had a positive relationship with investment performance. This means that as availability bias increases, investment performance also increases. It is recommended that individual investors should not simply prefer to invest in stocks of local firms over foreign ones, in companies whose names they easily remember, or in stocks of firms currently performing well. These decisions should be accompanied by proper evaluation of investment opportunities to support better decision-making. As such, their investment performance would be improved.

Overconfidence was found to have a positive relationship with investment performance. This means that as overconfidence increases, investment performance also increases. The study recommends that individual investors should be confident when trading in stocks after conducting thorough analysis and obtaining information that supports sound investment decisions. However, they should not overestimate their abilities or consider themselves better than other investors in the stock market, as this could lead to excessive trading, potentially harming their investment performance. In conclusion, confidence that stems from possession of analysed information about the stock market is beneficial for decision-making and likely to improve investment performance.

The results showed a negative relationship between public information and investment performance. Therefore, an increase in public information leads to a decrease in investment performance. Individual investors are advised to invest in stocks of companies with strong future profitability prospects, as indicated by financial statements and other profitability indicators, while avoiding those with bleak prospects.

Major Finding 6: Control Variable

The findings show that investment decisions do not have a significant effect on the model. After introducing investment decisions into the model, the effect on investment performance did not change. The variance explained remained 77.4%.

Interpretation of Findings

The investment decisions variable has no significant effect on investment performance. This is because the model remains unchanged even after including investment decisions as a control variable. Therefore, the decisions made in stock market investment do not alter the influence of behavioural and market factors on investment performance.

Conclusion

This section showed that there is no significant influence of investment decisions as a control variable on the effect of behavioural and market factors on investment performance. The kinds of decisions individual investors make do not change the influence of behavioural and market factors. Therefore, behavioural and market factors have a greater influence on investment performance. This influence should be addressed.

Implications

The findings of this study imply that the investment performance of individual investors is more influenced by behavioural factors. The decisions individual investors make are not significant. This suggests that behavioural factors influence investment performance and should be a cause for concern for the NSE management, investment advisors, and the Capital Market Authority.

Recommendations:

It is recommended that the NSE management, investment advisors, and the Capital Market Authority organise training and workshops for NSE investors. These sessions should focus on the influence of behavioural factors on decision-making and its effect on investment performance. The intention is to reduce noise in the stock market and, hence, improve the investment performance of individual investors.

Suggestions of the Study

Based on the findings of this study, there is evidence of individual investors at NSE exhibiting high levels of behavioural factors. There are high levels of herding, prospect factors, and heuristic factors. However, the study findings noted that there are low levels of market factors (public and expert information). The following recommendations are made:

Suggestions for Policy Makers and Investment Analysts

The policy makers should initiate awareness among the individual investors, since the results of the study show that the individual investors exhibit high levels of behavioural factors and low levels of market factors.

1. The Capital Market Authority and the NSE should introduce sensitisation, which can be done through the brokerage firms. The brokerage firms can be encouraged to organise seminars from time to time for their registered members so that they are trained in investment analysis and making investment decisions that are less affected by behavioural factors. The training for the individual investors may be organised through the media such as radio and television.
2. **Programmes to Promote Investor Education.** The policy makers should introduce training programmes for the individual investors of the stock market to enhance the culture of using market information, which will reduce the influence of behavioural factors in decision-making. The investment culture should be introduced in the early years of education programmes so that young people will grow up appreciating the importance and mechanism of investing from an informed position. The training for the individual investors may be organised through the media such as radio and television.
3. The investment advisors (brokerage firms) may be reached by producing research reports. They will use these research reports when advising the individual investors on the investment opportunities in the stock market.

Suggestions for Future Research

This study makes the following recommendations:

1. Future researchers may use different methodologies, such as the random sampling method, to identify respondents from the brokerage firms.
2. These findings will be published in peer-reviewed journal articles and, hence, form the basis of research design for future scholars.
3. The escalation of commitment as a prospect factor has been understudied. Therefore, it is recommended that exploratory studies should be conducted on this variable as it relates to investment decision-making and investment performance.
4. The link between market factors and investment performance needs to be explored further by researchers.
5. Future scholars may include rational factors in the model to determine the effect they have on investment performance. This study included only the irrational factors.

Appendices

A

Questionnaire

My Name is Jackson Oyaro Ong'eta, a PhD Candidate in Business at Adventist International Institute of Advanced Studies (AIIAS) in Philippines. I am in the process of writing my Book and I am kindly requesting for your participation in my research by filling this questionnaire. I will ensure anonymity and confidentiality as you will not be required to write your name on the questionnaire. All the information provided will be used for academic purposes only. Thank you.

SECTION A: *(Demographic Information)*

Please check (x) on the box that appropriately indicates your demographic characteristics.

1. Gender: Male [ ]Female [ ]
2. Age: 18 to 35 [ ] 36 to 52 [ ] 53 and above [ ]
3. Marital status: Single [ ] Married [ ] Divorced [ ]
4. Occupation: Employed [ ] Business [ ] Any Other (Specify) _____
5. Highest education level: High School [ ] College [ ] Post-graduate [ ] Other [ ]
6. Monthly income: Up to Kshs. 50, 000 [ ] Between Kshs. 50,001 and Kshs. 100,000 [ ]
Over Kshs. 100,000 [ ]
7. Experience investing in stock: up to 5 yrs [ ] Between 6 and 10 yrs [ ] 11 yrs and above [ ]

SECTION B: (Psychographic Characteristics)

Please check (x) on the box that appropriately indicates your psychographic characteristics.

1. Investment objective: Short-term [ ] Medium term [ ] Long-term [ ]
2. Frequency of investing: Daily [ ] Weekly [ ] Monthly [ ]
3. Investment lot size (number of shares) : 100-200 [ ] 201-1000 [ ] over 1000 [ ]
4. Type of sector invested in: Banking [ ] commercial [ ] others [ ]
5. Type of stock bought: Blue chip [ ] Income stocks [ ] Actively traded [ ]

SECTION C: (Behavioural Factors, Investment

Decisions and Investment Performance)
This section seeks to gather your perception on how the behavioural factors affect your investment decision that leads to investment performance. Please indicate your opinion by circling a number next to each of the statements below you think is most appropriate (Circle only one in each case. There are no right or wrong answer).

1 - Strongly disagree. 2 - Disagree. 3 - Neutral. 4 - Agree. 5 - Strongly agree.

	Behavioural Factors Herding	**Strongly disagree**	**Disagree**	**Neutral**	**Agree**	**Strongly agree**
1.	I follow the decisions of other investors while making investment decisions	1	2	3	4	5
2.	I follow the decisions of other investors without doing any analysis	1	2	3	4	5
3.	I follow the decisions of other investors so that I can be like them	1	2	3	4	5
4.	I immediately follow the decisions of other investors' whenever they do any changes in	1	2	3	4	5
5.	I follow the popular opinion in the selection of my stocks	1	2	3	4	5
6.	If my decision that turns out bad I immediately retreat to safer investments	1	2	3	4	5
7.	Loss Aversion					
8.	I make investment decisions which enables me to avoid losses	1	2	3	4	5
9.	A positive return in the past leads me to be more risk seeking	1	2	3	4	5
10.	A negative return in the past leads me to be more risk averse	1	2	3	4	5
11.	Regret Aversion					
12.	I am more than willing to sell stocks whose price is increasing	1	2	3	4	5
13.	I am less willing to sell stocks whose price is decreasing	1	2	3	4	5
14.	I feel bad when stocks that I did not choose turn out to perform better	1	2	3	4	5
15.	I believe that successful stock investments depend more on luck than on skill	1	2	3	4	5
16.	I buy stocks other people are buying to avoid regretting alone if it performs poorly.	1	2	3	4	5
17.	Escalating the commitment					
18.	I will still continue to invest in the stocks even if I lost in the previous period from the	1	2	3	4	5
19.	Even if I am not sure of attaining my goal I will still invest in the stocks.	1	2	3	4	5
20.	I will continue to invest in stock even if I become aware of it being a bad investment	1	2	3	4	5
21.	Availability Bias					
22.	I prefer investing in stocks of local companies rather than the foreign ones	1	2	3	4	5
23.	I invest in stocks that have performed well in the recent past	1	2	3	4	5
24.	I invest in stocks of companies whose name I can easily recall	1	2	3	4	5
25.	I like investing in the stocks whose information is in the public	1	2	3	4	5

26.	I do not change my stock investment portfolio I already have invested in.	1	2	3	4	5
27.	Overconfidence					
28.	My stock portfolio performs better than other people because of my better skills.	1	2	3	4	5
29.	I believe that stocks I have invested in the past performed poorly because of bad luck	1	2	3	4	5
30.	I am able to forecast future stock prices	1	2	3	4	5
31.	I am better placed than other investors to select good performing stocks	1	2	3	4	5
32.	I find it easy to trade in stocks	1	2	3	4	5
33.	I am able to trade in stocks without	1	2	3	4	5
34.	Public Information					
35.	I look at the printed financial statements of a firm before buying its shares	1	2	3	4	5
36.	I check the electronic financial statements of a firm before buying its shares	1	2	3	4	5
37.	I buy the shares of firms with reputation in	1	2	3	4	5
38.	I consider the status of the firm when deciding whether to buy its shares.	1	2	3	4	5
39.	Expert Information					
40.	I like to read expert information before making investment decisions	1	2	3	4	5
41.	I like to read expert information from the web before making investment decisions	1	2	3	4	5
42.	Expert information is helpful in investment decisions making	1	2	3	4	5
	INVESTMENT DECISIONS **I believe that my investment decision is made on the basis of trading:**	**Strongly disagree**	**Disagree**	**Neutral**	**Agree**	**Strongly agree**
43.	Stocks whose prices have always increased	1	2	3	4	5
44.	Stocks whose prices have always decreased	1	2	3	4	5
45.	Stocks other investors are also trading	1	2	3	4	5
46.	Stocks with relatively high returns	1	2	3	4	5
47.	Stocks with relatively low returns.	1	2	3	4	5
48.	Stocks that have good performance in the	1	2	3	4	5
49.	Stocks that have bad performance in the	1	2	3	4	5
50.	Stocks based on the need to diversify them for risk reduction	1	2	3	4	5
51.	Stocks with relatively high trading volumes	1	2	3	4	5
52.	Stocks that have been frequently announced in the news	1	2	3	4	5

	INVESTMENT PERFORMANCE I believe that the investment performance is influenced by my investment decision due to the following facts:	**Strongly disagree**	**Disagree**	**Neutral**	**Agree**	**Strongly agree**
53.	Stock prices reflect only past information	1	2	3	4	5
54.	Stock investments earn abnormal profits based on past information analysis	1	2	3	4	5
55.	Stock prices reflect both past and public available information	1	2	3	4	5
56.	Stock investment earns abnormal profits based on the financial statements analysis	1	2	3	4	5
57.	Sock investment earns abnormal profit based on the fundamentals of the company	1	2	3	4	5
58.	Stock prices reflect all information from the public and private sources	1	2	3	4	5
59.	Stock prices even reflect hidden insider information	1	2	3	4	5

B

A Framework of the Biblical Perspectives

Biblical Grand Themes	Biblical Principles	Biblical Reference	Variables Studied
Redemption	Followers of Jesus Christ	"As iron sharpens iron, so one person sharpens another." (Proverbs 27:17) NIV	Herding
Truth	Trust in God	"But store up for yourselves treasures in heaven, where moth and rust do not destroy, and where thieves do not break in and steal" (Mathew 6:20) NIV	Loss aversion
Truth	Perseverance	"After this, Job opened his mouth and cursed the day of his birth. He said: May the day of my birth perish, and the night it was said, 'A boy is born'!" (Job 3:1-3) NIV "And the Lord blessed the latter days of Job more than his beginning" (Job 42:12) ESV	Regret aversion
Justice	Patience	"Seek the LORD while he may be found; call on him while he is near" (Isaiah 55:6) NIV	Escalating the commitment
Redemption	Wisdom	"..Let not the wise man boast in his wisdom, let not the mighty man boast in his might, let not the rich man boast in his riches ." (Jeremiah	Availability bias

Creation		9: 23) ESV	Overconfidence
	Trust in God	"You are the light of the world. A city set on a hill cannot be hidden. Nor do people light a lamp and put it under a basket, but on a stand, and it gives light to all in the house." (Mathew 5: 14-15) ESV	
Justice	Knowledge		Public information
		"Go therefore and make disciples of all nations, baptizing them in the name of the father and of the son and of the holy spirit, teaching them to observe all that I have commanded you." (Mathew 28: 19-20) ESV	Expert information
Love	Fellowship	"Invest in seven ventures, yes, in eight; you do not know what disaster may come upon the land" (Ecclesiastes 11:2) NIV	Investment decisions
Truth	Prudence		
Creation	Stewardship	"Well then, you should have put my money on deposit with the bankers, so that when I returned I will have received it back with interest." (Mathew 25: 27) NIV	Investment performance

C

Significant Differences by the Demographic Characteristics

Behaviour	Demographic	F-value	T-value	P-value	Comment
Herding	Gender		-9.102	.000	Significantly differed
	Age		-.961	.337	Did not significantly differ
	Marital status	2.402		.092	Did not significantly differ
	Occupation		-3.511	.001	Significantly differed
	Education	5.599		.004	Significantly differed
	Income	5.566		.004	Significantly differed

	Investing experience	.386		.680	Did not significantly differ
Loss Aversion	Gender		-9.294	.000	Significantly differed
	Age		-1.759	.079	Did not significantly differ
	Marital status	2.448		.088	Did not significantly differ
	Occupation		-3.369	.001	Significantly differed
	Education	3.856		.022	Significantly differed
	Income	2.246		.107	Did not significantly differ
	Investing experience	.449		.638	Did not significantly differ
Regret Aversion	Gender		-5.492	.000	Significantly differed
	Age		-.534	.594	Did not significantly differ
	Marital status	.947		.389	Did not significantly differ
	Occupation		-2.770	.006	Significantly differed
	Education	10.870		.000	Significantly differed
	Income	11.380		.000	Significantly differed
	Investing experience	3.035		.049	Significantly differed
Escalating the Commitment	Gender		-9.093	.000	Significantly differed
	Age		-2.256	.054	Did not significantly differ
	Marital status	2.132		.067	Did not significantly differ
	Occupation		-3.831	.001	Significantly differed
	Education	3.342		.018	Significantly differed
	Income	1.987		.093	Did not significantly differ
	Investing experience	.367		.453	Did not significantly differ
Availability Bias	Gender		-8.948	.000	Significantly differed
	Age		-.279	.781	Did not significantly differ

	Marital status	4.722		.009	Significantly differed
	Occupation		-2.631	.010	Significantly differed
	Education	1.142		.320	Did not significantly differ
	Income	4.519		.011	Significantly differed
	Investing experience	.941		.391	Did not significantly differ
Overconfidence	Gender		-7.509	.000	Significantly differed
	Age		.850	.395	Did not significantly differ
	Marital status	4.006		.019	Significantly differed
	Occupation	.033		.974	Did not significantly differ
	Education	15.156		.000	Significantly differed
	Income	.541		.583	Did not significantly differ
	Investing experience	6.919		.001	Significantly differed
Public Information	Gender		9.365	.000	Significantly differed
	Age		-1.857	.064	Did not significantly differ
	Marital status	7.497		.001	Significantly differed
	Occupation		-.691	.490	Did not significantly differ
	Education	13.304		.000	Significantly differed
	Income	1.232		.293	Did not significantly differ
	Investing experience	8.507		.000	Significantly differed
Expert Information	Gender		7.295	.000	Significantly differed
	Age		-2.310	.021	Significantly differed
	Marital status	6.298		.002	Significantly differed
	Occupation		-.843	.400	Did not significantly differ
	Education	11.854		.000	Significantly differed
	Income	1.820		.163	Did not significantly differ

	Investing experience	8.350		.000	Significantly differed

D

Significant Differences by the Psychographic Characteristics

Behaviour	Psychographic	F-value	T-value	P-value	Comment
Herding	Investment objective	18.474		.000	Significantly differed
	Frequency of investment	8.894		.000	Significantly differed
	Investment size		-.918	.359	Did not significantly differ
	Sector of investment	6.619		.001	Significantly differed
	Type of stock	14.968		.000	Significantly differed
Loss Aversion	Investment objective	28.061		.000	Significantly differed
	Frequency of investment	14.783		.000	Significantly differed
	Investment size		-.853	.394	Did not significantly differ
	Sector of investment	5.609		.004	Significantly differed
	Type of stock	8.148		.000	Significantly differed
Regret Aversion	Investment objective	2.626		.073	Did not significantly differ
	Frequency of investment	1.238		.291	Did not significantly differ
	Investment size		-.940	.348	Did not significantly differ
	Sector of investment	8.060		.000	Significantly differed
	Type of stock	19.736		.000	Significantly differed
Escalating the commitment	Investment objective	18.752		.023	Significantly differed
	Frequency of investment	12.654		.012	Significantly differed
	Investment size		-.817	.296	Did not significantly differ
	Sector of investment	4.996		.028	Significantly differed
	Type of stock	6.987		.031	Significantly differed

Availability Bias	Investment objective	16.098		.000	Significantly differed
	Frequency of investment	10.929		.000	Significantly differed
	Investment size		1.426	.155	Did not significantly differ
	Sector of investment	8.888		.000	Significantly differed
	Type of stock	22.700		.000	Significantly differed
Overconfidence	Investment objective	13.857		.000	Significantly differed
	Frequency of investment	13.142		.000	Significantly differed
	Investment size		2.738	.008	Significantly differed
	Sector of investment	19.454		.000	Significantly differed
	Type of stock	7.602		.001	Significantly differed
Public Information	Investment objective	11.027		.000	Significantly differed
	Frequency of investment	16.244		.000	Significantly differed
	Investment size		-3.318	.002	Significantly differed
	Sector of investment	14.921		.000	Significantly differed
	Type of stock	8.774		.000	Significantly differed
Expert Information	Investment objective	8.578		.000	Significantly differed
	Frequency of investment	17.410		.000	Significantly differed
	Investment size	-3.568		.001	Significantly differed
	Sector of investment	18.915		.000	Significantly differed
	Type of stock	7.394		.001	Significantly differed

E

Literature Review Search Summary Matrix

Database	Search Terms	Results	Relevant
Google Scholar	Behavioural Factors + Investment Performance	349,000	4
	Investor behaviour + Investment Decisions	166,000	12
	Investor Behaviour + Investment performance	161,000	7
	Behavioural Factors + Investment Decisions	298,000	11
	Demographics + Investor Behaviour	20,800	13
	Psychographics + Investor Behaviour	4,270	2
	Herding + Investment Performance	35,800	3
	Prospect + Investment Performance	499,000	8
	Heuristic + Investment performance	168,000	5
	Market factors + Investment Performance	3,040,000	1
	Public Information + Expert information + Investment Performance	973,000	2
ProQuest	Behavioural Factors + Investment Performance	25	8
	Investor behaviour + Investment Decisions	27,203	20
	Investor Behaviour + Investment performance	23,157	13
	Behavioural Factors + Investment Decisions	12,907	12
	Demographics + Investors Behaviour	576	10
	Psychographics + Investor Behaviour	0	0
	Herding + Investment Performance	24,978	5
	Prospect + Investment Performance	27,254	9
	Heuristic + Investment performance	57,987	8
	Market factors + Investment Performance	45,576	0

	Public Information + Expert information + Investment Performance	32	1
Ebscohost	Behavioural Factors + Investment Performance	12,456	13
	Investor behaviour + Investment Decisions	236	5
	Investor Behaviour + Investment performance	784	7
	Behavioural Factors + Investment Decisions	23	6
	Demographics + Investors Behaviour	56	7
	Psychographics + Investor Behaviour	3	1
	Herding + Investment Performance	258	12
	Prospect + Investment Performance	8356	9
	Heuristic + Investment performance	3478	11
	Market factors + Investment Performance	46	3
	Public Information + Expert information + Investment Performance	9	1
BOOKs	Investments	1	1

F

Questionnaire Validation Grid

VARIABLE 1 HERDING Investors are influenced by the public opinion Selden (1912). The habit of following or imitating the decision of others (Bikhchandani & Sharma, 2001)					
Indicator	**Theory Statement [References to Specific Theory]**	**Questionnaire Items/Statements**	**Reliability Score**	**References**	**Pilot Study Test**
Herding	The individual investor will follow the actions of other investors Intentional copying of other investors behaviour The individual investors follow the public opinion	I follow the decisions of other investors while making my investment decisions I follow the decisions of other investors without doing any analysis I follow the decisions of other investors so that I can be like them I immediately follow the decisions of other investors' whenever they do any changes in their portfolio I follow the popular opinion in the selection of my stocks If I follow the decision that turns out to be bad I immediately retreat to safer investments	.895	Rekik, Y. M., & Boujelbene, Y. (2013) Bikhchandani, S., & Sharma, S. (2001) Vijaya, E. (2014 Das, S. K. (2012) Mackay, 1841.	100 individual investors in Nakuru county, Kenya

VARIABLE 2 PROSPECT					
Prospect theory notes that "people underweight outcomes that are merely probable in comparison with outcomes that are obtained with certainty" (Kahneman & Tversky, 1979, p. 263). People are "less willing to gamble with profit than with losses" (Vijaya, 2014, p.298)					
Indicator	**Theory Statement [References to Specific Theory]**	**Questionnaire Items/Statements**	**Reliability Score**	**References**	**Pilot Study Test**
Loss aversion	people underweight outcomes that are merely probable in comparison with outcomes that are obtained with certainty	I make investment decisions which enables me avoid losses	0.896	Kahneman, D., & Tversky, A. (1979)	100 individual investors in Nakuru county, Kenya
		A positive return in the past leads me to be more risk seeking			
		A negative return in the past leads me to more risk averse attitude towards stock investments			
Regret aversion	Investors avoid regret by refusing to sell decreasing shares and willing to sell increasing one	I am more than willing to sell stocks whose price is increasing	0.897	Luong, P. Le, Thu Ha, D. T., & Owe, H. R. (2011)	100 individual investors in Nakuru county, Kenya
		I am less willing to sell stocks whose price is decreasing.			
		I feel bad when stocks that I did not choose turn out to perform better			
		I believe that successful stock investments depend more on luck than on skill			
		I buy stocks other people are buying to avoid regretting alone if it performs poorly.			
Escalating the commitment	Escalation of commitment refers to situations in which individuals refuse to abandon losing strategies and in fact invest more time, money, manpower, and other resources	I will still continue to invest in the stocks even if I lost in the previous period from the stock	0.896	Lin, Y.-E., Fan, W.-M., & Chih, H.-H. (2014)	100 individual investors in Nakuru county, Kenya
		Even if I am not sure of attaining my goal I will still invest in the stocks.			
		I will continue to invest in stock even if I become aware of it being a bad investment			
Availability bias	People will use excessively the easily available information	I prefer investing in stocks of local companies rather than the foreign ones	0.894	Luong, P. Le, Thu Ha, D. T., & Owe, H. R. (2011)	100 individual investors in Nakuru county, Kenya
		I invest in stocks that have performed well in the recent past			

VARIABLE 2 PROSPECT Prospect theory notes that "people underweight outcomes that are merely probable in comparison with outcomes that are obtained with certainty" (Kahneman & Tversky, 1979, p. 263). People are "less willing to gamble with profit than with losses" (Vijaya, 2014, p.298)					
Indicator	**Theory Statement [References to Specific Theory]**	**Questionnaire Items/Statements**	**Reliability Score**	**References**	**Pilot Study Test**
Availability bias	People will use excessively the easily available information	I prefer investing in stocks of local companies rather than the foreign ones I invest in stocks that have performed well in the recent past	894	Luong, P. Le, Thu Ha, D. T., & Owe, H. R. (2011)	100 individual investors in Nakuru county, Kenya

VARIABLE 3 HEURISTICS People reduce complex tasks to simple judgmental tasks but which may lead to biases or errors (Tversky & Kahneman, 1974). This concept is useful when making complex decisions because it enables the individuals to arrive at decisions which may take longer.					
Indicator	**Theory Statement [References to Specific Theory]**	**Questionnaire Items/Statements**	**Reliability Score**	**References**	**Pilot Study Test**
		I invest in stocks of companies whose name I can easily recall I like investing in the stocks whose information is in the public I do not change my stock investment portfolio I already have invested in.			

VARIABLE 3 HEURISTICS People reduce complex tasks to simple judgmental tasks but which may lead to biases or errors (Tversky & Kahneman, 1974). This concept is useful when making complex decisions because it enables the individuals to arrive at decisions which may take longer.					
Indicator	**Theory Statement [References to Specific Theory]**	**Questionnaire Items/Statements**	**Reliability Score**	**References**	**Pilot Study Test**
Overconfidence	Investors presume to be more experienced than the average investor and hence, will make above average returns	My stock portfolio performs better than other people because of my better skills. I believe that stocks I have invested in the past performed poorly because of bad luck I am able to forecast future stock prices accurately I am better placed than other investors to select good performing stocks I find it easy to trade in stocks I am able to trade in stocks without incurring much risks	.893	Ngoc, L. T. B. (2013)	100 individual investors in Nakuru county, Kenya

VARIABLE 4 MARKET FACTORS Vijaya (2014) & Das (2012) Investors will seek information from the published financial statements and the web for investment purposes Satti, S. L., Din, S. U., & Ali, N. (2013). Investors will seek expert information when making investment decisions.s					
Indicator	**Theory Statement [References to Specific Theory]**	**Questionnaire Items/Statements**	**Reliability Score**	**References**	**Pilot Study Test**
Public information	Published financial statements in the print media. Published Financial statements in the electronic media	I look at the printed financial statements of a firm before buying its shares I check the electronic financial statements of a firm before buying its shares I buy the shares of firms with reputation in the industry I consider the status of the firm when deciding	.912	Vijaya, E. (2014)	100 individual investors in Nakuru county, Kenya

VARIABLE 4 MARKET FACTORS Vijaya (2014) & Das (2012) Investors will seek information from the published financial statements and the web for investment purposes Satti, S. L., Din, S. U., & Ali, N. (2013). Investors will seek expert information when making investment decisions.s					
Indicator	**Theory Statement [References to Specific Theory]**	**Questionnaire Items/Statements**	**Reliability Score**	**References**	**Pilot Study Test**
		whether to buy its shares.			
Expert Information	Seek expert information from financial experts Seek expert information from the web	I like to read expert information before making investment decisions I like to read expert information from the web before making investment decisions Expert information is helpful in investment decisions making	.910	Satti, S. L., Din, S. U., & Ali, N. (2013)	100 individual investors in Nakuru county, Kenya

VARIABLE 5: INVESTMENT DECISIONS Selling decisions by decreasing selling decisions for stocks that have recorded a loss due to the decline in its current price in comparison to the initial purchase price, Shefrin & Statman, 1985. Odean (1998) noted that investors "may sell winners to rebalance their portfolios. Or they may refrain from selling losers due to the higher transactions costs of trading at lower prices". Luong, Thu Ha, and Owe (2011), momentum in stock returns also influences the investors in selling stocks that have gained capital. In addition, the pressure to sell will reduce the share price but increase returns later. In contrast, the investor may make selling decisions when given an expected price which may increase but may lower returns later.					
Indicator	**Theory Statement [References to Specific Theory]**	**Questionnaire Items/Statements**	**Reliability Score**	**References**	**Pilot Study Test**

VARIABLE 5: INVESTMENT DECISIONS					
Selling decisions by decreasing selling decisions for stocks that have recorded a loss due to the decline in its current price in comparison to the initial purchase price, Shefrin & Statman, 1985. Odean (1998) noted that investors "may sell winners to rebalance their portfolios. Or they may refrain from selling losers due to the higher transactions costs of trading at lower prices". Luong, Thu Ha, and Owe (2011), momentum in stock returns also influences the investors in selling stocks that have gained capital. In addition, the pressure to sell will reduce the share price but increase returns later. In contrast, the investor may make selling decisions when given an expected price which may increase but may lower returns later.					
Indicator	**Theory Statement [References to Specific Theory]**	**Questionnaire Items/Statements**	**Reliability Score**	**References**	**Pilot Study Test**
Investment decisions	Selling winners too soon Holding losers too long	Stocks whose prices have always increased. Stocks whose prices have always decreased. Stocks other investors are also trading. Stocks with relatively high returns. Stocks with relatively low returns. Stocks that have good performance in the past. Stocks that have bad performance in the past. Stocks based on the need to diversify them for risk reduction. Stocks with relatively high trading volumes. Stocks that have been frequently announced in the news.	.895	Shefrin & Statman (1985) Luong, Thu Ha, & Owe (2011) Odean (1998)	100 individual investors in Nakuru county, Kenya

Indicator	Theory Statement [References to Specific Theory]	Questionnaire Items/Statements	Reliability Score	References	Pilot Study Test
Weak efficiencies Semi-strong efficiencies Strong form efficiencies	Prices always fully reflect all available information Investors will not earn excess return by analyzing past information Investors will not earn excess return by analyzing past and public available information Investors will not earn return by analyzing public and private information	Stock prices reflect only past information. Stock investments earn abnormal profits based on past information analysis. Stock prices reflect both past and public available information. Stock investment earns abnormal profits based on the financial statements analysis. Sock investment earns abnormal profit based on the fundamentals of the company. Stock prices reflect all information from the public and private sources. Stock prices even reflect hidden insider information.	.895	Fama (1970)	100 individual investors in Nakuru county, Kenya

References

i. Abdellaoui, M., Bleichrodt, H., & Paraschiv, C. (2007). Loss aversion under prospect theory: A parameter-free measurement. Management Science, 53(10), 1659–1674. https://doi.org/10.1287/mnsc.1070.0711

ii. Abreu, D., & Brunnermeier, M. K. (2003). Bubbles and crashes. Econometrica, 71(1), 173–204. http://www.jstor.org/stable/3082044

iii. Aduda, J., Oduor, O. E., & Onwonga, M. (2012). The behaviour and financial performance of individual investors in the trading shares of companies listed at the Nairobi Stock Exchange, Kenya. Journal of Finance and Investment Analysis, 1(3), 33–60.

iv. Águila, N. (2009). Behavioral finance: Learning from market. Revista de Instituciones, Ideas y Mercados, 50(May 2009), 47–104.

v. Ahmed, A. H., Bwisa, H., Otieno, R., & Karanja, K. (2014). Strategic decision making: Process, models, and theories. Business Management and Strategy, 5(1), 78–104. https://doi.org/10.5296/bms.v5i1.5267

vi. Al-Matari, E. M., Al-Swidi, A. K., & Fadzil, F. H. B. (2014). The measurements of firm performance's dimensions. Asian Journal of Finance & Accounting, 6(1), 24. https://doi.org/10.5296/ajfa.v6i1.4761

vii. Almeida, R. P. De, Costa, H. C., Newton, C. A., Jr, C., Porto, R., Costa, H. C., ... Jr, C. (2017). Herd behavior in Latin American stock markets. Journal of Behavioral Finance, 8526(August). https://doi.org/10.1080/10978526.2012.700271

viii. Alrabadi, D. W. H., Al-Abdallah, S. Y., Ibrahim, N., & Aljarayesh, N. I. A. (2018). Behavioral biases and investment performance: Does gender matter? Evidence from Amman Stock Exchange. Jordan Journal of Economic Science, 5(1), 77–92.

ix. Anjum, S. (2011). An overview of financial ratios from 1900s till present days. International Journal of Research in Commerce and Management, 1(8), 126–130.

x. Ariely, D., Loewenstein, G., & Prelec, D. (2006). Tom Sawyer and the construction of value. Journal of Economic Behavior & Organization, 60(1), 1–10. https://doi.org/10.1016/j.jebo.2004.10.003

xi. Ashraf, N., Camerer, C. F., & Loewenstein, G. (2005). Adam Smith, behavioral economist. Journal of Economic Perspectives, 19(3), 131–145. https://doi.org/10.1257/089533005774357897

xii. Bakar, S., & Yi, A. N. C. (2016). The impact of psychological factors on investors' decision making in Malaysian stock market: A case of Klang Valley and Pahang. Procedia Economics and Finance, 35, 319–328. https://doi.org/10.1016/S2212-5671(16)00040-X

xiii. Baker, H. K., & Nofsinger, J. R. (2002). Psychological biases of investors. Financial Services Review, 11(2), 97–116.

xiv. Barber, B. M., & Odean, T. (2000). Trading is hazardous to your wealth: The common stock investment performance of individual investors. The Journal of Finance, 55(2), 773–806.

xv. Barber, B. M., Odean, T., & Zhu, N. (2009). Do retail trades move markets? Review of Financial Studies, 22(1), 151–186. https://doi.org/10.1093/rfs/hhn035

xvi. Barberis, N. (2013). Thirty years of prospect theory in economics: A review and assessment. Journal of Economic Perspectives, 27(1), 173–196. https://doi.org/10.2139/ssrn.2177288

xvii. Barberis, N., & Thaler, R. (2003). A survey of behavioral finance. In Handbook of the Economics of Finance (pp. 1052–1121). https://doi.org/10.2139/ssrn.327880

xviii. Bell, D. E. (1982). Regret in decision making under uncertainty. Operations Research, 30(5), 961–981. https://doi.org/10.1287/opre.30.5.961

xix. Biais, B., Hilton, D., Mazurier, K., & Pouget, E. (2005). Judgemental overconfidence, self-monitoring, and trading performance in an experimental financial market. Review of Economic Studies, 72, 287–312.

xx. Bikhchandani, S., & Sharma, S. (2000). Herd behavior in financial markets. IMF Staff Papers, 47(3), 279–310. https://doi.org/10.2139/ssrn.228343

xxi. Bikhchandani, S., & Sharma, S. (2001). Herd behavior in financial markets. International Monetary Fund, 47(3), 279–310. https://doi.org/10.2307/3867650

xxii. Bodie, Z., Kane, A., & Marcus, J. A. (2014). Investments (10th ed.). New York, NY: McGraw-Hill.

xxiii. Brockner, J. (1992). The escalation of commitment to a failing course of action: Toward theoretical progress. Academy of Management Review, 17(1), 39–61. https://doi.org/10.5465/AMR.1992.4279568

xxiv. Capital Market Authority. (2015). Quarterly statistical bulletin. https://www.cma.or.ke/index.php?option=com_phocadownload&view=category&id=81:work-2015&Itemid=259

xxv. Capital Market Authority. (2017). Quarterly statistical bulletin. Retrieved from https://www.cma.or.ke/index.php?option=com_phocadownload&view=category&id=81:work-2015&Itemid=259

xxvi. Chandra, A., & Kumar, R. (2012). Factors influencing Indian individual investor behaviour: Survey evidence. Decision (0304-0941), 39(3), 141–167. Retrieved from http://search.ebscohost.com/login.aspx?direct=true&db=bth&AN=87340154&site=ehost-live&scope=site&authtype=shib&custid=s8000044

xxvii. Chen, T. (2013). Do investors herd in global stock markets? Journal of Behavioral Finance, 14(3), 230–239. http://doi.org/10.1080/15427560.2013.819804

xxviii. Christie, W. G., & Huang, R. D. (1995). Following the pied piper: Do individual returns herd around the market? Financial Analysts Journal, 51(4), 31–37. http://doi.org/10.2469/faj.v51.n4.1918

xxix. Cipriani, M., & Guarino, A. (2014). Estimating a structural model of herd behavior in financial markets. American Economic Review, 104(1), 224–251. http://doi.org/10.1257/aer.104.1.224

xxx. Creswell, J. W. (2009). Research design: Quantitative, qualitative, and mixed methods (3rd ed.). Los Angeles, CA.

xxxi. Dalbar. (2015). 21 annual quantitative analysis of investor behavior.

xxxii. Das, S. K. (2012). Small investor's behaviour on stock selection decision: A case of Guwahati stock exchange. International Journal of Advanced Research in Management and Social Sciences, 1(2), 59–78.

xxxiii. Decision-making. (2018). In Merriam-WebsterDictionary.com. Retrieved from https://www.merriam-webster.com/dictionary/decision-making

xxxiv. Dietrich, C. (2010). Decision making: Factors that influence decision making, heuristics used, and decision outcomes. Inquiries Journal/Student Pulse, 2(02).

xxxv. Eklund, J. E. (2013). Theories of investment: A theoretical review with empirical applications. Retrieved from http://entreprenorskapsforum.se/wp-content/uploads/2013/03/WP_22.pdf

xxxvi. Ert, E., & Erev, I. (2003). On the descriptive value of loss aversion in decisions under risk. Judgment and Decision Making, 8(3), 214–235. http://doi.org/10.2139/ssrn.1012022

xxxvii. Etikan, I. (2016). Comparison of convenience sampling and purposive sampling. American Journal of Theoretical and Applied Statistics, 5(1), 1–4. http://doi.org/10.11648/j.ajtas.20160501.11

xxxviii. Fama, E. F. (1970). Efficient capital markets: A review of theory and empirical work. The Journal of Finance, 25(2), 383–417.

xxxix. Fama, E. F. (1998). Market efficiency, long-term returns, and behavioral finance. Journal of Financial Economics, 49(3), 283–306. http://doi.org/10.1016/S0304-405X(98)00026-9

xl. Fleming, M. J., & Remolona, E. M. (1999). Price formation and liquidity in the U.S. treasury market: The response to public information. The Journal of Finance, 54(5), 1901–1915. http://doi.org/10.1111/0022-1082.00172

xli. Gigerenzer, G. (2001). Decision making: Nonrational theories. International Encyclopedia of the Social & Behavioral Sciences, 5, 911–916. http://doi.org/10.1016/B978-0-08-097086-8.26017-0

xlii. Glaser, M., & Weber, M. (2007). Overconfidence and trading volume. Geneva Risk and Insurance Review, 32(1), 1–36. http://doi.org/10.1007/s10713-007-0003-3

xliii. Goel, S. (2014). Investor's herding behavior and investment performance: An empirical evidence from Delhi. The International Journal of Business & Management, 2(12), 56–59.

xliv. Gyamfi, E. N., Kyei, K. A., & Gill, R. (2017). Market efficiency of African stock markets: A meta-analysis. The Journal of Developing Areas, 51(4), 69–80.

xlv. Hair Jr., J. F., Black, W. C., Babin, B. J., & Anderson, R. E. (2014). Multivariate data analysis (7th ed.). London, UK: Pearson Education.

xlvi. Hammond, R. C. (2015). Behavioral finance: Its history and its future. Southeastern University - Lakeland.

xlvii. Imenda, S. (2014). Is there a conceptual difference between theoretical and conceptual frameworks? Journal of Social Sciences, 38(2), 185–195. http://doi.org/10.1080/09718923.2014.11893249

xlviii. Ishaq Bhatti, M., & Awan, H. M. (2014). The key performance indicators (KPIs) and their impact on overall organisational performance. Quality and Quantity, 48(6), 3127–3143. http://doi.org/10.1007/s11135-013-9945-y

xlix. Jagongo, A., & Mutswenje, V. S. (2014). A survey of the factors influencing investment decisions: The case of individual investors at the NSE. International Journal of Humanities and Social Science, 4(4), 92–102.

l. Javed, H., Bagh, T., & Razzaq, S. (2017). Herding effects, overconfidence, availability bias and representativeness as behavioural determinants of perceived investment performance: An empirical evidence from Pakistan stock exchange (PSX). Journal of Global Economics, 6(1), 1–13. http://doi.org/10.4172/2375-4389.1000275

li. Kahneman, D. (2003). Maps of bounded rationality: A perspective on intuitive judgement and choice. American Economic Review, (December), 449–489. https://doi.org/10.1037/0003-066X.58.9.697

lii. Kahneman, D., & Tversky, A. (1979). Prospect theory: An analysis of decision under risk. Econometrica, 47(2), 263–292. https://doi.org/10.1017/CBO9781107415324.004

liii. Kalima, E., Shukla, J., & Mbabazize, M. (2016). Effect of credit management system on financial performance of Development Bank in Rwanda: Case study of

Development Bank of Rwanda. The International Journal of Business & Management, 4(5), 2321–8916. Retrieved from http://www.theijbm.com

liv. Kaur, M., & Vohra, T. (2012). Understanding individual investors' behavior: A review of empirical evidences. Pacific Business Review International, 5(6), 10–18.

lv. Kengatharan, L., & Kengatharan, N. (2014). The influence of behavioral factors in making investment decisions and performance: Study on investors of Colombo Stock Exchange, Sri Lanka. Asian Journal of Finance & Accounting, 6(1), 1. https://doi.org/10.5296/ajfa.v6i1.4893

lvi. Khan, H. H., Naz, I., Qureshi, F., & Ghafoor, A. (2017). Heuristics and stock buying decision: Evidence from Malaysian and Pakistani stock markets. Borsa Istanbul Review, 17(2), 97–110. https://doi.org/10.1016/j.bir.2016.12.002

lvii. Khan, M. H. (2014). An empirical investigation on behavioral determinants of perceived investment performance: Evidence from Karachi Stock Exchange. Research Journal of Finance and Accounting, 5(21), 2222–2847.

lviii. Kharb, A., & Malik, M. (2014). Behavioural finance: An impact of investors' unpredictable behaviour on stock market. Tactful Management Research Journal, 3(1), 34–38.

lix. Kirkman, B. L., & Shapiro, D. L. (1998). The impact of cultural values on escalation of commitment. International Journal of Organizational Analysis, 6(2), 165–176. https://doi.org/10.2307/3069370

lx. Kishore, R. (1979). Theory of behavioural finance and its application to property market: A change in paradigm. In Twelfth Annual Pacific Rim Real Estate Society Conference, January 22–25, Auckland, New Zealand (pp. 1–17).

lxi. Kofarbai, H. Z., & Zubairu, M. (2016). Efficient market hypothesis in emerging market – A conceptual analysis. European Scientific Journal, 12(25), 260–270. https://doi.org/10.19044/esj.2016.v12n25p260

lxii. Konstantinidis, A., Katarachia, A., Borovas, G., & Voutsa, M. E. (2012). From efficient market hypothesis to behavioural finance: Can behavioural finance be the new dominant model for investing? Scientific Bulletin – Economic Sciences, 11(2), 16–26.

lxiii. Kramer, M., & Lensink, R. (2012). The impact of financial advisors on the stock portfolios of retail investors (pp. 1–39). https://doi.org/10.2139/ssrn.2021883

lxiv. Kumar, S., & Goyal, N. (2015). Behavioural biases in investment decision making – A systematic literature review. Qualitative Research in Financial Markets, 7(1), 88–108. https://doi.org/10.1108/QRFM-07-2014-0022

lxv. Latif, M., Arshad, S., Fatima, M., & Farooq, S. (2011). Market efficiency, market anomalies, causes, evidences, and some behavioral aspects of market anomalies. Research Journal of Finance and Accounting, 2(9), 1–14.

lxvi. Le Bon, G. (1896). The crowd: A study of the popular mind.

lxvii. Lee, Y., Wang, G.-L., Kao, K.-S., Chen, C.-Y., & Zhu, F.-P. (2010). The investment behavior, decision factors and their effects toward investment performance in the Taiwan stock market. Journal of Global Business Management, 6(2), 1–12.

lxviii. Lin, Y.-E., Fan, W.-M., & Chih, H.-H. (2014). Throwing good money after bad? The impact of the escalation of commitment of mutual fund managers on fund performance. Journal of Behavioral Finance, 15(1), 1–15. https://doi.org/10.1080/15427560.2013.849706

lxix. Loomes, G., & Sugden, R. (1982). Regret theory: An alternative theory of rational choice under uncertainty. The Economic Journal, 92(368), 805–824. https://doi.org/10.2307/2232669

lxx. Lunenburg, F. C. (2010). Escalation of commitment: Patterns of retrospective rationality. International Journal of Management, Business and Administration, 13(1), 1–5.

lxxi. Luong, P. Le, Thu Ha, D. T., & Owe, H. R. (2011). Behavioral factors influencing individual investors' decision-making and performance.

lxxii. Mackay, C. (1841). Popular delusions and the madness of crowds. London: Richard Bentley.

lxxiii. Malkiel, B. G. (1989). Is the stock market efficient? Science, New Series, 243(4896), 1313–1318.

lxxiv. Masry, M. (2017). The impact of technical analysis on stock returns in an Emerging Capital Markets (ECM's) country: Theoretical and empirical study. International Journal of Economics and Finance, 9(3), 91. https://doi.org/10.5539/ijef.v9n3p91

lxxv. Mertler, C. A., & Vannatta, R. A. (2017). Advanced and multivariate statistical methods (6th ed.). NY: Routledge.

lxxvi. Morris, S., & Shin, H. (2002). Social value of public information. American Economic Review, 92(5), 1521–1534. Retrieved from http://www.ingentaconnect.com/content/aea/aer/2002/00000092/00000005/art00012

lxxvii. Ngoc, L. T. B. (2013). Behavior pattern of individual investors in stock market. International Journal of Business and Management, 9(1), 1–16. https://doi.org/10.5539/ijbm.v9n1p1

lxxviii. Nwude, E. C. (2012). Return on investment: Conceptions and empirical evidence from banking stocks. Research Journal of Finance and Accounting, 3(8), 2222–2847. Retrieved from file:///C:/Users/Aliff/Downloads/2829-4847-1-PB.pdf

lxxix. Nyamute, W. I. (2016). Investor behaviour, investor demographic characteristics, investment style and individual investor portfolio performance at the Nairobi Securities Exchange. Jomo Kenyatta University of Agriculture and Technology.

lxxx. Nyamute, W., Lishenga, J., & Oloko, M. (2015). The relationship between investor behavior and portfolio performance at the Nairobi Securities Exchange. International Journal of Multidisciplinary Research and Development, 2(5), 548–551.

lxxxi. Odean, T. (1998). Are investors reluctant to realize their losses? The Journal of Finance, 53(5), 1775–1798. http://doi.org/10.1111/0022-1082.00072

lxxxii. Oliveira, A. (2007). A discussion of rational and psychological decision-making theories and models: The search for a cultural-ethical decision-making model. Electronic Journal of Business Ethics and Organization Studies, 12(2), 12–17. http://doi.org/10.1111/j.1572-0241.1998.00467.x

lxxxiii. Park, J., & Kim, M. (2014). Investment performance of individual investors: Evidence from the Korean stock market. Emerging Markets Finance and Trade, 50(s1), 194–211. http://doi.org/10.2753/REE1540-496X5001S113

lxxxiv. Patrick, I. D. Z., Tavershima, A., & Eje, E. B. (2017). Effect of financial information on investment decision making by shareholders of banks in Nigeria. IOSR Journal of Economics and Finance, 8(3), 20–31. http://doi.org/10.9790/5933-0803032031

lxxxv. Petrusheva, N., & Jordanoski, I. (2016). Comparative analysis between the fundamental and technical analysis of stocks. Journal of Process Management – New Technologies, 4(2), 26–31. http://scindeks-clanci.ceon.rs/data/pdf/2334-735X/2016/2334-735X1602026P.pdf

lxxxvi. Polič, M. (2009). Decision making: Between rationality and reality. Interdisciplinary Descriptions of Complex Systems, 7(2), 78–89.

lxxxvii. Prosad, J. M., Kapoor, S., & Sengupta, J. (2015). Behavioural biases of Indian investors: A survey of Delhi-NCR region. Qualitative Research in Financial Markets, 7(3), 230–263.

lxxxviii. Ranjbar, H. M., Abedini, B., & Jamali, M. (2014). Analysing the effective behavioural factors on the investors' performance in Tehran stock exchange (TSE). International Journal of Art & Humanity Science, 8(8), 80–86.

lxxxix. Reed, F., & Johnson, W. (2012). Philosophical documents in education (4th ed.). Pearson.

xc. Rekik, Y. M., & Boujelbene, Y. (2013). Determinants of individual investors' behaviours: Evidence from Tunisian stock market. Journal of Business and Management, 8(2), 109–119.

xci. Rutledge, R. W. (1994). Escalation of commitment in groups and the moderating effects of information framing. Management Research News, 17(1–2), 12–24. http://doi.org/10.1108/eb028334

xcii. Sadi, R., Asl, H. G., Rostami, M. R., Gholipour, A., & Gholipour, F. (2011). Behavioural finance: The explanation of investors' personality and perceptual biases effects on financial decisions. International Journal of Economics and Finance, 3(5), 234–241. http://doi.org/10.5539/ijef.v3n5p234

xciii. Sahi, S. K., Arora, A. P., & Dhameja, N. (2013). An exploratory inquiry into the psychological biases in financial investment behaviour. Journal of Behavioral Finance, 14(2), 94–103. http://doi.org/10.1080/15427560.2013.790387

xciv. Satti, S. L., Din, S. U., & Ali, N. (2013). Investor knowledge, risk aversion, and investment decision. Actual Problems of Economics, 146(8), 380–389.

xcv. Saunders, M., Lewis, P., & Thornhill, A. (2007). Research methods for business students (4th ed.). Edinburg: Prentice Hall.

xcvi. Selden, G. C. (1912). Psychology of the stock market. New York: Ticker Publishing Company.

xcvii. Sewell, M. (2010). Behavioural finance. University of Cambridge, (April), 1–13. http://doi.org/10.1111/j.1468-036X.2007.00365.x

xcviii. Sharma, A. J. (2014). The behavioural finance: A challenge or replacement to efficient market concept. The SIJ Transactions on Industrial, Financial & Business Management, 2(6), 273–277.

xcix. Shefrin, H. (2001). Behavioural corporate finance. Santa Clara University, (September), 1–17. http://doi.org/10.2139/ssrn.288257

c. Shefrin, H., & Statman, M. (1985). The disposition to sell winners too early and ride losers too long: Theory and evidence. The Journal of Finance, 40(3), 777–790.

ci. Shiller, R. J. (1998). Human behaviour and the efficiency of the financial system. Cowles Foundation Papers, (N.1025), 1–34. http://doi.org/10.3386/w6375

cii. Shiller, R. J. (2003). From efficient markets theory to behavioural finance. Journal of Economic Perspectives. http://doi.org/10.2139/ssrn.349660

ciii. Singer, J. D. (1982). Variables, indicators, and data. Social Science History, 6(2), 181–217.

civ. Spyrou, S. (2013). Herding in financial markets: A review of the literature. Review of Behavioral Finance, 5(2), 175–194. http://doi.org/10.1108/RBF-02-2013-0009

cv. Sukheja, G. M. (2016). The impact of behavioural psychology in individual investment decision-making. Journal of Insurance and Financial Management, 1(3), 67–81.

cvi. Tabachnick, B. G., & Fidell, L. S. (2013). Using multivariate statistics (6th ed.). NJ: Pearson Education.

cvii. Tang, M.-J. (1998). An economic perspective on escalating the commitment. Strategic Management Journal, 9(5), 79–92. http://doi.org/10.1111/1468-0327.00107

cviii. Ton, H. T. H., & Dao, T. K. (2014). The effects of psychology on individual investors' behaviours: Evidence from the Vietnam stock exchange. Journal of Management and Sustainability, 4(3), 125–134. http://doi.org/10.5539/jms.v4n3p125

cix. Turino, H. K., & Soetjipto, B. W. (2012). The effect of image compatibility and escalation of commitment on decision performance. The South East Asian Journal of Management, 6(1), 23–32. Retrieved from http://search.proquest.com/docview/1348129132?accountid=10297%0Ahttp://sfx.cranfield.ac.uk/cranfield?url_ver=Z39.88-2004&rft_val_fmt=info:ofi/fmt:kev:mtx:journal&genre=article&sid=ProQ:ProQ:abiglobal&atitle=The+Effect+of+Image+Compatibility+and+Escalation

cx. Tversky, A., & Kahneman, D. (1974). Judgment under uncertainty: Heuristics and biases. Science, 185(4157), 1124–1131. http://doi.org/10.1097/00001888-199907000-00012

cxi. Tversky, A., & Kahneman, D. (1986). Rational choice and the framing of decisions. The Journal of Business, 59(S4), S251. http://doi.org/10.1086/296365

cxii. Valsecchi, I. (2013). The expert problem: A survey. Economics of Governance, 14(4), 303–331. http://doi.org/10.1007/s10101-013-0129-y

cxiii. Veeraraghavan, K., & Anbalagan, M. (2011). Heuristic behavior of the investors. International Journal of Enterprise Innovation Management Studies, 2(2), 142–149.

cxiv. Velumoni, D. (2017). Analysis of prospect theory on equity investment decision making—A behavioural perspective. Indian Journal of Science Research, 14(1), 211–215.

cxv. Vijaya, E. (2014). An empirical analysis of influential factors on investment behaviour of retail investors in Indian stock market: A behavioural perspective. International Journal in Management and Social Science, 2(12), 296–308.

cxvi. Wadongo, B., Odhuno, E., Kambona, O., & Othuon, L. (2010). Key performance indicators in the Kenyan hospitality industry: A managerial perspective. Benchmarking: An International Journal, 17(6), 858–875. http://doi.org/10.1108/14635771011089764

cxvii. Waweru, N. M., Mwangi, G. G., & Parkinson, J. M. (2014). Behavioural factors influencing investment decisions in the Kenyan property market. Afro-Asian J. of Finance and Accounting, 4(1), 26. http://doi.org/10.1504/AAJFA.2014.059500

cxviii. Weible, C. M. (2008). Expert-based information and policy subsystems: A review and synthesis. Policy Studies Journal, 36(4), 615–635. http://doi.org/10.1111/j.1541-0072.2008.00287.x

cxix. Wilson, T. D. (1999). Models of information behaviour research. The Journal of Documentation, 55(3), 249–270.

cxx. Zeelenberg, M. (1999). Anticipated regret , expected feedback and behavioral decision-making. Journal of Behavioural Decision Making, 12(2), 93–106.

www.ingramcontent.com/pod-product-compliance
Lightning Source LLC
Chambersburg PA
CBHW041754220926
51847CB00014B/202
* 9 7 8 9 3 4 7 3 9 7 7 3 8 *